DANGER TO ELIZABETH

DANGER TO ELIZABETH

THE CATHOLICS UNDER ELIZABETH I

ALISON PLOWDEN

SUTTON PUBLISHING

First published in 1973 by Macmillan Ltd

This edition first published in 1999 by
Sutton Publishing Ltd · Phoenix Mill · Stroud · Gloucestershire

A catalogue record for this book is available from the British Library

ISBN 0-7509-2196-X

*Cover illustration: Elizabeth I by an unknown artist, c. 1575 (by courtesy of
the National Portrait Gallery, London)*

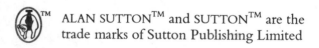
Printed and bound in Great Britain by
The Guernsey Press Company Limited,
Guernsey, Channel Islands.

For My Mother
With My Love

Contents

ALISON PLOWDEN was born in India and was formerly a script writer and editor for the BBC. Her television credits include *Mistress of Hardwick*, for which she won a Writers Guild Award. She is the author of many successful historical books including *The House of Tudor*, acclaimed by the great historian A.L. Rowse as 'Simply excellent on every count ... impossible to fault in scholarship or writing'. This has recently been re-published by Sutton, where it joins others of her works, including *Two Queens in One Isle: The Deadly Relationship of Elizabeth and Mary Queen of Scots*, *Tudor Women*, *The Stuart Princesses*, and *Women all on Fire: The Women of the English Civil War*. Alison Plowden lives near Wantage in Oxfordshire.

This lady and princess

'This lady and princess is a notable woman.'
Francis Knollys, Carlisle, 11 June 1568

At seven o'clock in the evening of Sunday, 16 May 1568 housewives in the 'lytle prety fyssher town' of Workington, which lay near the mouth of the River Derwent on the coast of Cumberland, were indoors preparing supper; but those people still out and about enjoying the Sabbath air had been able to watch the progress of a small vessel edging into the harbour and tying up at the quayside. The unexpected visitor turned out to be a rough little craft of the type used for inshore fishing and carrying coals and lime across the Solway Firth, but the idlers on the waterfront could see at a glance that her passengers – sixteen of them in all – were neither colliers nor Galloway fishermen. Although tired and travel-stained, these were clearly people of consequence among them an unusually tall young woman, muffled in cloak and hood, who stumbled and fell as she came ashore.

The strangers sought shelter for the night at Workington Hall, their spokesman (he was John Maxwell, Lord Herries) giving out that he had carried off an heiress whom he was hoping to marry to the son of his old friend Sir Henry Curwen; but by the time darkness had fallen the whole neighbourhood was buzzing with the news that the tall young woman was none other than the already legendary Mary Queen of Scots, deposed and imprisoned by her ungrateful subjects and now fleeing for her life. Henry Curwen happened to be away from home but one of his servants, a Frenchman, had recognised the Queen as soon as she crossed the threshold and told a member of her entourage that he had formerly seen Her Majesty in better plight than now.

The reasoning which lay behind Mary's rash decision to throw herself on the protection of her cousin, Elizabeth of England, remains obscure. It was a decision taken, as she herself later admitted, against the advice of her best friends. In the six and a half years which had passed since her return to her northern kingdom it was by no means the first time that the Queen of Scots had refused to listen to advice. Certainly the stubborn determination to go her own way was characteristic enough, as was her gambler's instinct to stake all on a single throw.

During her brief period of freedom – it was just over a fortnight since she had escaped from Lochleven Castle with the assistance of Willy Douglas – Mary had sent Elizabeth a full account of her predicament. Now she wrote again from Workington Hall on Monday, 17 May, ending with a moving plea for help: 'I entreat you to send for me as soon as possible, for I am in a pitiable condition, not only for a Queen but even for a gentlewoman, having nothing in the world but the clothes in which I escaped, riding sixty miles the first day and not daring to travel afterwards except by night, as I hope to be able to show you, if it please you to have compassion on my great misfortunes and permit me to come and bewail them to you.'

Mary can scarcely have finished this letter before she was ceremoniously waited on by a deputation of local gentry, who conducted her a few miles inland to the town of Cockermouth. There Sir Richard Lowther, deputy governor of Carlisle, 'made his attendance' upon her and it was agreed that she should spend that night in the house of a well-to-do merchant, one Master Henry Fletcher. When Mary told the Queen of England that she had nothing but the clothes she stood up in, she had, it seems, been speaking the literal truth. Richard Lowther noted that 'her grace's attire is very mean, and as I can learn, hath not any better, neither other wherewith to change'. Henry Fletcher is said to have presented his guest with thirteen ells of crimson velvet, and a black cloth gown was hastily made up for her on credit.

Anxious not to be outdone in matters of hospitality, Richard Lowther 'ordered her charges at Cockermouth to be defrayed', and himself provided horses to carry her and her train on the remainder of the journey to Carlisle. Lowther was not at all certain about the protocol governing the reception of refugee queens who had made their own realms too hot to hold them – especially a queen who represented the sort of political dynamite that Mary Stuart did – and he begged Sir William Cecil for instructions. Meanwhile, he intended to keep the fugitive safe at Carlisle Castle with such entertainment as he could provide 'on such sudden'.

Mary had been considerably cheered by the kindness of her welcome. The warm-hearted (and predominantly Catholic) North Country folk were touched by her plight, besides being naturally curious to catch a glimpse of so romantic a figure as the Queen of Scots, and they came flocking in to Carlisle to pay their respects. Mary's naturally buoyant spirits rose and, in a letter dated 20 May, she told the Earl of Cassilis that she expected to be back in Scotland at the head of an army, French if not English, by the middle of August.

By 20 May the news of her arrival had reached London. It cannot have been entirely unexpected. Queen Elizabeth had known for at least a week about her cousin's escape from captivity and the possibility that Mary might be driven to cross the border must certainly have occurred to her. Elizabeth Tudor had in the past been given small reason to feel any personal affection for Mary Stuart but, as she had already made abundantly clear to the Scots, she held strong views on subjects who, whatever the provocation, forced their sovereign to abdicate, held her prisoner and threatened her very life. According to the French and Spanish ambassadors, Elizabeth's first impulse had been to take Mary's part and receive her at Court, but a majority on the Council quickly over-ruled their mistress's instinctive desire to show solidarity with the afflicted Queen of Scotland. 'Although these people are glad enough to have her in their hands,' wrote the Spanish ambassador, 'they have many things to consider. If they keep her as in prison, it will probably scandalise all neighbouring princes, and if she remain free and able to communicate with her friends, great suspicions will be aroused. In any case,' added Guzman de Silva with studied understatement, 'it is certain that two women will not agree very long.'

The English Council, only too conscious of the many things they had to consider, at once 'entered into serious deliberation' as to what should be done with the Queen of Scots – Elizabeth's Catholic, *de facto* if unacknowledged heir, who had 'heretofore openly challenged the crown of England, not as a second person after the Queen's majesty, but afore her'.

At the age of twenty-five Mary had already succeeded in leaving a quite considerable trail of havoc behind her. Widely suspected of complicity in the assassination of her second husband at Kirk o'Field the year before, she had not improved matters by marrying again, three months later, 'the principal murderer' James Hepburn, Earl of Bothwell. It was this unconventional course of action which had led to her downfall and Scotland was now controlled by her bastard half-brother, the Earl of Moray, ruling in the name of her infant son and the Protestant Kirk. Moray, strongminded and capable, showed every sign of being able to provide his country-men with some much needed stability and, if he was left undis-turbed, of pursuing a policy of peaceful co-existence with England. He had, after all, been accepting an English pension for some years.

In the circumstances, therefore, Mary's sudden eruption into their midst presented the English government with an embarrassing problem. 'If she were detained in England,' says William Camden, 'they reasoned lest she (who was as it were the very pith and marrow of sweet eloquence) might draw many daily to her part which favoured her title to the crown of England, who would kindle the coals of her ambition, and leave nothing unassayed whereby they might set the crown upon her head. Foreign ambas-sadors would further her counsels and designs; and the Scots then would not fail her, when they should see so rich a booty offered them.' Besides this, Camden observed, 'the trust of keepers was doubtful'.

If Mary were to die in England, even though from natural causes, it would be made a 'matter of calumniation' and Elizabeth would be 'daily molested with new troubles'. If she were allowed to go over to France, her powerful kinsmen there would stir up a hornets' nest on her behalf in both Scotland and England. On the other hand, for Elizabeth to attempt to restore her to her Scottish throne by force of arms would be to invite civil war in Scotland, disruption of the precious, none too secure 'amity' with that country, and a possible revival of the old Franco-Scottish alliance which had been the cause of so much ill-feeling and blood-shed in the past. In any case, it was unthinkable that a Catholic monarch should be re-imposed on a Protestant kingdom with the help of other Protestants. At the same time, it had to be remembered that Mary had sought refuge in England of her own volition, trusting in Elizabeth's many previous – and public – promises of help. She could not now with any appearance of decency be handed back to her enemies.

It was a situation calling for the most careful handling in the long term, but some action had to be taken quickly. On 22 May, therefore, Elizabeth sent her Vice-Chamberlain, Sir Francis Knollys, an old and trusted friend, to take charge at Carlisle. He found Mary recovering rapidly from the rigours of her escape and flight, and full of an articulate sense of grievance over the wrongs she had suffered in Scotland. Knollys, an ardent left-wing Protestant, was immediately impressed both by her charismatic personality and her other formidable qualities. She had 'an eloquent tongue and a discreet head', he reported, 'and it seemeth by her doings she hath stout courage and liberal heart adjoined thereto.'

After an uneasy fortnight in her company, Knollys saw no reason to change his opinion. 'This lady and princess is a notable woman,' he wrote on 11 June. 'She seemeth to regard no ceremonious honour beside the acknowledging of her estate regal. She showeth a disposition to speak much, to be bold, to be pleasant, and to be very familiar. She showeth a great desire to be avenged of her enemies. She showeth a readiness to expose herself to all perils in hope of victory. She delighteth much to hear of hardiness and valiancy, commending by name all approved hardy men of her country, although they be her enemies, and she concealeth no cowardice even in her friends. The thing that most she thirsteth after is victory, and it seemeth to be indifferent to her to have her enemies diminished either by the sword of her friends, or by the liberal promises and rewards of her purse, or by division and quarrels raised among themselves: so that for victory's sake pain and peril seemeth pleasant to her: and in respect of victory, wealth and all things seemeth to her contemptible and vile. Now what is to be done with such a lady and princess?' enquired Francis Knollys, with a certain rhetorical flourish, of his friend William Cecil.

No one, least of all either of the rival queens, could have foretold that it would be eighteen years before history provided its inexorable answer to that question.

CHAPTER ONE

A wise and religious Queen

'We have a wise and religious Queen'
John Jewel, London, 22 May 1559

WHEN Elizabeth Tudor succeeded to her sister's throne in November 1558 she was the same age as Mary Stuart at the time of her flight into England, but Elizabeth at twenty-five was still very much of an unknown quantity. This was partly due to the fact that she had spent most of the previous five years either in prison or living in rural retirement under some form of surveillance, and partly to the habits of discretion and dissimulation acquired during her precarious adolescence. However, as it became obvious that the ailing, unhappy Mary Tudor would leave no other heir, international curiosity about the young Elizabeth had intensified, and in 1557 the Venetian ambassador included a detailed description of the Princess in his report on his tour of duty in England. Her face, wrote Giovanni Michiel, was comely rather than handsome, but she was tall, well-formed and with a good skin, although sallow. She had fine eyes and very beautiful hands which she took care to display.

Even in her early twenties, the pale, sharp-featured, red-haired Elizabeth had never been able to compete with her Scottish cousin's fabled beauty, but she possessed other attributes which were to prove of greater value in the long-drawn-out battle between them. As early as 1557, Michiel could comment respectfully on the excellence of her mind and on the wonderful intellect and understanding she had shown when facing danger and suspicion. She was proud, too, and haughty, he declared, in spite of the fact that her birth was regarded as illegitimate by most of Christian Europe and that her mother, the great-granddaughter of a London mercer, had once been commonly referred to as that goggle-eyed whore Nan Bullen. Nevertheless, Elizabeth it seemed did not regard herself as being of inferior degree to her half-sister the Queen, whose mother had been a Spanish princess of irreproachable lineage and virtue. 'She prides herself on her father and glories in him', wrote Michiel, adding that her resemblance to Henry VIII was remarked by everybody.

Elizabeth's greatest source of strength in the dismal days of her sister's reign had always been her immense popularity, especially with the Londoners, and her accession was greeted with a spontaneous outburst of public rejoicing which has seldom been equalled. The uninhibited warmth of her welcome cannot be explained away by mere desire for a change, or relief that the transition had been accomplished peacefully. In the decade which had passed since King Henry's death, the nation had suffered from the rule of greedy, factious juntas during the minority of Edward VI and the unpopular, inefficient government of a Queen accused of loving Spaniards and hating Englishmen. Mary Tudor had indeed leaned heavily on Spanish advisers and on her Spanish husband, who had ended by dragging the country into a ruinous war with France, culminating in the loss of Calais, last outpost of England's once great Continental empire.

Some people doubted whether another woman ruler would be much of an improvement, but there seems to have been a widespread, intuitive feeling that Henry VIII's younger daughter was a genuine chip off the old block. Elizabeth was at least a full-blooded Englishwoman, unencumbered by foreign ties. Most important of all, she was young and healthy and with any luck would bear healthy sons. That apart, in the winter of 1558, she looked like being England's last hope of peace and good government for a long time to come, and one senses an undercurrent of rather desperate optimism in the cheers, the pealing bells and salutes of guns which greeted the new Queen as she rode in procession through the City to the Tower on 28 November.

Among the legacy of problems Elizabeth had inherited from her sister were a restive, divided kingdom, an empty Treasury and a mountain of debt. The international situation, too, looked grim, with 'steadfast enmity but no steadfast friendship abroad'. Technically England was still at war with France – 'the French King', in Armagil Waad's picturesque phrase, 'bestriding the realm, having one foot in Calais and the other in Scotland'. The first task facing the new administration, therefore, was to make peace on the best terms it could get, and it did not seem as if they would be very good. As well as possessing all the military and strategic trumps, the French held a strong political card in their control of young Mary Stuart, granddaughter of Henry VIII's elder sister Margaret who had married James IV of Scotland.

In the eyes of the Catholic world which, of course, had never recognised the King of England's famous divorce, Mary had a far better legal claim to the English throne than Henry's daughter, born during the lifetime of his first wife. Elizabeth had, after all, been bastardised and disinherited by her own father in a still unrepealed Act of Parliament, and her present title was based on another Act of 1544 restoring her to the succession. The English Catholics, led by the Lord Chancellor, Nicholas Heath, had accepted her on the strength of her parliamentary title. The French, however, were less convinced of either Henry's or Parliament's competence to manipulate the natural laws of inheritance, and in December 1558 Lord Cobham reported from Brussels that they 'did not let to say and talk openly that Her Highness is not lawful Queen of England and that they have already sent to Rome to disprove her right'. A few weeks later, Sir Edward Carne was writing from Rome that 'the ambassador of the French laboreth the Pope to declare the Queen illegitimate and the Scottish Queen successor to Queen Mary'.

The King of France had every reason to take a close interest in this matter, since Mary Stuart, who had been brought up in France, was now married to the Dauphin while her mother, Mary of Guise, ruled Scotland with French support. If the Queen of Scots' right to the English throne could be established, it opened up a tempting prospect of French hegemony. So at least it seemed to several experienced English politicians, among them Nicholas Wotton, one of the Commissioners at the preliminary peace talks being held at Cercamp.

Wotton was pessimistic about their prospects of coming away with anything more than 'a piece of paper only containing the words of a treaty of peace', and he wrote to William Cecil gloomily outlining the various causes which moved him to doubt the sincerity of the French. These included 'the ancient and immortal hatred they bear unto us ... the pretence they make now by the Scottish Queen's feigned title to the crown of England; the occasion and commodity they have now to invade us by land on Scotland side ... the most dangerous divisions in religion among ourselves ... the poor state the crown of England is in for lack of money, which I fear they understand too well; the lack of good soldiers, captains and of all kind of munition that we have; the nakedness of all our country, having almost never a place well fortified to sustain a siege; the great commodity which they look to have thereby, if they may subdue England to them; for, bringing once that to pass, (which God forbid) and having England, Scotland and Ireland, no doubt they would look shortly after to be monarchs of almost all Europe; and so were they like to be indeed.' Wotton also regarded Mary Stuart's ambitious Guise relations with the gravest misgivings, 'considering that the House of Guise's greatness and authority dependeth chiefly upon the great commodity that France hath and looketh to have by this marriage of Scotland. And therefore, whatsoever they shall say, sing or pipe, their meaning and intent can be none other but to seek all the means possible to increase the power and honour of their niece the Queen of Scots and of her posterity.'

The fact that the sixteen-year-old Mary was now quartering the royal arms of England with her own and was styled Queen of England in official documents, appeared to reinforce Wotton's forebodings. As it turned out, however, the King of France was not so much interested in embarking on military adventures on behalf of his daughter-in-law as in using her potential status as a lever to extort concessions from the English Commissioners. For example, when the question of the restitution of Calais was raised at the conference table, the French were able to enquire blandly: to whom should Calais be restored? Was not the Queen of Scotland true Queen of England?

This sort of talk naturally infuriated Queen Elizabeth, but she and her advisers knew that without Spanish assistance there was not the slightest chance of recovering Calais. They also knew — as did the King of France — that Philip II, King of Spain, Naples and Sicily, Lord of the Netherlands and widower of Mary Tudor, while showing no disposition to help England in the matter of Calais, would go to considerable lengths to prevent France from interfering in the matter of the succession. Philip might be a zealous Catholic, but he was also a practical statesman who infinitely preferred to see an English queen of doubtful orthodoxy on the English throne, than one half-French by birth and wholly French in sympathy.

Nevertheless, although for the time being, Mary Stuart's very Frenchness was paradoxically a safeguard, the question of her claim remained a source of anxiety and possible danger. The 'auld alliance' between France and Scotland had been a running sore in England's side for generations. It was unfortunate that just now, when the body politic seemed least able to deal with it, this complaint should be present in an acute form.

The other immediate task facing the new Queen of England and her government was the particularly delicate one of making a religious settlement at home. Ironically enough, it had been to ensure her own birth in wedlock that Elizabeth's father, a quarter of a century earlier, had separated England from the body of the Roman Church and had thus helped to destroy the unity of Christendom – that seamless garment of common discipline and belief which had covered the whole of mediaeval Western Europe. Henry's Reformation had been a deliberate political act and, although explicitly denying the authority of the Pope, his Church retained many of the basic tenets of Roman Catholicism.

As long as he lived, the old King had ridden both conservative spirits and more radical reformers with a tight rein, but after his death the radicals quickly took the bit between their teeth. Doctrinal and liturgical innovations followed one another thick and fast. Old rites and ceremonies were abolished, the clergy were permitted to marry, heresy laws were swept away, it was ordained that the laity should henceforward communicate in both kinds, and on Whitsunday 1549 Cranmer's first English Book of Common Prayer became the official and obligatory order of service in every parish church. Based on the old Sarum use, Cranmer's prayer book was still something of a compromise between old and new and worded loosely enough to be acceptable, it was hoped, to both old and new. The new liturgy was, however, rejected by certain ungrateful and reactionary West Countrymen as 'a Christmas game', while others of a more progressive turn of mind did not scruple to refer to it as 'a Popish dunghill'. Three years later a second, more radical version was introduced. The Prayer Book of 1552 completed the process of transforming the sacrifice of the ancient Latin Mass into a communion or commemorative service. The words of the administration: 'Take and eat this in remembrance that Christ died for thee, and feed on him in thy heart by faith with thanksgiving' could no longer be interpreted, even by the most elastic conscience, as anything but a denial of the Real Presence.

Then, in 1553, Edward VI, enthusiastically hailed by the reformers as 'a young Josiah', died in his sixteenth year and Mary Tudor, after unexpectedly defeating the *coup d'état* in favour of Lady Jane Grey, succeeded to the throne. Henry VIII's elder daughter had never made any secret of her devout Catholicism. Indeed she had suffered for it repeatedly, both at her father's hands and the hands of her brother's ministers. She made no secret either of the fact that she believed herself to have been specially called by God to save her unhappy and deluded subjects from the forces of darkness.

There can be no question about Mary's sincerity, but her gallant rearguard action was foredoomed to failure. Had she been content merely to restore the Anglo-Catholic settlement of her father's day, she might well have succeeded. The Protestant left-wingers, although noisy and well-organised, represented as yet only a small minority of the nation, the great bulk of which would have been glad enough to return to the more seemly ritual of the Henrician Church – as in fact was demonstrated by the Parliament of October 1553. Unfortunately this could not satisfy one of Mary's uncompromising spirit. The following year it seemed as if she had won her victory when, on 30 November, England was officially absolved from the sin of schism and received back into the bosom of Mother Church. The Edwardian ecclesiastical legislation had already gone, the married clergy had been ordered to put away their wives and Mass was again being celebrated in all its old panoply; now the mediaeval heresy laws were revived once more and all the Henrician statutes denying papal authority repealed.

But Mary's victory proved a hollow one. The contemporary habit of obedience to the sovereign's will was strong. It was not strong enough to persuade any of those who had profited from the plunder of the Reformation to part with an inch or a pennyworth of their loot. Watertight safeguards for the holders of Church property had had to be devised before Parliament was prepared to accept the Pope's forgiveness. Worse than this, it soon became depressingly clear that the Queen was losing the battle for hearts and minds. Many prominent Protestants found it prudent to go abroad to wait for better times but many others, in less fortunate circumstances, were showing a disconcerting readiness to suffer for their faith. Serious heresy hunting began in February 1555 and continued spasmodically until Mary's death; by which time nearly three hundred men and women, nearly all of them humble people and nearly all of them from London and the south-eastern counties, had been burnt alive.

It is often predicated that the persecution of a minority for the sake of an ideology is invariably a self-defeating exercise; this is a fallacy. There have been instances in history when persecution has been extremely successful. In order to succeed, however, such persecution must be carried out with utter conviction and single-minded ruthlessness. It must also have at least passive support from the bulk of the population in the country concerned. The Marian persecution fulfilled neither of these conditions and therefore had the inevitable effect of strengthening the persecuted. The Edwardian reformers, hitherto quite widely regarded as a loud-mouthed gang of troublemakers, grew immeasurably in dignity and stature and, in Bishop Latimer's immortal words to Ridley as they stood bound to the stake in the dry ditch outside the walls of Oxford, they did indeed light such a candle, by God's grace, in England as never was put out.

In the sixteenth century violent and painful death was too much of a commonplace to be regarded with the same revulsion as it is today, but on those people who witnessed the fortitude of their neighbours – poor widows, journeymen and apprentices, agricultural labourers, weavers, clothworkers, artisans and tradesmen – dying in agony for what they believed to be God's truth, the burnings made an impression disproportionate to the numbers who actually suffered. From the ashes of the Marian martyrs rose the phoenix of that bitter, ineradicable fear and hatred of Rome which had begun to spread its wings even before John Foxe published his famous best-seller, and which was to brood over the national consciousness for centuries to come.

Although public sympathy for Mary's victims was immediate, it has also to be remembered that for every Protestant who took his conscience to the more congenial climate of Germany or Switzerland, or who lit a candle of martyrdom in the local market-place, there were many thousands more who stayed at home, going about their business, obeying the law and keeping their opinions to themselves. The most notable of these conformers was the heir to the throne. During Edward's reign Elizabeth had come in for a good deal of praise from Protestant divines who commented approvingly on her 'maiden shamefastness' and devotion to godly learning; and, as the Holy Roman Emperor's ambassador reported rather sourly on the occasion of one of her visits to Court, 'she was most honourably received by the Council who acted thus in order to show the people how much glory belongs to her who has embraced the new religion and is become a very great lady.' Elizabeth, however, was not the stuff of which religious martyrs are made. After little more than a token show of resistance she had asked for instruction in the Catholic faith and was soon accompanying the Queen to Mass. She unblinkingly assured her anxious sister that 'she went to Mass and did as she did because her conscience prompted and moved her to it; that she went of her own free will and without fear, hypocrisy or dissimulation'. While she was living under restraint at Woodstock, her custodian reported that she had received 'the most comfortable sacrament', and after her release she had joined the rest of the Court in a three-day fast to qualify for indulgence from Rome.

To the outward eye Elizabeth's Catholicism was difficult to fault, and yet somehow nobody had ever believed for a moment in her conversion. Count de Feria, the King of Spain's ambassador who arrived in England in the autumn of 1558, had an interview with her a few days before Mary's death and reported to Philip that he was afraid the new Queen would be unreliable over religion. She appeared to favour those councillors who were suspected of heresy and he was told that all her ladies were similarly inclined. In fact, it seemed to the ambassador that there was not a traitor or heretic in the country who had not risen, as if from the tomb, to welcome her accession.

This jubilation was not confined to England. In such centres of advanced Protestant thought as Strasbourg, Frankfurt, Zurich, Basle and Geneva, the English exiles were already packing their bags preparatory to returning home to assist in rebuilding the walls of Jerusalem. To these enthusiasts the removal of Mary Tudor came as a sign from heaven comparable to the deliverance of the children of Israel from Egyptian bondage, and Sir Anthony Cooke, William Cecil's father-in-law and once tutor to Edward VI, wrote hopefully from Strasbourg on 8 December to the Swiss reformer Heinrich Bullinger: 'If the Queen, mindful of the great mercy she has received, will but place her confidence in God; if she will daily say unto the Lord, Thou art my fortress, my rock, and my refuge, there will neither be wanting to herself the spirit of a Judith or a Deborah, nor wisdom to her councillors, nor strength to her army.'

De Feria in London continued to take a gloomy view of the situation, and on 14 December he told Philip that the Queen was every day standing up against religion more openly. The kingdom, he wrote, was entirely in the hands of young folks, heretics and traitors. The old people and Catholics were dissatisfied but dared not open their lips. Elizabeth seemed incomparably more feared than her sister and gave her orders and had her way as absolutely as her father had done. Certainly, remembering some of King Henry's ways, this hardly looked a good augury for Rome.

Nevertheless, in spite of de Feria's pessimism, Elizabeth was in no hurry to show her hand and refused to be drawn about her intentions by either side. Shortly after the accession an amnesty was granted to some classes of offenders and a bold courtier reminded the Queen that there were four or five more innocent men in prison, 'the four evangelists and the apostle Paul, who have long been shut up in the prison of an unknown tongue'. The prisoners would have to be asked first if they wanted to be let out, retorted Elizabeth. When de Feria took the first available opportunity to beg her to be very careful about religious affairs, she answered demurely 'that it would indeed be bad for her to forget God who had been so good to her', and with this 'equivocal' reply the ambassador had to be content.

A number of Protestants had been included in the newly constituted Privy Council and Protestant influence was growing in Court and government circles, but the weeks passed and England remained officially a Catholic country, in full communion with Rome, with the doctrines and rites of the Church still being carefully observed. There were certain obvious advantages to be derived from keeping it that way. The Pope would be only too pleased to rectify the little matter of the Queen's illegitimacy in return for assurances of her continued orthodoxy. The menace of Mary Stuart would be effectually neutralised and England assured of the friendship and protection of Spain. Yet it seemed unthinkable that Elizabeth, idol of the Protestant Londoners, who owed her very existence to the English Reformation, could be contemplating such a course. There is, in fact, no evidence that she ever did contemplate it.

The grass within the Roman fold might look temptingly green, but Elizabeth was far too astute a politician not to sense the quagmire which lay beneath it: even if it had been in her nature to be content to acquiesce in the undoing of her father's work, to accept her throne at the Pope's hands, and to allow her country to sink to becoming a client state of the Hapsburg empire.

She gave the world its first definite clue as to the course she meant to follow on Christmas Day 1558 by sending a message to Owen Oglethorpe, Bishop of Carlisle, ordering him not to elevate the Host at High Mass. The bishop, reported de Feria, answered stoutly 'that Her Majesty was mistress of his body and life, but not of his conscience, and accordingly she heard the Mass until after the gospel, when she rose and left, so as not to be present at the canon and adoration of the Host which the bishop elevated as usual'. The Queen's next move was to issue a proclamation forbidding all preaching and teaching, thus silencing hotheads on both sides and putting an end to 'unfruitful dispute in matters of religion'. The proclamation laid down that the gospel, epistle and ten commandments were to be recited in the vernacular 'without exposition or addition'. There was to be no other 'public prayer, rite, or ceremony in the church, but that which is already used and by law received; or the common litany used at this present in Her Majesty's own Chapel, and the Lord's Prayer and the Creed in English; until consultation may be had by parliament, by Her Majesty, and her three estates of this realm, for the better conciliation and accord of such causes as at this present are moved in matters and ceremonies of religion.' After this it was obvious that the forthcoming session of Parliament would be a crucial one.

But even before Parliament met, the Queen had given further and unmistakable signs of what her policy was likely to be. During her triumphant procession through the City on the day before the Coronation she was presented with an English Bible which she ostentatiously kissed and clasped to her breast. The Coronation ceremony itself was performed by Owen Oglethorpe – the only bishop who could be persuaded to officiate – and again Elizabeth withdrew before the elevation of the Host. Neither did she receive communion, which was administered in one kind only according to the Catholic rite.

On 25 January, after an early dinner, the Queen went in state to Westminster for the opening of Parliament wearing a robe of crimson velvet, with an ermine cape 'like the one worn by the Doge of Venice', and on her head 'a cap of beaten gold covered with very fine oriental pearls'. 'On arriving at Westminster Abbey,' wrote an Italian observer, 'the Abbot, robed pontifically, with all his monks in procession, each of them having a lighted torch in his hand, received her as usual, giving her first of all incense and holy water; and when Her Majesty saw the monks who accompanied her with the torches, she said, "Away with those torches, for we see very well"; and her choristers singing the litany in English, she was accompanied to the high altar under her canopy. Thereupon, Dr Cox, a married priest who has hitherto been beyond the sea, ascended the pulpit and preached the sermon, in which, after saying many things freely against the monks, proving by his arguments that they ought to be persecuted and punished by Her Majesty, as they were impious for having caused the burning of so many poor innocents under pretext of heresy, on which he expatiated greatly; he then commenced praising Her Majesty, saying among other things that God had given her this dignity to the end that she might no longer allow or tolerate the past iniquities; exhorting her to destroy the images of the saints, the churches, the monasteries, and all other things dedicated to divine worship; proving by his own arguments that it is very great impiety and idolatry to endure them; and saying many other things against the Christian religion.' Dr Cox thundered on for an hour and a half and it is scarcely surprising that the Spanish ambassador should have reported on 31 January that the Catholics were 'very fearful of the measures to be taken in this Parliament'.

With the benefit of four hundred years of hindsight, Elizabeth's actions during the first few months of 1559 have an air of inevitability about them. But in the political climate of the time it seemed an astonishingly bold, even foolhardy proceeding for a young, inexperienced Queen whose title to her throne would not stand up to too close an examination, deliberately to cut off her small, ramshackle kingdom once again from the community of Christendom. The Continental Catholic Church was now beginning to shake off its late mediaeval torpor and was gathering its still formidable resources to combat the creeping plague of heresy. Once those two colossi France and Spain had settled their differences, England might well find herself alone in a ring of hostile powers.

Elizabeth was playing a dangerous game, but national unity and national independence were prizes worth gambling for and this was just the kind of diplomatic poker she excelled at. Besides, she could feel reasonably confident that political considerations would continue to outweigh Philip's crusading fervour. It had always been a cardinal principle of Hapsburg foreign policy to maintain an alliance with England. Philip's father had, after all, swallowed a quite remarkable number of insults from Elizabeth's father to safeguard his maritime communications with the Netherlands. Even when peace was concluded between France and Spain the old mutual distrust would remain – it might even be possible to foster it – and both countries had enough problems of their own to keep them occupied at home with any luck for some little time to come.

All the same, Elizabeth knew she was trying Philip pretty high. Since his marriage with Mary Tudor he had felt a special responsibility for the English Catholics, and de Feria reminded him at frequent intervals that they were looking to him for protection. It would also be embarrassing at the least for one who liked to regard himself as the eldest son of the Church to be seen to be openly condoning heresy, however compelling his worldly reasons. Elizabeth quite saw the King of Spain's difficulty and did her best to make things easier for him by leaving, or at any rate appearing to leave, the door of reconciliation if not open, at least ajar. She had refused his half-hearted offer of marriage, no doubt greatly to his relief, but she allowed him to suggest his equally orthodox cousins, the Austrian Archdukes Ferdinand and Charles, as possible alternatives, and she continued to move with circumspection over the religious settlement.

She told de Feria on one occasion that she wanted to restore religion as her father had left it and became 'so disturbed and excited' that the ambassador at last said soothingly that he did not consider she was heretical. Another time she declared that she did not mean to call herself Head of the Church. On yet another occasion she said she wanted the Lutheran Augustanean or Augsburg confession to be maintained in her realm, and when de Feria marshalled arguments to dissuade her, she shifted her ground again, telling him that it would not be the Augsburg confession but something else like it. According to de Feria, she then went on to say that she herself differed very little from the Catholics, 'as she believed that God was in the sacrament of the Eucharist, and only dissented from three or four things in the Mass'.

One way and another the Queen was contriving to create enough uncertainty about her intentions, both religious and matrimonial, to give Spain an excuse for staying friendly, although de Feria was personally convinced that she was going to perdition and complained mournfully about the difficulties he was experiencing in negotiating with a woman so naturally changeable. Philip, however, continued to be nervous of possible French machinations and while de Feria lost no opportunity of trying unsuccessfully to impress Elizabeth with a proper sense of her dependence on his master, his instructions remained doggedly conciliatory. The King was for some time to cling pathetically to the belief that his unpredictable sister-in-law could be controlled if she could only be persuaded into marriage with one of his archducal cousins.

Meanwhile Parliament had embarked on the work of a stormy and momentous session. The first measure introduced by the government was a bill confirming the Queen's title. Unlike her sister in similar circumstances, Elizabeth did not take the trouble to have her birth re-legitimised. Advised by Nicholas Bacon, she took her stand firmly on the 1544 Act of Succession and on the principle 'that the Crown once worn quite taketh away all defects whatsoever'. Another government measure was a bill restoring clerical first fruits and tenths to the Crown. These had first been annexed from the Pope by Henry VIII and subsequently renounced by Mary. The bill made rapid progress in the Lords, although the spiritual peers all voted against it – an unwelcome portent of the unco-operative attitude to be adopted by the Marian bishops. On 9 February the Commons began the first reading of a bill 'to restore the supremacy of the Church of England to the Crown of the realm', and it was at this point that the government began to encounter serious opposition to its plans.

During the two months which had passed since her accession, Elizabeth had been presented with several detailed memoranda of advice on religious matters. All except one – the anonymous 'Device for the Alteration of Religion' which urged the immediate setting-up of a national Protestant Church and the avoidance of 'a cloaked papistry or a mingle-mangle' – were in favour of caution. The lawyer Richard Goodrich, much as he hated Rome, was even prepared to accept the retention of papal supremacy for a time. It is now generally believed that the Queen had made up her mind to proceed by stages – thus following the precedents set by her father and sister – and that to begin with she had intended to go no further than an Act of Supremacy, in which a clause permitting communion in both kinds for the laity was to be inserted as a sop to Protestant opinion. A Catholic order of service would thus have been maintained, at any rate until the next Parliament, by which time those bishops who refused to take the Oath of Supremacy could have been removed and foreign reaction assessed more accurately.

If this was, in fact, the Queen's intention, she and her advisers had seriously misjudged the mood of the House of Commons in general, and the determination and tactical skill of the returned Marian exiles in particular. There was a caucus of at least a dozen of these earnest individuals sitting in the Commons led by Anthony Cooke, Nicholas Bacon and Francis Knollys – all men of ability and influence and all impatient of playing politics with the Word of God.

'We are now busy in parliament about expelling the tyranny of the Pope and restoring the royal authority and re-establishing true religion,' wrote Anthony Cooke to Peter Martyr on 12 February. Busy they certainly were. When the Supremacy bill emerged from its committee stage it had been virtually redrafted. Although the actual text has not survived, it would appear from other evidence that the second Edwardian Act of Uniformity, the 1552 Prayer Book and the Act allowing the clergy to marry – a matter of close personal interest to the *émigré* Protestant divines, most of whom had wives – were all resuscitated and provision made to stiffen the penalties for refusing the Oath of Supremacy. The bill in its amended form was sent up to the Lords on 25 February and there followed a fortnight's pause, during which time presumably the Queen and Council considered what action to take.

Elizabeth was not yet prepared to climb down. Like all her family she strongly resented being hustled, and at this stage she was still apparently hoping to move gradually towards a far more conservative settlement than that envisaged by her obstreperous House of Commons. At all events, the bill was given a second reading by the Lords on 13 March and then went into committee, where it was stripped of its amendments and restored more or less to its original form. Although this was undoubtedly done on instructions from above, it was the House of Lords and especially the bishops who got the blame. 'The Queen,' wrote John Jewel, another returned exile, 'though she openly favours our cause, yet is wonderfully afraid of allowing innovations.... She is, however, prudently and firmly and piously following up her purpose, though somewhat more slowly than we could wish.'

The militants in the Commons did not wait for the emasculated Supremacy bill to be returned to them. On 17 March they launched a counter-attack, introducing a measure of their own 'that no persons shall be punished for using the religion used in King Edward's time'. This demand for non-conformity ran directly counter to government policy and its sponsors could scarcely have expected to get it through the Lords. It seems to have been intended both as a propaganda gesture and a warning to the government of the strength of left-wing feeling in the Lower House. Outside Parliament Protestant propagandists were keeping up an active campaign against official pusillanimity. According to the Mantuan envoy, they were 'clever, loquacious and fervent, both in preaching and in composing and printing squibs and lampoons, or ballads as they entitle them, which are sold publicly'. The shocked Italian considered these of 'so horrible and abominable a description' that he wondered their authors did not perish by act of God. The Almighty, however, was to remain strictly neutral in the contest being carried on in his name.

Nevertheless, as Easter approached and with it the expected dissolution of Parliament, it began to look very much as though the activists were going to lose this particular round. The pressure group in the Commons was not yet prepared to risk open defiance of the government, and anyway if they had refused to accept royal supremacy without a Protestant service, they would have been left with continued papal supremacy, and that was not to be contemplated. Accordingly they passed the bill as re-amended and by 22 March it was ready for the royal assent. The Queen had intended to go to Westminster on Good Friday, 24 March, and de Feria noted with some satisfaction that the heretics were very downcast. Then, at the last moment, Elizabeth changed her mind. Instead of ending the session, she adjourned Parliament until 3 April and thus dramatically foreshortened the whole course of her religious policy.

Exactly what had brought about this apparent *volte-face* is not known, but several reasons can be surmised. The reformers had powerful allies on the Council and no doubt some pretty intensive lobbying had been going on at Court. The unexpectedly aggressive unity displayed by the House of Commons had probably also led to second thoughts about the political wisdom of leaving the question of public worship more or less in abeyance. Added to this, the intransigent behaviour of the bishops (who had voted against royal supremacy in the Lords) made it plain that the government was going to have to rely on the ministers among the returning exiles to lead their reorientated Church. Another important contributory factor was the news which had reached London on 19 March that the English Commissioners had concluded a reasonably satisfactory peace treaty with France at Câteau Cambresis. These were all solid, practical considerations in helping the Queen to come to a decision, but Elizabeth possessed an almost uncanny flair for gauging the drift of public opinion. Once she had sensed that the country at large wanted the matter settled and would be ready to accept a moderate form of Protestantism, it seems as if she made up her mind to act.

During the Easter recess a public disputation was staged between a contingent of Protestant leaders – all except one returned exiles, all except one future bishops – and a contingent of Catholic bishops and theologians. This disputation was a propaganda exercise pure and simple; its object, according to John Jewel, being to deprive the Catholic bishops of any excuse for saying they had been put down only by the power and authority of the law – in other words, that they had never been given a chance to put their case. The result was a foregone conclusion. The Catholics refused to accept the conditions of debate imposed upon them, as the government had known they would. The proceedings came to an abrupt end and the Protestants were able to make useful capital out of the apparent obstinacy and obscurantism of the Catholics. However, when Parliament reassembled, the Queen made it clear that although she had yielded in principle, she was not prepared to go all the way with the radical party. The Supremacy bill was now redrafted for a third time.

Elizabeth had decided, just as she told de Feria she would,

not to accept the title of Supreme Head of the Church. She was instead to be styled Supreme Governor – a fine distinction possibly, but it was nevertheless a rejection of Henry VIII's caesaro-papalism and came as a relief to radicals and conservatives alike. Masculine prejudice did not find it easy to reconcile the idea of a woman occupying such a position with the views forcibly expressed by St Paul; neither did Elizabeth's own tastes run to the sort of personal intervention in matters of dogma and ritual which her father had found so stimulating. Not that she intended to give her bishops a free hand. Her influence was to make itself decisively felt, but she preferred to exercise it indirectly.

The Supremacy bill in its final form had a relatively smooth passage through both Houses of Parliament; it was over the new bill for the Uniformity of Common Prayer and Service in the Church and Administration of the Sacraments, that the last round in the battle for the Elizabethan settlement was fought. Again, when the Queen told de Feria that she wanted the confession of Augsburg, or something like it, maintained in her realm and that she herself believed in a Real Presence, there is every likelihood that she was speaking the plain truth. (It is ironical that so often when Elizabeth was being most sincere, she was taken least seriously.) She had after all been brought up in the High Anglicanism of the latter part of her father's reign; she had been educated by the Cambridge humanists and strongly influenced by the intellectual Lutheranism of her last step-mother, Katherine Parr. Elizabeth may have been a politique to her fingers' ends, but that is no justification for saying she had no religious convictions.

A Protestant order of service grounded on the 1549 Prayer Book and retaining some at least of the externals of Catholic practice would not only have chimed in with the Queen's personal preferences, but would also have opened up a prospect of alliances with Lutheran states abroad and compromise with conservatives at home. Unfortunately for such hopes, the inescapable fact remained that the Church of England could not be made a going concern without the active co-operation and assistance of the returning radical exiles, and they would accept nothing less than the 1552 Prayer Book. Many of them, indeed, would have liked to move still further to the left. During the diaspora they had had the opportunity of seeing at first-hand some of the 'best-reformed' Churches abroad – that is those modelled on the Swiss pattern – and they had all drunk more or less deeply of the heady waters of Calvinism. Fortunately for the government's peace of mind, the 'wolves' from Geneva itself did not, in fact, arrive home in time to take any direct part in the settlement. Elizabeth would certainly not have tolerated any attempt to impose a system which would seriously have undermined the principle of royal supremacy. There was no room in her Church for ministers of religion claiming a mandate straight from heaven; neither had she forgiven John Knox, that sturdy disciple of Calvin, for his singularly tactless remarks on 'the monstrous regimen of women'.

When the Queen agreed to negotiate on the basis of the second Edwardian Prayer Book, she had gone every inch of the way she intended to go and still hoped to salvage something from the wreck of her original plans. In the event, she won several small but significant victories. The phrase: 'The body of our Lord Jesus Christ, which was given for thee, preserve thy body and soul into everlasting life', taken from the 1549 Prayer Book, was prefaced to the administration of the communion in the new liturgy, thus allowing a certain amount of latitude in eucharistic belief. The so-called 'Black Rubric' of 1552 which explicitly denied the existence of a Real Presence was deleted, as was the offensive reference to 'the tyranny of the Bishop of Rome'. Elizabeth also insisted on the inclusion of a proviso concerning the retention of church ornaments and vestments which was to lead to a controversy of quite remarkable bitterness. But this lay in the future. When Parliament finally dispersed on 8 May 1559 a compromise had been hammered out, not – as has sometimes been said – between Catholicism and Protestantism, but rather between the Queen's and the Commons' conceptions of Protestantism.

As is usually the way with compromises, no one was particularly pleased. Elizabeth had been outmanoeuvred by the revolutionary tactics of the clique in the Commons and was irritated and alarmed by their success – certainly she was to resist all further attempts at encroachment by the left-wing with bulldog tenacity. The left-wingers, for their part, felt they had achieved little more than a 'leaden mediocrity'. John Jewel in particular regretted the survival of so much of 'the scenic apparatus of divine worship'. He was saddened that those in authority should have clung to the old-fashioned notion that 'the Christian religion could not exist without something tawdry', although he loyally excepted the 'wise and religious' Queen from this reproach. Foreign Catholic observers, on the other hand, did not hesitate to voice their conviction that all questions of religion in the island kingdom would henceforward go to ruin. De Feria's informants told him that everything was now even worse than it had been in King Edward's time, and he wrote to Philip in a fit of petulance that England had fallen into the hands of a woman who was a daughter of the devil, and the greatest scoundrels and heretics in the land.

What the people of England thought about their new Church is more difficult to discover, but all the evidence points to the conclusion that the silent majority accepted it with a placidity bordering on indifference. A cynical foreigner had once remarked that the English would turn Mohammedan if commanded by their prince, and it seems fair to postulate that a nation which had to all intents and purposes been content to change its religion three times in the space of thirty years was not unduly preoccupied with the quality of its spiritual life. The committed Protestants, whose vigour and efficient organisation did so much to gain their party its victory in 1559, still represented a very small section of the total population – at a generous estimate the Marian martyrs and exiles put together only account for some 1200 souls. The fact that their strength was concentrated in London, the south-east and the great seaports – the most prosperous and forward-looking parts of the country – had of course helped considerably in the conduct of their campaign. So had the undoubted fact that the Marian counter-reformation had failed to kindle any spark of enthusiasm amongst the laity as a whole. This seems to have been very largely due to the ineptitude with which it was presented and carried out. Mary Tudor's politically disastrous Spanish marriage, coinciding as it did with one of England's periodic attacks of xenophobia, had polluted the whole of her regime with the taint of foreign interference and oppression. Fairly or unfairly, Roman Catholicism was not to lose that taint for centuries.

There were, of course, committed Catholics in both Houses of Parliament, but lacking leadership or active support in the country they could make little headway against their opponents in the Commons. In the Lords, the depleted ranks of Mary's bishops – notably Heath of York and Scott of Chester – fought a losing battle with courage and dignity, but without government backing their position had been hopeless from the start.

All the same, even after the Acts of Supremacy and Uniformity the situation remained fluid and the lines had not yet been drawn. Despite the Queen's disappointing lack of godly zeal, the radicals had by no means given up hope of improving and consolidating their position. Despite her repeated protestations of reluctance, the conservatives were optimistic that she would soon be marrying a Catholic. No reasonable man ungifted by second sight could have been expected to foresee the astonishing epic of the Virgin Queen, or that the Church of England – which did not look an especially sturdy infant – would prove so tenacious of life. In 1559 neither side was willing or able to push matters to a crisis, but equally neither side believed for a moment that the final victory had been won.

CHAPTER TWO

There is nothing to be done

'There is nothing to be done, but everything to endure, whatsoever God may will.'
Nicholas Heath, London, May 1559

THE ease with which the English Catholics surrendered to the forces of reform has long been a source of sorrow to Catholic historians. It even came as something of a surprise to the Protestant reformers. 'The ranks of the papists have fallen almost of their own accord,' wrote John Jewel with a touch of awe. At first sight, the apparently spontaneous collapse of the Old Faith does seem a little odd, especially in view of the fact that de Feria, never one for looking on the bright side, had told King Philip in March 1559, 'I am sure that religion will not fall, because the Catholic party is two thirds larger than the other.' But in another dispatch, written two months later, the ambassador provides two important clues to the mystery. 'The Catholics are in a great majority in the country,' he declared, 'and if the leading men in it were not of so small account things would have turned out differently. It is quite impossible that the present state of affairs can last.'

The situation of the Catholics in 1559 was, in fact, not unlike that of a once-great political party which, having held office for generations, suffers an overwhelming defeat at the polls and retreats exhausted to lick its wounds in decent privacy while waiting for better days to return. Looking back over the upheavals of the past three decades, it was not unreasonable to assume that better days would return. After all, none of the three previous religious revolutions had survived the monarchs who had presided over them. The style of government in the sixteenth century depended to an enormous extent on the personality of the sovereign – especially in England with its tradition of a strong monarchy – and life in the sixteenth century was notoriously uncertain. Elizabeth might die. (She very nearly did die of smallpox in 1562.) If she lived, she would soon be getting married – her frequently expressed preference for a single life being very properly ignored by all sensible men – and when she married it was difficult to see how she could avoid choosing a Catholic consort.

Since the death of Edward Courtenay in Padua four years earlier, there was no Englishman of sufficiently exalted rank to make him acceptable to his fellows, and abroad there was as yet no Protestant ruling house which could be compared in importance with the English one. Mary Tudor had indignantly refused to demean herself by marrying a subject and it seemed unlikely that her younger sister would have any less an idea of her dignity. In one of her frequent conversations with de Feria on the subject he reported that she spoke like a woman who would only accept a great prince.

Elizabeth was very well aware of her value in the international marriage market and zestfully exploited the advantages attached to being the most eligible spinster in Europe, turning the apparent disability of her sex into a diplomatic weapon which for the next twenty years she was to wield with deliberate, ruthless feminine guile. However, it is scarcely surprising that her male contemporaries should have failed to recognise such an unnatural and unwomanly purpose, and during the early sixties the Catholics in England were able to cling to the comforting conviction that the facts of life would soon be catching up with the Queen. Her 'Catholic husband' (the Archduke Charles of Austria remained for some time the most favoured candidate) would then take up the reins of government while Elizabeth was occupied with her real business of bearing children.

From the point of view of the English Catholics in the early sixties, though, it was fatally unfortunate that they possessed no leaders with the foresight to realise that time might not after all be on their side, and who might have rallied the faithful to resist during that crucial period before the new national Church had become embedded in the national life. By the early seventies, when such leaders did begin to come forward, it was too late. This absence of initiative illustrates perhaps more clearly than anything else just how far Catholicism had decayed in mid-sixteenth century England. On the other hand, of course, it also saved England from the religious wars which were to ravage France.

Due in large measure to the ruthless policies pursued by her father and grandfather, Elizabeth had no over-mighty Catholic subjects to contend with. The Duke of Norfolk, England's premier nobleman and only duke, although sympathetic towards Catholicism was officially a Protestant; besides, Thomas Howard, while commanding the affection and respect of his friends, was no leader of men. In 1559, therefore, the only focal point to which the Catholic laity could turn for guidance and inspiration was the hierarchy appointed by Mary Tudor. But here again, although the surviving Marian bishops were, in the opinion of Count de Feria, excellent men who had borne themselves bravely and piously, there was no outstanding personality among them Their titular head, Reginald Pole, Cardinal Archbishop of Canterbury and the chief instrument of Mary's counter-reformation, had died on the same day as his Queen – as though to emphasise the fact that an era had ended. Even if he had lived, it is more than doubtful whether Pole, a frail, blue-blooded, middle-aged scholar who had spent most of his life in exile and understood the English people as little as Mary had done, could have influenced the course of events.

After his death, the leadership of the Catholic party had devolved on Nicholas Heath, but no crusading fire burnt in the veins of the Archbishop of York. Before de Feria left England in May 1559, he had visited Heath to ask his advice on what ought to be done for the cause of religion. 'There is nothing to be done,' the archbishop is said to have replied, 'but everything to endure, whatsoever God may will.' This may have shown a very proper spirit of Christian resignation. It was emphatically not the spirit which wins battles for souls. Nicholas Heath had been Mary's Lord Chancellor – the statesman whose prompt action had secured Parliamentary recognition of Elizabeth's title on the day of her sister's death. He would do nothing which might endanger the peace and unity of the nation, but he would not compromise his conscience by subscribing to the Oath of Supremacy or attending the new Protestant service. Nor would any of his brother bishops who were all, according to de Feria, firmly and steadfastly determined to die for their faith.

While Elizabeth had no intention of obliging any would-be candidates for martyrdom, their lordships' attitude was naturally a disappointment – especially as several of them had proved pliant enough under her father and brother – and the government seems to have made some effort to persuade them to change their minds. At the end of June, Alvaro de Quadra, de Feria's successor at the Spanish embassy, reported that five bishops had been summoned before the Council and proffered the Oath 'with great promises and threats'. Another attempt was made a few days later, after which they were released on bail of £500 each and ordered not to leave London until further notice. The support of even a few of the old hierarchy would have been valuable in giving the Anglican Church a broader base and in helping to undermine right-wing opposition, but the Queen could not afford to wait for long – her laws had to be seen to be obeyed – and by the end of the summer all the Catholic bishops (with the exception of Kitchin of Llandaff who conformed) had been removed from office.

Opinions as to the harshness or otherwise of their subsequent treatment differ according to point of view. John Strype, the eighteenth-century Protestant historian, observes that they were never burdened with any capital pains, 'nor yet deprived of any of their goods or proper livelihoods, but only removed from their ecclesiastical offices, which they would not exercise according to the laws'. On the other side, the contemporary Catholic writer Edward Rishton insisted gloomily that after being deprived of their dignities and 'committed either to prison or to the custody of divers persons', the bishops were all worn out by the weariness of their miserable treatment. The truth, as is usually the case, seems to have lain somewhere between these two extremes. Mary's bishops, together with a number of other senior members of the Catholic clergy, all suffered some degree of financial loss, personal incon-venience, humiliation and loss of liberty; but it also has to be remembered that they were all disobeying the law of the land, and there are indications that each case was decided more or less on its merits.

Nicholas Heath, a public figure respected in both camps, was allowed 'after a little trouble' (three years in the Tower to be exact) to retire to his house at Chobham in Surrey where he lived un-molested, even, it is said, receiving occasional friendly visits from Elizabeth herself. 'An example of gentleness never matched in Queen Mary's days,' remarks Strype with an air of righteousness. That rugged individual Edmund Bonner, Bishop of London, was a different proposition. Bonner's enthusiasm for the pursuit of heretics in the previous reign had earned him an unpleasant, though prob-ably rather exaggerated reputation for cruelty even among Catholics. As a result, he was so hated by the Londoners that he ran the risk of being lynched when he appeared in public. In the spring of 1560 he was committed to the old Marshalsea prison in Southwark where, although Strype assures us he 'lived daintily' and had the use of the garden and orchards when he was minded to walk abroad and take the air, he stayed until his death nine years later.

Owen Oglethorpe, Ralph Bayne of Coventry and Lichfield, and Cuthbert Tunstal of Durham all died before the end of 1559 of an apoplexy, the stone, and old age respectively. John White of Winchester, who had got into trouble very early on for preaching a provocative sermon at Queen Mary's funeral and would needs preach in his 'Romish pontifical vestments', spent some months in the Tower, but was released when he became ill, and died of a quartan ague at his sister's house in Hampshire in January 1560. Most of the other bishops did varying terms in gaol for 'obstinately' absenting themselves from public worship and actively opposing the new dispensation. Thomas Thirlby of Ely, 'a person of nature affable' but who also manifested an unfortunate tendency to preach against the Reformation, was later released into the custody of Dr Parker, Elizabeth's first Archbishop of Canterbury, and remained an involuntary house guest at Lambeth for ten years. Thomas Watson of Lincoln, described by Camden as being 'learned in deep divinity but surly with an austere gravity' and by Strype as 'altogether a sour and morose man', survived until 1584 but spent the rest of his life either in prison or in the custody of one or other of the new bishops. Released for a while in 1574, he came under suspicion of being 'too conversant' with 'certain Romish emissaries' and was sent to the concentration camp which had been set up to house refractory Catholics at Wisbech Castle near Ely.

For the rest, Gilbert Bourne of Bath and Wells ended his days with his friend Dean Carewe. James Turberville of Exeter, 'an honest gentleman but a simple bishop', was restricted to certain limits after his release from prison but allowed to live in his own home. David Poole of Peterborough, 'an ancient grave person and quiet subject', never actually went to prison but he, too, was ordered to remain within a three-mile limit of London and the suburbs. Cuthbert Scott, 'a rigid man', spent four years in the Fleet gaol and then skipped his bail and escaped to the Low Countries. Richard Pate of Worcester also went abroad, as did Thomas Goldwell of St Asaph. Goldwell, who had once shared Reginald Pole's exile, died in Rome in 1585, the last survivor of the old hierarchy.

The sixteenth century was not a comfortable epoch for anyone in holy orders and bishops, by the very nature of their office, found themselves in the front line of battle. Nearly all the Marian bishops had known previous experience of deprivation, imprisonment, exile and anxiety. All of them had done the state some service during the course of their careers, and when the final test came they were no longer young men: Heath and Bonner were both nearly sixty, Cuthbert Tunstal was well into his eighties, Thomas Thirlby over fifty. Their steadfastness, therefore, does them the more credit, but given the climate of the times and remembering what had happened to such conscientious objectors as Fisher of Rochester and the monks of the Charterhouse under Henry VIII – not to mention the fate of the Protestant bishops under Mary – it is difficult to agree that they were treated with particular severity.

1559 was a busy year. While the cases of the individual bishops were still pending, the government was pressing ahead with its plans for establishing the Church of England. The new Prayer Book came into use officially on Midsummer Day and by August a series of visitations had been organised, the Queen's Commissioners setting out on a tour of all the dioceses of England and Wales to enforce nationwide obedience to the provisions of the Acts of Supremacy and Uniformity, as well as the newly issued Royal Injunctions which dealt, among other things, with such important matters as the replacing of stone altars by communion tables. The commissioners were also supplied with a list of fifty-six 'Articles of Inquiry' – an alarmingly detailed questionnaire covering every aspect of clerical character and conduct.

In view of the pious example set by their former episcopate, it cannot be said that the rank and file of the clergy put up a very impressive defence of their faith. A great deal of patient research and scholarship has been devoted to this subject, but again conclusions tend to differ quite widely according to point of view. Catholic historians estimate that between six and seven hundred beneficed clergy out of a total of eight thousand were deprived of their livings for refusing to accept the new order. Protestants, beginning with Camden, put the number of non-conformers at between two and three hundred out of a total of nine thousand, although John Jewel maintained that 'if inveterate obstinacy was found anywhere, it was altogether among the priests'. In the absence of reliable statistics (it is not even known for certain how many priests there were in England and Wales in 1559) the discrepancy between the two estimates is never likely to be satisfactorily resolved.

What is certain, however, is that the overwhelming majority of parish priests did conform, at least outwardly, and really this is scarcely surprising. They were most of them poor men and they wanted to eat. They had become accustomed by this time to being told what to do by the central government, whatever its complexion, and their standard of education was generally low, a fact vigorously bemoaned by the new hierarchy. Nor was illiteracy the worst of the shortcomings uncovered by the Visitors. According to Strype, not only were superstition, absenteeism and corruption rife, but many parsons, vicars and curates had got into the habit of haunting taverns and alehouses, giving themselves to drinking, rioting and playing at unlawful games. Another frequent accusation made against incumbents ('almost in every parish' says Strype) concerned fornication, keeping other women besides their wives and having bastard children.

No doubt this was a time for the settling of scores and the Visitors also heard the complaints of many clergymen 'that had been turned out of their livings under Queen Mary for being married, whom they restored'. Queen Elizabeth never became entirely reconciled to the idea of clerical marriage and popular prejudice was against it, but the reformers got their way – although it was laid down that in future a would-be parson's wife must be honest, sober and approved by the bishop and two justices of the peace. What with hardly knowing from one year to the next if they were legally married or not and having to put up with disparaging remarks from old-fashioned parishioners, the pioneer generation of vicarage ladies led a precarious and harassed existence.

In spite of the regrettable tendency of so many clergy to neglect their cures for the more congenial pastimes of ale-swilling and bastard-begetting, John Jewel felt able to allow himself a certain cautious optimism when he returned to London at the end of October after his trip through the western group of dioceses. 'We found everywhere the people sufficiently well disposed towards religion, and even in those quarters where we expected most difficulty,' he wrote. 'It is however hardly credible what a harvest, or rather what a wilderness of superstition had sprung up in the darkness of the Marian times. We found in all places votive relics of saints, nails with which the infatuated people dreamed that Christ had been pierced, and I know not what small fragments of the sacred cross. The number of witches and sorceresses had everywhere become enormous. The cathedral churches were nothing else but dens of thieves, or worse, if anything worse or more foul can be mentioned.'

Allowing for a certain amount of natural exaggeration by the new Protestant brooms, there can be no doubt that they found the Church in a bad way. In those sees which had been left vacant by Reginald Pole abuses of various kinds flourished unchecked, and the convulsions of the past ten years had not been exactly conducive to good order and management anywhere. The low morale of the clergy was reflected in an acute shortage of parish priests – so acute, in fact, that the authorities were obliged to continue to employ many of the old priests whose conformity was doubtful to say the least, and to fill the gaps with laymen pressed into service as readers.

Strype says that 'these readers had been tradesmen, or other honest, well-disposed men, and they were admitted into inferior orders to serve the church in the present necessity by reading the common prayer and the homilies, and orders unto the people'. This expedient was defended on the grounds that it was better to supply some small cures with 'honest artificers exercised in the scriptures' – at any rate until the universities were able to produce enough men of learning to fill their places – rather than leave the people either with no pastor at all or to the care of ignorant 'mass-mongers', a popish Sir John Mumblemattins, Dr Dicer or Mr Card-player.

James Pilkington, the new Bishop of Durham, was thoroughly depressed by the 'negligent forgetfulness of God' which he saw all around him. 'Worldly wise men,' he wrote, 'see so many things out of order, and so little hope of redress, that they cannot tell which to correct or amend first; and therefore let the whip lie still, and every one to do what him list, and sin to be unpunished.' Certainly the new hierarchy had a formidable task before it, and the new Archbishop of Canterbury had to contend with indifference from the masses, who were understandably losing respect for the institutions of public worship – according to Bishop Pilkington the churches were half empty on Sundays, even when there was the added attraction of a sermon, while 'the ale-house is ever full'

— as well as active hostility from the militant left wing and passive resistance from the right. It was a prospect to make the boldest quail and Matthew Parker, a moderate, scholarly man of retiring disposition who had once been Anne Boleyn's chaplain, did quail. He had to take the job on, however, and turned out to be an inspired choice. It was due very largely to his tact and patience that by the end of the 1560s the Anglican Church had taken hold, and by the seventies and eighties was strong enough to withstand determined attacks from both within and without.

The question of just how many of the English people could properly be counted as Catholics in 1559 will again probably never be answered with real accuracy. Much detailed research has been done and is still being done into local records but no statistics, however detailed, can show the way into the human heart. Catholic sympathisers, both native and foreign, continued to insist naturally enough that their party was in the majority. Nicholas Sander, the English Catholic apologist, in a report drawn up for Cardinal Moroni some time in the spring of 1561, declared that 'the English common people consist of farmers, shepherds and artisans. The two former are Catholic. Of the others none are schismatics except those who have sedentary occupations, as weavers and shoemakers, and some idle people about the court. The remote parts of the kingdom are still very averse from heresy as Wales, Devon and Westmorland, Cumberland and Northumberland. As the cities in England are few and small, and as there is no heresy in the country, nor even in the remoter cities, the firm opinion of those capable of judging is that hardly one per cent of the English people is affected.'

Sander, of course, is a highly prejudiced witness but he may not have been so very far out in his estimate. Technically, every Englishman and woman over the age of thirty-five had been baptised and brought up in the Church of Rome. It was still only fourteen years since Henry VIII's death and his Church had retained so many of the elements of Catholic practice that the ordinary layman might have been excused for hardly noticing the difference. The Edwardian revolution had lasted a bare six years before the pendulum swung back again, so that the great majority were still far more accustomed to the Catholic form of service than to any other. It was also true that in the more remote and conservative parts of the country people had as yet scarcely begun to think of themselves as 'Catholics' or 'Protestants'. Terms like 'papist', 'heretic', 'mass-monger' and 'schismatic', which were freely banded about among the initiates in London, had little currency in the Yorkshire Dales, the Welsh mountains or the Cumberland fells where life was harder and more primitive and the farmers and shepherds, unlike all those sedentary weavers and shoemakers in the south-east, had little surplus energy to spare for the heady intellectual delights of theological debate.

Nevertheless, all the evidence points to the fact that committed Catholics were in a small minority. It has been argued that after the defection of the priesthood and with it the disappearance of their church as an organised body, the laity had little choice but to conform to the new scheme of things. This is true, but it can also be argued *a posteriori* that if the laity in general had been less apathetic the priesthood might have stood firm. Certainly an untried Queen and government could never have imposed a Protestant settlement on a nation of convinced Catholics. In the event, the great majority of the laity, like the priesthood, did conform, at least outwardly. They continued to attend their parish church partly in order to keep out of trouble with the law, partly from sheer force of habit and, habit being what it is, gradually became absorbed as communicating members of the new Church.

There were positive as well as negative reasons for this. Many people much preferred to worship in their native tongue – a significant number of Catholics had been reluctant to part with their English bibles during Mary's reign. Also no reasonable man could deny that some measure of reform was long overdue. The moribund state of the Church of Rome in the first half of the sixteenth century was by no means confined to England, but by the time that revivifying force known to history as the Counter-Reformation had crossed the Channel, the process of absorption had gone too far and the English people had finally turned their backs on Rome.

Perhaps the strongest underlying cause of this rejection was the fact that Roman Catholicism had become un-English. For reasons connected with both history and geography, England's ties with Rome had never been quite as binding as those of other European countries, and English Protestantism at the grass roots level was closely connected with the growth of nationalism. The mediaeval polity of Church and State existing side by side as interdependent but separate bodies, each exacting their own due measure of allegiance, had been destroyed by Henry VIII. It was Henry who first equated Roman Catholicism with treason, introducing the novel concept that allegiance to the Bishop of Rome – that is to a foreign power – could no longer be regarded as compatible with the subject's duty of allegiance to the Crown.

The perplexity facing patriotic Elizabethan Catholics in 1559 was neatly summarised in the Oath of Supremacy by which everyone holding office in Church or State had to 'utterly testify and declare in my conscience that the Queen's highness is the only supreme governor of this realm ... as well in all spiritual or ecclesiastical things or causes, as temporal, and that no foreign prince, person, prelate, state or potentate has, or ought to have, any jurisdiction, power, superiority, pre-eminence or authority ecclesiastical or spiritual within this realm; and therefore I do utterly renounce and forsake all foreign jurisdictions, power, superiorities and authorities, and do promise that from henceforth I shall bear faith and true allegiance to the Queen's highness, her heirs and lawful successors.' This oath, rejecting as it did the spiritual authority of Rome, was one which no true Catholic could conscientiously swear, but the stigma of implied disloyalty attached to refusing it was to prove too much for most Englishmen.

The Old Faith did not disappear. It went underground as other old faiths had done before it; those who clung to the old ways from conviction or from affection being divided roughly into three groups. At one end of the scale were the irreconcilables like Sir Richard Shelley, the last prior of the English Knights of Malta, Sir John Gage, who had been Queen Mary's Lord Chamberlain, and Sir Francis Englefield, one of her most devoted servants. These men, who could not accept the authority of a Protestant state and – perhaps even more to the point – could not bring themselves to accept Anne Boleyn's daughter as their Supreme Governor in matters spiritual, sought refuge abroad, some in Spain and some in Italy. More serious was the exodus from the universities. Edward Rishton declared that 'the very flower of the two universities Oxford and Cambridge, was carried away as it were by a storm and scattered into foreign lands'. Rishton was overstating the case but Oxford was certainly to prove a fertile breeding ground for Catholic thought and already had a bad reputation among the reformers. John Jewel, writing to his friend Bullinger in 1559, lamented that whatever had been planted there by Peter Martyr had now been 'so wholly rooted out, that the Lord's vineyard was turned into a wilderness'. Jewel could not recommend sending any Protestant youths to be educated at the senior university in case they should be corrupted by popery and return home 'wicked and barbarous'.

The scholars who fled from Oxford and to a lesser extent from Cambridge in the early sixties gathered in various towns in Northern France and the Spanish Netherlands, but their chief centre was Louvain near Brussels which had a long-standing connection with the family and friends of Sir Thomas More. Like their counterparts in Mary's reign, the Elizabethan exiles were a minority of a minority, probably never exceeding more than a few thousand; also like their Marian counterparts, they were men of ability and initiative who exerted an influence out of proportion to their numbers and who represented a considerable loss to their native land, for the Elizabethan refugees were to be condemned to a lifetime of exile. Not that the colony at Louvain was content to wait in idleness. Under the leadership of Nicholas Sander and his principal lieutenants and fellow-Wykehamists, Thomas Stapleton and Thomas Harding, they were to miss no opportunity of attempting to further their cause by whatever means appeared most promising. They at once embarked on a vigorous propaganda campaign and between the years 1559 and 1570 produced getting on for sixty books, tracts and broadsheets stating the Catholic case and refuting the arguments of their Protestant opponents. Titles such as *Harding Against the Apology of the English Church*; Sander's *The Rock of the Church Wherein the Primacy of St. Peter and of His Successors the Bishops of Rome is Proved out of God's Word* and Sander's *Rock of the Church Undermined by W. Fulke*; not to mention Sander's *Treatise of the Images of Christ and of his Saints: and that it is unlawful to break them and lawful to honour them* and Thomas Stapleton's *Counterblast to Mr. Horne's Vain Blast against Mr. Feckenham ... touching the Oath of Supremacy* became the ammunition for a series of briskly conducted paper skirmishes.

This war of words kept its participants happily employed and at least had the advantage of not actually hurting anyone. All the same, the Elizabethans were fully alive to the power of propaganda and by the mid-sixties the importation of 'seditious and slanderous books' into England had begun to cause the government a measure of concern. As most of this undesirable literature was apparently finding its way in through the Port of London, the bishop, John Aylmer, received a directive from the Queen in January 1566 ordering him 'specially to have regard thereunto'. Aylmer was authorised to appoint 'one or more persons of discretion ... to resort to our custom house of London, as any ship or vessel shall come in from time to time, and there to sit with our customers and other officers for the search and perfect understanding of the state of such books'. Despite the vigilance of the port authorities, the output of the printing presses at Louvain and other places in the Netherlands continued to be smuggled in and found a ready market among English Catholics, for whom it represented virtually their only contact with the outside world.

In 1565 John Jewel wrote that 'the Popish exiles are disturbing us and giving us all the trouble in their power' but, in fact, during the first dozen years of Elizabeth's reign the exiles had little more than nuisance value. In the early days the government adopted what might be described as a 'good riddance' policy towards them, even allowing them to take money out of the country. Francis Englefield was given permission to live abroad, providing he undertook not to reside in Rome itself, and Thomas Stapleton remained legally a prebendary of Chichester Cathedral until 1563. Later, as attitudes hardened, it was to be a different story.

Among the Catholics who stayed at home, either by choice or necessity, two distinct sub-divisions had begun to emerge by the middle of the 1560s. The first and largest consisted of those who attempted, not unreasonably in the circumstances, to have things both ways. They were to become known as 'Church papists' by the Protestant establishment and as 'schismatics' by their more resolute co-religionists; they attended services at the parish church often enough to avoid unwelcome notice from the authorities, while continuing to practise their own religion as and when they could. The hard core Catholics – or 'recusants' – rejected this form of compromise, and it was they who suffered the brunt of the approaching storm.

A graphic general picture of the sort of shifts to which the faithful were resorting is provided by Edward Rishton. 'At the same time,' he wrote, 'they had Mass said secretly in their own houses by those very priests who in church publicly celebrated the spurious liturgy, and sometimes by others who had not defiled themselves with heresy; yea, and very often in those disastrous

times were on one and the same day partakers of the table of our
Lord and of the table of devils, that is, of the blessed Eucharist
and the Calvinistic supper. Yea, what is still more marvellous and
more sad, sometimes the priest saying Mass at home, for the sake
of those Catholics whom he knew to be desirous of them, carried
about him Hosts consecrated according to the rite of the Church,
with which he communicated them at the very time in which he
was giving to other Catholics more careless about the faith the
bread prepared for them according to the heretical rite.'

All the same, in those early days even strict Catholics saw no
harm in simply being present at the Protestant service. The thin end
of the wedge dangers inherent in this attitude were soon obvious,
and in the summer of 1562 a deputation of English Catholics,
lacking any other guidance, approached the Spanish ambassador
to ask for a ruling on whether or not it was lawful for them to
attend their parish church. De Quadra referred the matter to
Rome and in due course it was considered by a committee of the
Council of Trent. The answer which came back that October was
definite: no Catholic might lawfully be present at the heretical
service, not even to avoid the penalties for recusancy. For some this
was the parting of the ways. The Duke of Norfolk's mother-in-law
had been 'accustomed to have the Protestant service read to her by a
chaplain in her house and afterwards to hear Mass said privately by
a priest. But as soon as she understood the unlawfulness of this
practice, she would never be present at the Protestant service any
more.' Others, for example the eminent lawyer Edmund Plowden,
were able to hold for a few more years that the Pope had not yet
explicitly condemned the Protestant ritual.

It is generally accepted – at least by Protestant historians – that
the English Catholics were treated with comparative leniency by
the Elizabethan government until attempts to overthrow it, sponsored by international Catholicism, forced it to adopt harsher
measures. Certainly the penal legislation passed at the beginning
of Elizabeth's reign was mild enough by sixteenth-century standards
– mild in comparison with that of Mary's reign and mild in
comparison with that of the 1580s. At the same time it was severe
enough, even in 1559, to prove quite a powerful deterrent, at least
on paper.

Anyone who refused to take the Oath of Supremacy was deprived
of office and barred from holding office for life. The Oath could

be administered to all ecclesiastics, judges and mayors, to anyone taking holy orders or university degrees, to all office-holders under the Crown. Non-jurors, therefore, faced loss of livelihood, and for conscientious Catholic youth the way to advancement was closed. The Act of Supremacy also laid down that anyone who 'by writing, printing, teaching, preaching, express words, deed or act' maintained and defended the spiritual or ecclesiastical jurisdiction of any foreign prince or prelate (i.e. the Pope) could lose all his goods and chattels for a first offence, lose all his property and go to prison for life for a second offence, and suffer the penalties of high treason for a third offence.

By the terms of the Act of Uniformity, any beneficed clergyman who refused to use the new Prayer Book, who used any other form of service – in other words, who said Mass – or who spoke 'in derogation' of the Prayer Book, could lose a year's income and go to prison for six months for a first offence, lose all his benefices and go to prison for a year for a second offence, and suffer life imprisonment for a third offence. Any layman who spoke in derogation of the Prayer Book, or who caused any clergyman to use any other form of service – in other words, who heard Mass – could be fined 100 marks and 400 marks respectively for a first and second offence (the mark was worth thirteen shillings and fourpence), lose all his goods and go to prison for life for a third offence. Anyone absent from church on Sundays and holy days without a sufficient reason could be fined twelve pence for each offence or suffer 'censure of the church'. This could involve lesser or greater excommunication which, in its turn, could involve the loss of certain civil rights. For example, an excommunicated person's evidence was considered worthless in a court of law – a serious handicap in a litigious age.

While none of these penalties was exactly comparable to burning at the stake, and while they were by no means systematically or universally enforced, their mere presence on the Statute Book was an uncomfortable weight on the minds of those people they were intended to deter – clergymen, country gentlemen and justices of the peace, squires and small landowners. These were the leaders of the local community whose example would be followed by their tenants and dependants. These were the people least able to face with equanimity the prospect of a prison sentence, the loss of a modest property, or a career and reputation. It is small wonder, therefore, that the majority were prepared to pay lip service at least to the Church of England.

Lip service was really all that was required of the majority. 'The Queen and her ministers,' observed Edward Rishton, 'considered themselves most fortunate in that those who clung to the ancient faith, though so numerous, publicly accepted, or by their presence outwardly sanctioned in some way the new rites they had prescribed. They did not care so much about the inward belief of these men, or if they did, they thought it best to dissemble for a time.' Elizabeth was not, in fact, particularly interested in her subjects' inward beliefs which, as long as they did not affect their outward conduct, she regarded as being their own business. Her government claimed, and was to continue to claim, that provided the Queen's subjects obeyed the law, they would not suffer molestation 'by way of examination or inquisition of their secret opinions in their consciences'.

One modern Catholic historian has summed up the position in words not so very different from Edward Rishton's. 'The Queen's subjects may continue to be Catholics so long as they pretend to be Protestants, and to live as Protestants and to use the new rites as though they are Protestants. They do not need to believe anything of what they profess to believe.' This may have been doubtful ethics, but it was sound political common sense.

The Queen's distaste for the practice of making windows into men's souls and the fact that her subjects were to be exempt from inquisition of their secret opinions in their consciences did not, however, mean that she was prepared for a moment to allow them liberty of conscience. No sixteenth-century state could have contemplated such a course and expected to retain any semblance of national unity. When, in 1563, the Emperor Ferdinand asked Elizabeth to let the English Catholics have the use of at least one church in every city in which 'without molestation or hindrance' they might celebrate the divine offices and sacraments, he received a polite but firm refusal which can scarcely have surprised him very much.

'This request,' wrote the Queen, 'is of such a kind and beset with so many difficulties that we cannot without hurt alike to our country and our own honour, concede it.... To found churches expressly for diverse rites, besides being only repugnant to the enactments of our Supreme Parliament, would be but to graft

religion upon religion, to the distraction of good men's minds, the
fostering of the zeal of the factious, the sorry blending of the
functions of church and state, and the utter confounding of all
things human and divine in this our now peaceful state: a thing
evil in itself, of the worst example pernicious to our people, and
to those themselves in whose interest it is craved, neither advantageous nor indeed without peril.' Oddly enough, the King of
Spain thought it a poor plan, too, as it might give the Queen an
opportunity of identifying the most devout and then punishing
them!

There might be no question of giving the Catholics their own
places of worship, but Mass continued to be quite widely available
for those who knew where to look for it: in quiet country houses
where a sympathetic gentleman had given shelter to a deprived
priest; in remote districts where, once the Queen's Visitors had
ridden away, priest and people continued to do just as they had
always done; in London in the chapels of the French and Spanish
embassies, where from time to time government agents arrived
to take the names of those present.

The Spanish embassy at Durham House was (not without
reason) an object of particular suspicion to the English government and a caretaker was installed to make a note of comings
and goings. The Council, however, was by no means satisfied
with this arrangement and in January 1563 took advantage of a
disturbance at the embassy, caused by an armed quarrel between
two Italians, to increase their surveillance. 'At the hour when
certain people were coming hither to hear Mass,' reported de Quadra
indignantly, 'some locksmiths were sent, without any respect or
consideration, to change the locks and keys on the doors and hand
the new keys to the custodian.' The Council was unimpressed by
the ambassador's protests at this violation of his diplomatic
immunity. He had allowed his house to become a resort of criminals,
they said; a breach of the peace might have resulted endangering
the lives of innocent passers-by and, anyway, there had been complaints from the neighbours.

The Council had complaints of its own, too, which it proceeded
to set out in detail. 'It is a notorious fact,' de Quadra was informed,
'that by the back door leading to the water there has been for a
long time past public access to your house given to a great number
of persons, subjects of Her Majesty the Queen, both citizens of

London and elsewhere, who come every Sunday and feast day to hear your Mass, which has been a means of keeping them obstinate in their disobedience and disregard for the laws of this realm. In order that these persons might not be recognised when they resorted to your house on such days, the doors of the hall towards the street are closed and the custodian himself detained outside.' Worse than this, it could be proved that 'certain traitors' had been slipping in and out of the embassy by the river door and had been encouraged and advised by the ambassador.

Certainly, the previous year, on de Quadra's own admission, the Irish rebel Shane O'Neill 'and ten or twelve of his principal followers ... received the holy sacrament in my house with the utmost secrecy'. He was also using his servants to bring in consecrated oils from the Netherlands, 'as Catholics come to me for them'. The English government clearly had a shrewd idea of what was going on, for their reply continued: 'To speak plainly, it is believed that, under cover of religion, your lordship is the cause of a large number of Her Majesty's subjects being disposed to sedition and disobedience who otherwise would have been good and loyal.'

The Spanish ambassador was not, in fact, the only person encouraging the Queen's Catholic subjects in disobedience. In 1564, the bishops were ordered to consult the leading figures in their dioceses known to be reliable Protestants and with their assistance to conduct a survey of justices of the peace, classifying them according to their religious proclivities. The bishops' labours revealed that opposition to the Government's policy was strongest in the north and west – the dioceses of Carlisle, Durham, York, Worcester, Hereford and Exeter containing the largest numbers of 'hinderers of religion'. There were pockets of resistance, too, in Staffordshire, Buckinghamshire and, in fact, wherever the most influential local family clung to Catholicism. Out of a total of 852 justices listed by the bishops, 264 were marked as unfavourable or at best indifferent, while 157 were actively hostile.

It was naturally difficult to enforce the law on a nationwide basis when approximately half the local magistrates were either persistently turning a blind eye to infringements or committing infringements themselves. There were clearly many occasions when the justice of the peace knew very well that the middle-aged man living in a neighbour's house and being passed off as a tutor or perhaps a poor relation was one of those 'popish and perverse priests which, misliking religion, have forsaken the ministry and yet live in corners'. Clearly there were many villages where the inhabitants knew very well that if you knocked on the side door of a certain house at a certain time, you would find Mass being discreetly celebrated in an upper room with, most probably, the justice of the peace among the worshippers – even if later that same day he might be seen sitting in the family pew at the parish church, listening unblinkingly to a godly Protestant sermon.

Queen Elizabeth undoubtedly knew this too, but on the whole she was apparently not dissatisfied with the progress of her religious settlement; at any rate no drastic measures were taken as a result of the bishops' survey. Justices of the peace with the requisite legal and local knowledge did not, after all, grow on trees and in several cases the bishops themselves had been obliged to recommend that the services of some 'noted adversaries of religion' be retained because there was no one suitable to replace them.

So far as it is possible to generalise, it seems fair to say that throughout the 1560s the Catholic population was allowed a good deal of rope. Every now and then an example would be made. For instance, in 1561 Sir Edward Waldegrave and his wife, Sir Thomas Wharton and several other prominent Catholics were sentenced to the statutory penalty for hearing Mass. Every now and then an embassy chapel would be raided and the congregation arrested en bloc.

In March 1568, the current Spanish ambassador, Don Diego Guzman de Silva, was telling King Philip that the Catholics in England were numerous but much molested and that news had recently arrived from the Duchy of Lancaster, 'where nearly all the people are Catholics', that many people of position had been arrested for refusing to take the Protestant communion or to attend the services and also, so he heard, because Mass was celebrated in their houses. But apart from these occasional drives – noticeably directed at the most prominent people in a given neighbourhood – the Queen at least was content to leave her Catholic subjects in peace, providing they kept their activities within decent bounds and, most important, providing there was no immediate prospect of any foreign intervention on their behalf.

Elizabeth seems to have been hoping that when the old generation of priests on whom the English Catholics were forced to rely had died out, and when a new generation of schoolchildren reared on sound Protestant principles (after 1563 all schoolmasters were required to take the Oath of Supremacy) had grown up, the problem would go away by itself. The fact that it did not was due in large measure to two people. One was Mary Stuart, Queen of Scotland. The other was William Allen.

CHAPTER THREE

A beginning has been made

'...by God's goodness a beginning has been made.'
Jean Vendeville, Douai, October 1568

IN the year 1568 two events took place which were effectually
to destroy the English government's hopes of reaching a peaceful
solution to the problem of their Catholic minority. The first of
these events was Mary Stuart's escape from her Scottish prison
and flight across the Solway Firth. The second was the renting
of a modest house in the university quarter of Douai to accom-
modate a handful of English theological students under the director-
ship of Dr William Allen. The Queen of Scots' dramatic descent
on the coast of Cumberland naturally attracted most attention
at the time, but the less well-publicised activities of Dr Allen were
to have equally if not more far-reaching results.

The Allens of Rossall Grange in the County of Lancaster were
typical of those ancient gentry families, intensely, innately conservative, who clung stubbornly to the old ways; families as rooted
in their native soil as the oak trees growing on their demesnes, who
were to suffer not only the physical and material consequences of
their steadfastness to the faith of their ancestors, but who more
tragically were to become increasingly divorced from the mainstream
of English national life. William Allen was born in 1532 – the
year which saw the death of the last pre-Reformation Archbishop
of Canterbury, the year in which Henry VIII and Thomas Cromwell were putting the finishing touches to their plans for the break
with Rome. Young William was educated at home, in a sheltered,
happy family atmosphere, where there was no room for any new-
fangled ideas and where the seven Allen children imbibed all the
comfortable convictions, prejudices and old-fashioned piety of their
parents, untouched as yet by the social upheaval going on around
them.

William was only four at the time of the so-called Pilgrimage of Grace – that ill-fated movement of popular revulsion against the new order by the conservative North Country – and the Allens were not personally involved in the rising. But the hanging of the abbot of the nearby Cistercian house of Whalley in front of his own monastery, together with two of his monks – one of whom was William Haydock of the Haydocks of Cottam Hall, close friends and neighbours of the family at Rossall Grange – can only have impressed the young Allens with the truth of their parents' teaching that an evil force had been let loose in the world.

In 1547, the year of King Henry's death, William Allen went up to Oriel College, Oxford. Unlike Cambridge, Oxford had never become a centre of advanced thought, and Oriel College in particular was regarded as being a stronghold of popery. William's tutor was a Welshman, Dr Morgan Philipps, an ardent Catholic nicknamed 'the Sophister' because of his skill in disputation. The fifteen-year-old boy made rapid progress under Philipps' guidance and although the three years he spent reading for his BA was a time of uncertainty and stagnation in the university, his studies do not seem to have been unduly affected, nor is there any record of his coming into conflict with the reforming authorities.

In 1554, the year of the Wyatt rebellion and Mary Tudor's marriage to Philip of Spain, William Allen, already a Fellow of his College, took his Master of Arts degree. Two years later he was appointed Principal of St Mary's Hall and elected to the office of Proctor. It was in this year, 1556, that Thomas Cranmer was at last brought out of Bocardo gaol to be burnt at the stake for heresy. It would be interesting to know whether Allen was among the crowd of spectators outside St Mary's Church on that wet March morning. All Oxford was there, so it seems likely enough. It would also be interesting to know what his feelings were as one of the chief architects of the English Reformation made his last, and probably most telling contribution to the future of English Protestantism.

Now that the nation had been officially taken back into the bosom of Mother Church, Allen's own future looked bright. He was a man who responded to the discipline and security of academic life. He possessed all the attributes of brains, energy, good looks and personal charm. He was well-born, well-connected, well-liked and respected. His orthodoxy was irreproachable. He was, in fact, just the kind of recruit that a renascent Catholic establishment in

England was going to need. At the age of twenty-four William Allen could reasonably hope that an honoured and profitable career of service to his country and his Church lay before him.

Then came the new Queen, closely followed by the new Queen's religious settlement. Allen's faith was not of the kind which admitted compromise. There could be no question of his taking the Oath of Supremacy and in 1560 he resigned his post at St Mary's Hall, although he stayed on at Oxford for a time. The conservative element in the university remained strongly entrenched – according to Nicholas Sander, 'on the Visitors going to the Colleges severally, they did not obtain oath or subscription from one in twenty' – and it was still possible for even such a well-known and recalcitrant Catholic as William Allen to live and study privately without being molested. But by the following year the climate had become so uncongenial that Allen joined that 'flower of the two universities' which was being scattered into foreign lands and crossed over to Flanders, where he made a welcome addition to the English colony at Louvain.

Louvain was a famous university town where there was every facility for study, and Allen would have found many of his friends already established there. In fact, the exiles, with all the Englishman's passion for club life and facility for creating a little bit of home in the most unpromising surroundings, had lost no time in organising themselves into two communities, christened Oxford and Cambridge. William Allen played his part in the propaganda campaign, writing his *Treatise on Purgatory* which defended the Catholic practice of saying prayers for the dead. In order to support himself, he took on the job of tutoring young Christopher Blount – the same who forty years later was to die on the scaffold for his part in the Essex rebellion. Allen also went on with his theological studies, trying to keep usefully occupied during what he hoped would be a period of only temporary set-back.

Nevertheless, those early months of exile were a bitterly unhappy time. His lodgings at Louvain were a poor substitute for Oriel College; the flat, insipid landscape of Flanders not to be compared with the hills of his native North Country or the sight and smell of Morecambe Bay lapping the edges of the Rossall estate. Nor was tutoring and the writing of tracts much compensation for the brilliant career which had been snatched away from him. Some time that year Allen's pupil became ill with what is ominously described as 'an atrophy, or perishing away of his body'. Allen was similarly afflicted, but in his case the trouble seems to have been largely psychosomatic in origin – a fact recognised by the Flemish doctor who told him he must go home if he wanted to save his life. So, in the late summer or autumn of 1562, William Allen returned unobtrusively to England to 'lie hidden among his own people'.

The reunion with his family and the invigorating Atlantic breezes soon restored him to health, but in other directions there was little comfort to be found. The people of Lancashire were still predominantly Catholic, but Allen was shocked and saddened by the evidence of apathy and decay he saw everywhere about him. He at once embarked on a one-man crusade, visiting his friends and kinsmen in the vicinity of Rossall – the Haydocks at Cottam, Thomas Hoghton, John Westby at Mowbreck Hall, John Talbot at Salesbury and Edward Osbaldeston – doing his best to stiffen their resistance to the new laws. But Allen was too well-known a local figure to be able to stay close to his home for long, and presently he shifted the field of his operations to the Oxford area, where he moved about from one 'safe house' to another and where, as he later told his friend Dr Vendeville: 'I demonstrated by irrefragable notes and tokens the authority of the Church and the Apostolic See, and I proved by popular but invincible arguments that the truth was to be found nowhere else save with us Catholics.'

As he travelled about the country, Allen became increasingly worried over the number of Catholics 'who believed the faith in their hearts and heard mass at home when they could' but who 'frequented the schismatical churches and ceremonies, some even communicating in them'. Worse than this, he, like Edward Rishton, had come across many instances of priests who said mass secretly and then 'celebrated the heretical offices and supper in public, thus', wrote Allen, 'becoming partakers often on the same day, O horrible impiety! of the chalice of the Lord and the chalice of devils'. These pernicious practices had, of course, arisen from 'the false persuasion that it was enough to hold the faith interiorly while obeying the Sovereign in externals, especially in singing psalms and parts of scripture in the vulgar tongue, a thing which seemed to them indifferent and, in persons otherwise virtuous, worthy of toleration'.

William Allen set his face firmly against such complacency. According to his biographer, Nicholas Fitzherbert, he went 'vehemently to exhort at various meetings and to enforce with many arguments that so great was the atrocity of this crime that whosoever was contaminated by it could on no account remain in the Catholic communion'. Allen knew that the recent ruling from Rome forbidding the faithful to attend Church of England services had not been entirely well received – 'many worldly-wise men' giving it as their opinion that in the circumstances any attempt to enforce strict ecclesiastical discipline would only result in considerably reducing the number of Catholics who did still 'hold the faith interiorly'. Allen had no patience with this defeatist attitude and fifteen years later he was to write: '... we have now more confessors and genuine Catholics than with all our indulgence and connivance we then had concealed Christians; a class of men, moreover, whose inward faith would have furthered neither their own salvation nor that of others, while their outward example would have led many to ruin; and thus, without giving a thought to the damnable sin of schism, or to the restoration of the true religion, but flattering themselves with their good will and pleading in excuse for their unlawful acts the Sovereign's laws, they would have plunged themselves and theirs, unrepentant, into the miserable abyss of destruction'. Thus, in a nutshell, William Allen summed up the basic, irreconcilable conflict between the laws of his God and his Queen.

Allen was to spend two and a half years in England labouring at his self-appointed task; writing and circulating his 'notes, rules or motives for distinguishing with certainty the Catholic faith from heresy' (which were later to be published at Douai in expanded form), rallying the faint-hearted, admonishing back-sliders and bringing as many wandering sheep as he could reach back into the fold. 'He both kept to their duty the family in which he resided,' says Fitzherbert, 'and often visited Oxford which was near and there soon converted not a few.'

It is a commentary on the generally relaxed attitude of the early sixties that Allen, who had lived in Oxford for fourteen years and would have been known by sight to the majority of the citizens, was apparently able to go about openly encouraging people to break the law. All the same, he evidently felt it would be unwise to push his luck and after a time sought shelter under the hospitable roof of the Duke of Norfolk. In spite of the fact that he had once been tutored by the redoubtable John Foxe of martyrology fame, Thomas Howard had many Catholic connections and his East Anglian estates offered sanctuary to a number of those 'stragling doctors and priests who have liberty to stray at their pleasure within this realm and do much harm secretly and in corners'.

It is said that Allen subsequently went back to Oxford, but now the relatives of one of his young converts were after his blood; one man in particular, who knew his face, having undertaken to find him and denounce him to the magistrates. This man, so the story goes, actually sat opposite to Allen at dinner at an inn and either providentially failed to recognise him or was suddenly struck by remorse and remained silent. There is a distinct flavour of St Elizabeth and the roses about this episode, but it may well reflect the healthy English dislike of laying information and also something of the astonishing indifference of the English – until they begin to feel personally threatened.

William Allen left for the Low Countries again in the spring of 1565. He made his way to Malines where he was at last ordained priest and was appointed lecturer in theology at the Benedictine college in the city. At the age of thirty-three he had become a man with a mission in life – from now on there would be no more time for homesickness. His *Certain Brief Reasons concerning Catholic Faith* had already appeared in print. In May 1565 his *Treatise on Purgatory* was published at Antwerp, to be followed in 1567 by further treatises on such controversial matters as the authority of the priesthood to remit sins, the duty of confession and 'the Churches meaninge concerning Indulgences, commonlie called the popes pardons'.

By 1567 in England there were signs of a general stiffening of attitudes on both sides of the religious divide. The Catholics had by this time shed most of their dead wood and the Established Church, having survived the critical years of its infancy, was growing in stature and self-confidence. The government still clung to its gradualist policy, but the obstinate survival, even resurgence, of Catholicism in parts of the North was giving cause for concern, especially in view of the remarkable events currently taking place in Scotland. Strype records that 'religion in Lancashire and the parts thereabouts went backwards, papists about this time showing themselves to be numerous, Mass commonly said, priests harboured, the Book of Common Prayer and the church established by law laid aside, many churches shut up and cures unsupplied, unless with such popish priests as had been ejected'.

William Allen's work in his native county had been followed and supplemented by a visit from his fellow Lancastrian and fellow exile Laurence Vaux, who came to spread the militant word of the new Pope; and now reports were reaching London of groups of gentlemen taking oaths not to attend the Protestant communion and of leading families becoming reconciled to Rome. Slowly but inexorably the tragedy was beginning to unfold.

In February 1568 a writ went out under the Queen's name to Edward Holland, Sheriff of Lancashire. 'Whereas we have been credibly informed,' it ran, 'that certain persons, who having been late ministers in the Church were justly deprived of their offices of ministery for their contempts and obstinacy, be yet or lately have been secretly maintained in private places in that our county of Lancaster (whose names are here subscribed) where they do not only continue their former doings in contempt, as it seemeth, of our authority and good orders provided for an uniformity, but also do seditiously pervert and abuse our good subjects to our no small grief: like as we think it convenient for the service of Almighty God and for the love we bear to our good and obedient subjects to have such evil members rooted out to the end the good may the better prosper: so have we thought good to will and command you forthwith upon the receipt hereof, to the end that none may pretend ignorance herein, to take order and cause to be openly published in the chief market towns of that our county in times and places of most resort thither, that our pleasure is to have the said persons and every of them apprehended and committed to ward.' The list of the half-dozen wanted men subscribed was headed by 'Allen who wrote the late book of Purgatory'.

By the time the warrant for his arrest was out in Lancashire, William Allen was in Rome. He had made the journey apparently hoping there might be an opening for him as chaplain at the English Hospice in the city, but the job did not materialise and later that spring Allen returned to Flanders in the company of his friend Jean Vendeville. Both men were in a despondent frame of mind. Dr Vendeville had spent the winter in Rome trying to interest the Pope in an ambitious project for the conversion of all infidels, but Pius V had more immediate matters on his mind and Vendeville had failed to get a hearing. As they travelled across Europe together, he poured out his disappointment to William Allen and William Allen promptly seized what looked like a heaven-sent opportunity to try and divert this missionary zeal into more practical channels by propounding a scheme of his own – a scheme which may well have been in his mind ever since his trip to England.

Allen and his fellow propagandists had found it convenient to lay the blame, at least in public, for the dismal collapse of English Catholicism on 'the terrible rigour of the law'. But Allen had had personal experience of the degree of latitude being allowed to even such a determined proselytiser as himself. He was far too intelligent a man not to have realised that it was not persecution but isolation – the absence of leadership and hope for the future – which had demoralised the English Catholics. Quite as clearly as Queen Elizabeth he could see that once the old generation of priests had died out, 'no seed would be left hereafter for the restoration of religion, and that heresy would thus obtain a perpetual and peaceful possession of the realm'. Unless, of course, something was done to prevent it.

He therefore suggested that a college should be founded where the exiled scholars, then scattered in various towns throughout the Low Countries, 'might live and study together more profitably than apart'. In this way, he hoped, their energies might be concentrated and conserved, so that a body of learned men would always be ready and waiting 'to restore religion when the proper moment should arrive'. Such a college would also provide a much needed centre and refuge for future exiles and offer a means of snatching from the jaws of death 'as many souls of our countrymen as in a very few years might be educated in this society of ours'.

Allen does not at this stage seem to have envisaged the active missionary work for which Douai was to become so famous. On the contrary, he felt it would be hopeless to attempt anything 'while the heretics were masters'. His plan was simply to keep the flame alight and be prepared to seize whatever opportunity might be offered by the death of the Queen or some similar cataclysm. But Dr Vendeville, who took up the idea with enthusiasm, did envisage it. His thoughts, as Allen put it, took a wider range and he saw no reason why, after a few years preparation, the students should not be employed in promoting the Catholic cause in England 'even at the peril of their lives'.

As soon as the two men got back to Belgium, Dr Vendeville went into action on his friend's behalf. The recently established university at Douai in the province of Artois, now in northern France but then forming part of the King of Spain's Burgundian heritage, seemed the most promising site for the new venture. Vendeville himself held the position of Regius Professor of Canon Law and was able to win the support of the Chancellor, Dr Galen. William Allen was appointed Public Catechist which gave him some standing in the university, but the most pressing need was money, and Vendeville set about raising the necessary funds by appealing to 'four or five devout and pius men who possessed the means and from their piety seemed unlikely to refuse'. He also petitioned the Duke of Alva for a grant of 300 crowns, with what success is not recorded.

The idea of an English college did not meet with universal approval, but Vendeville refused to be discouraged and by October he was able to write to Dr Viglius, President of the Council of the Netherlands, that 'by God's goodness a beginning has been made; for from St Michael's feast a house has been rented of sufficient size, and very convenient, nigh to the theological schools, and there are already living in it five or six Englishmen of great ability and promise, some of whom are men, while others are youths of twenty-three or twenty-four, and also two of our countrymen'.

If it was Jean Vendeville's practical enthusiasm which brought the English College at Douai into being, its immediate and continuing success was undoubtedly due to the character of its first president. William Allen was a born schoolmaster, with the gift of inspiring genuine personal affection as well as respect. Political refugees are a notoriously touchy and cantankerous breed and the English Catholic exiles were no exception to this rule, but Douai was to remain noticeably free from the internecine feuds which afflicted later foundations. John Pitts, himself a one-time student, was to write: 'Allen presided over everything, and with wonderful dignity, constancy and authority governed the whole college, yea, through the college almost all the Catholics of our nation, and by his firm and prudent rule kept them all to the fulfilment of their duties in the greatest charity, peace and concord.' Dr Worthington, another student in the early days of the college, recalled that 'there was no need of any written law to keep the members in discipline.... If a question arose about anything, it was decided by the president, Allen, whose will was a law to all.... He alone prescribed the laws of study and piety. He taught his people by example, word of mouth and in every way. Everyone depended on his will like sons, and that too most readily.' Dr Humphrey Ely, the Welsh priest, added to the generally idyllic picture when he wrote that the students at Douai lived 'very quietly without rigorous rules and penances ... governed and ruled by the countenance and look of one man whom all from highest to the lowest did love and highly reverence'.

William Allen had had the commonsense to realise that it would be impossible to attempt to subject his students – men of widely differing ages and backgrounds – to conventional college discipline. 'A little government there is and order,' he was to write, 'but no bondage nor straitness in the world. There is neither oath nor statute nor other bridle nor chastisement; but reason and every man's conscience in honest superiority and subalternation each one towards others.' This wise and liberal policy paid handsome dividends. It was work after Allen's heart and in later years, when his feet were set on murkier paths, he always remembered Douai with affectionate nostalgia.

Not that it was easy; apart from the battle with the common adversary, Allen, like all successful pioneers, had to contend with jealousy and prejudice from his own side. But his most urgent problems were connected with money, or rather lack of it. During the first seven years of its existence the college was entirely dependent on voluntary contributions, supplemented after 1570 by its President's salary as Professor of Divinity at the university. Even when a regular allowance began to come from Rome money continued to be a problem, for Allen steadfastly refused to turn away anyone who came to his door. As a result, conditions at Douai were spartan – so much so that the two Belgians who formed part of the original intake soon took themselves off – but to the zealous and idealistic a life of poverty made its own appeal. In 1575, a visitor reported seeing nearly sixty men and youths of the greatest promise seated at three tables, 'eating so pleasantly a little broth, thickened merely with the commonest roots, that you could have sworn they were feasting on stewed raisins and prunes, English delicacies'.

The living may have been plain, but the thinking at Douai was high. Although Allen wrote that 'our students, being intended for the English harvest, are not required to excel or be great proficients in theological science' and laid down that, above all, 'they must abound in zeal for God's house, charity and thirst for souls', he did not make the mistake of underrating the opposition. He knew that if the new generation of priests he was hoping to create were to have any chance of reversing current trends in England, they must be educated and trained to meet and beat the enemy on his own ground.

'In the first place,' he told Jean Vendeville in a long apologia for the college and its work, written about 1578, 'since it is of great consequence that they should be familiar with the text of holy Scripture and its more approved meanings, and have at their fingers' ends all those passages which are correctly used by Catholics in support of our faith or impiously misused by heretics in opposition to the church's faith, we provide for them, as a means by which they may gain this power, a daily lecture on the New Testament, in which the exact and genuine sense of the words is briefly dictated to them. . . .

'At suitable times they take down from dictation with reference to the controversies of the present day all those passages of holy Scripture which make for Catholics or are distorted by heretics, together with short notes concerning the arguments to be drawn from the one and the answers to be made to the other. A disputation is held once a week on these passages, in which the students defend in turn not only the Catholic side against the texts of Scripture alleged by heretics, but also the heretical side against those which Catholics bring forward, that they may all know better how to prove our doctrines by argument and to refute the contrary opinions.'

On Sundays and feast days the advanced students took it in turn to preach a sermon in English, 'in order to acquire greater power and grace in the use of the vulgar tongue, a thing on which the heretics plume themselves exceedingly and by which they do great injury to the simple folk'. Allen was well aware of the importance of this advantage which the heretics, 'however ignorant they may be in other points', had over the more learned Catholics, 'who having been educated in the universities and the schools do not commonly have at command the text of Scripture or quote it except in Latin'. 'Our adversaries, on the other hand,' wrote Allen, 'have at their fingers' end all those passages of Scripture which seem to make for them, and by a certain deceptive adaptation and alteration of the sacred words, produce the effect of appearing to say nothing but what comes from the Bible.'

As well as realising the need for a Catholic version of the Bible in English – a need which Douai was later to supply – Allen knew it was vital that his students should not only be able to preach fluently and persuasively to the 'unlearned' in their own language, but should also have no difficulty in holding their own in any scriptural quoting match. (It was a favourite scoring point of the reformers to demonstrate that there was no justification for Catholic dogma in Holy Writ.) Every day, therefore, at dinner and supper, three or four chapters of the Bible were read aloud and before they left their places at table the students heard 'a running explanation' of one chapter of the Old and another of the New Testament, this being in addition to daily private study beforehand. By this method the Old Testament was gone through twelve times and the New Testament sixteen times during the three years which the course at Douai normally lasted, and it proved, not surprisingly, to be 'a great help towards acquiring a more than common familiarity with the text'.

But although he was prepared to take on the opposition at their own game where necessary, in drawing up his training programme William Allen never lost sight of the fundamental issues. Since the budding missionaries were to be employed in administering the sacraments and hearing confessions, they had to be carefully instructed in the catechism and pastoral matters. They must also know as much as possible about ecclesiastical penalties and censures, and 'of the way to deal with their people in such cases'. It was Allen's ambition not merely to restore 'a real and true observance of church discipline' among the afflicted English Catholics, but to see every aspect of the Faith – especially the power and authority of the Pope – 'better known and more devoutly and purely honoured than it used to be; for it is the exceeding neglect and contempt with which this was treated by pastors and people alike that God has punished with the present miserable desolation'. This was, of course, the only possible, the only bearable explanation.

Even the most optimistic well-wishers of the small experiment begun at Douai on 29 September 1568 knew that results, if any, could not be expected for some time. The startling reappearance on the scene of Mary Queen of Scots was another matter altogether. The fact that Queen Elizabeth's Catholic subjects now had not only a potential leader but a potential alternative to their present sovereign actually in their midst was to produce immediate, if unfortunate results, and for nearly twenty years was to cast an ever darkening shadow across English political life.

The relative positions of the two Queens had changed radically during the past decade. Elizabeth had survived the first critical years of her reign and come safely through a major crisis in her emotional life. 'Queen Elizabeth,' wrote an admiring Venetian, 'owing to her courage and to her great power of mind ... declines to rely upon anyone save herself, although she is most gracious to all.' Her stature as a ruler had increased slowly but steadily and at thirty-four she was firmly established on her throne – a force to be reckoned with in international affairs.

Mary's fortunes, by contrast, had fluctuated violently. In November 1558 she had stood on the threshold of a career which promised to be of unexampled brilliance. By the following summer, the freakish death of Henri II had brought her to the French throne beside her youthful husband – a Queen twice over at sixteen and a half. By December 1560 the sickly Francois II was dead, leaving 'as heavy and dolorous a wife as of right she had good cause to be'. The Venetian ambassador, Michel Surian, took a sympathetic view of Mary's altered circumstances. 'The thoughts of widowhood at so early an age,' he wrote, 'and of the loss of a consort who was so great a King, and who so dearly loved her, and also that she is dispossessed of the Crown of France, with little hope of recovering that of Scotland which is her sole patrimony and dower, so afflict her that she will not receive any consolation, but, brooding over her disasters with constant tears and passionate and doleful lamentations, she universally inspires great pity.'

Not quite universally, though, for Nicholas Throckmorton, Queen Elizabeth's representative in Paris, could only regard Mary's dispossession from the French crown as providential. 'And yet, my lord,' he warned Robert Dudley, 'this I trust shall be no occasion to make her Majesty less considerate, or her counsel less provident, for assuredly the Queen of Scotland, her Majesty's cousin, doth carry herself so honourably, advisedly, and discreetly, as I cannot but fear her progress.'

When Throckmorton saw Mary on 31 December, she had recovered her spirits and begun to take stock of her situation. Her ten-year-old brother-in-law was now King of France and effective power had passed into the hands of the Queen Mother, that formidable matriarch Catherine de Medici, whose chief pre-occupation lay in defending the rights of her remaining Valois sons against the predatory House of Guise. As a childless dowager Mary's immediate usefulness to her Guise relations was at an end and their star had gone into temporary eclipse. Meanwhile, the new Regent was making no particular secret of the fact that she would prefer the Queen of Scots' room to her company. All the same, Mary could have stayed on in France, living in com-fortable retirement on her dower lands while awaiting future developments. Not surprisingly, this unexciting course held no appeal for a full-blooded, optimistic young woman of eighteen.

Mary had been brought up to regard her Scottish kingdom as a mere appanage of France (at the time of her marriage she had signed a secret deed of gift making over Scotland and, incidentally, her rights to the English succession unconditionally to the crown of France in the event of her death without heirs), but in the early spring of 1561 Scotland appeared in a rather different light, offer-ing a challenge and a promise of adventure with perhaps more glittering triumphs to come. The only question was, would Scotland have her back?

Two years earlier the Protestant nobility, banded together under the title of the Lords of the Congregation and egged on by John Knox, newly returned from the fountain-head at Geneva, had risen in revolt against the Catholic and alien government of the Queen Regent, Mary of Guise. 'Everything is in a ferment in Scotland,' wrote John Jewel happily to Peter Martyr. 'Knox, surrounded by a thousand followers, is holding assemblies throughout the whole kingdom. The old Queen has been compelled to shut herself up in garrison. The nobility, with united hearts and hands, are restoring religion throughout the country, in spite of all opposition. All the monasteries are everywhere levelled with the ground: the theatrical dresses, the sacrilegious chalices, the idols, the altars, are consigned to the flames; not a vestige of the ancient superstition and idolatry is left. What do you ask for? You have often heard of drinking like a Scythian; but this is churching it like a Scythian.' Unfortunately, though, the military capabilities of the Lords of the Congregation did not match their iconoclastic fervour and they were forced to turn to the Queen of England for help. 'If the occasion is lost,' Kirkcaldy of Grange told William Cecil, 'ye may thirst for, yet not find another.'

The English Secretary of State scarcely needed reminding that this might well be a unique opportunity to get the French out of Scotland, neither did his mistress. Both, however, fully realised the risks involved. To interfere in Scottish internal affairs would be a direct violation of the four-month-old Treaty of Câteau-Cambresis and would be to invite retaliation by one of the greatest military powers in Europe. If things went badly, Elizabeth could easily find herself with a victorious French army sitting on the border and only the Catholic North Country between it and the vulnerable, undefended South. Cecil, always a careful man, weighed up the pros and cons and finally came to the conclusion that the game was worth the candle. The Queen agreed with him, up to a point, and in August 1559 Sir Ralph Sadler was sent north with £3,000 in gold to be distributed among the rebels under conditions of elaborate secrecy.

Thus, within a year of her accession, Elizabeth first found herself cast in the role of Protestant champion. It was never a role she enjoyed as, quite apart from the risk and expense it invariably carried with it, she never lost her reservations about the ultimate wisdom of encouraging other people's rebels. In the case of Scotland, these reservations were strengthened by the fact that she could not stand John Knox and his revolutionary Calvinism at any price. The long-suffering Cecil soon discovered that the mere mention of the name of Knox was enough to provoke an explosion.

As the winter drew on, it became distressingly apparent that the Scots were not going to be able to dislodge the Regent and her three thousand or so French veterans from their stronghold at Leith without more visible assistance than surreptitious subsidies, but here Elizabeth balked. Cecil, now irrevocably committed to a policy of intervention, had to resort to threats of resignation to shift her. In December, a fleet under the command of William Winter was despatched to lie in the Firth of Forth, with orders to annoy the French and blockade the garrison at Leith. At the same time, any action Winter took was to appear to come 'of his own head and of himself, as though he had no commission therefore' from the Queen. William Winter performed his delicate task with skill and imagination, and has the distinction of being the first Elizabethan naval commander to weigh anchor with instructions of this kind.

It was beyond even Elizabeth's ingenuity to disclaim responsibility for an army, but by the time her land forces did eventually arrive under the walls of Leith in the spring of 1560, a number of external factors were beginning to make it look as if God might by a Protestant after all. Storms in the Channel the previous autumn had scattered and partially destroyed a French fleet carrying reinforcements for Scotland. The French government was now having serious trouble with its own heretics and in consequence had become demonstrably less eager to embroil itself with the Scottish variety. The death in June of that gallant warrior Mary of Guise took the heart out of the resistance at Leith, and news that Philip of Spain had been heavily defeated by the Turks in the Mediterranean removed any immediate fears of interference from that quarter.

William Cecil, therefore, found himself in an unexpectedly strong position at the peace talks which opened in Edinburgh on 19 June, and during the course of a fortnight's hard bargaining extracted a series of major concessions from the French Commissioners acting on behalf of the young Queen and her husband. Among other things, it was agreed that all French troops should be withdrawn from Scotland, the fortifications at Leith dismantled and that in future the country should be governed by a council of Scottish nobles. France also formally recognised the Queen of England's right to occupy her own throne and undertook that the King and Queen of France would give up their provocative use of the English royal arms and title. The burning question of religion was tactfully left in abeyance but when the Scots Parliament met in August they at once proceeded to abolish the Pope's authority and adopt a Calvinistic form of Protestantism as the national religion. Thomas Randolph, the English agent in Edinburgh, told Cecil that he had never seen 'so important matters sooner dispatched, or agreed to with better will'.

In these circumstances it was hardly surprising that the Lords of the Congregation should regard the prospect of the return of their Catholic sovereign with something less than enthusiasm. 'I believe here will be a mad world!' remarked William Maitland of Lethington. 'Our exactness and singularity in religion will never concur with her judgement; I think she will hardly be brought under the rule of our discipline, of the which we can remit nothing to any estate or person.'

Mary, as Queen of France, had refused to ratify the Treaty of Edinburgh and in the autumn of 1560 had expressed herself forcibly on the proceedings in the Scottish Parliament to Nicholas Throckmorton. ' "My subjects of Scotland do their duty in nothing, nor have they performed one point that belongeth to them. I am their Queen," quoth she, "and so they call me, but they use me not so. They have done what pleaseth them, and though I have not many faithful there, yet those few that be there of my party, were not present when these matters were done, nor at this assembly. I will have them assemble by my authority, and proceed in their doings after the laws of the realm, which they so much boast of, and keep none of them.... I am their sovereign, but they take me not so. They must be taught to know their duties." '

In the spring of 1561 she was no longer in a position to take this high tone and had the sense to realise it. Guided by the advice of those experienced operators her Guise uncles to 'repose most upon them of the reformed religion' and who now held power, she set herself out to charm the English and Scottish envoys who came to France to look her over. It was noticeable that since her widowhood she had stopped using the English royal arms, but all the efforts of Nicholas Throckmorton and the Earl of Bedford to get her to ratify the Treaty of Edinburgh were unsuccessful. She must first take the advice of the Estates and nobles of her own realm, said Mary demurely. It was only right and proper that they should be consulted before she took such an important step. She hoped Queen Elizabeth would understand and repeatedly declared her earnest desire to live in peace and amity with her 'good sister and tender cousin'.

To the Scots she indicated that she was ready to let bygones be bygones and accept the status quo in Scotland. Not, of course, that she could have done anything else but she did it gracefully, insisting only that she must be given the right to practise her own religion in private. 'I will be plain with you,' she told Throckmorton. 'The religion that I profess I take to be most acceptable to God, and indeed neither do I know, nor desire to know, any other. Constancy doth become all folks well, but none better than Princes and such as have rule over realms, and especially in the matter of religion. I have been brought up in this religion, and who might credit me in anything if I should show myself light in this case?' Having made her position clear, adding rather pointedly that she was 'none of those who would change their religion every year', Mary repeated that she had no intention of constraining her subjects in matters of conscience and trusted in return that no one would attempt to constrain her. This sounded reasonable enough – evidently Mary Stuart was no Mary Tudor – and as it began to dawn on the Scots that their Queen's dynastic potentialities would now work in favour of Scotland rather than France, they cheered up and got ready to welcome her home.

Mary in fact was winning golden opinions all round and Nicholas Throckmorton's despatches were full of her virtue and discretion, her good judgement, her 'wisdom and kingly modesty' and her willingness to 'be ruled by good counsel'. It may not have been entirely tactful to praise one Queen to another in quite such glowing terms, but Throckmorton had not yet forgiven his mistress for the acute embarrassment she had caused him the previous autumn when, for a few nerve-wracking weeks, it had looked very much as if she meant to marry a man strongly suspected of having done away with his wife.

Elizabeth, for her part, was clearly disconcerted and not a little alarmed by the siren-like propensities being displayed by her eighteen-year-old cousin. If Mary could so captivate Nicholas Throckmorton, a hardheaded diplomat and man-of-the-world, there was no knowing what sort of havoc she might create among the hot-headed, restless Scottish warlords. Who could tell how many simple men might be 'carried away with vain hope, and brought abed with fair words'?

When Mary made a formal application for the Queen of England's safe conduct for her journey, her envoy met with a flat refusal. Let the Queen of Scots first ratify the Treaty of Edinburgh, as she was in honour bound to do. Then would be the time to start talking about passports. This was a pretty devastating public snub, but irritatingly Mary kept both her nerve and her temper. She was only sorry, she said, that she had demeaned herself by asking for something she did not need. The English had not been able to prevent her voyage to France thirteen years ago. They could not prevent her from returning home now. Mary only wanted to be friends but, she told Nicholas Throckmorton, it was beginning to look as if the Queen of England was more interested in 'the amity of her disobedient subjects than of their Sovereign'. Elizabeth had called her young and inexperienced. Yet, said Mary, she hoped she knew how to behave uprightly towards her friends and kinsfolk and would not allow *her* passion to betray her into using unbecoming language of another Queen and her nearest kinswoman. She was not without allies, she added pointedly, and Elizabeth would find she was not to be bullied.

In the first round of the personal contest between the cousins, Mary had won on points. Elizabeth, realising that she had over-reacted and was getting bad publicity as a result, did finally send the safe conduct with its implicit offer of an amicable meeting – a meeting which might have had such incalculable results – but it was too late. Mary had already sailed for Scotland. The long journey to Fotheringay had begun.

For the next two years all Mary's efforts in the field of foreign policy were directed towards obtaining formal recognition of her status as heiress presumptive to the English throne. Within a fort-night of her return home, Maitland of Lethington, ablest of her Scottish councillors, was despatched to London with instructions to approach the Queen of England on the subject. He met with no success but, in the course of several interviews, Elizabeth talked very freely about her attitude to Mary and the whole delicate matter of the succession.

She knew that Mary was 'of the blood of England', her cousin and next kinswoman, so that she was bound by nature to love her. 'And as my proceedings have made sufficient declaration to the world,' she went on, 'that I never meant evil towards her person nor her realm, so can they that knew most of my mind bear me accord that in time of most offence and when she, by bearing my arms and acclaiming the title of my crown, had given me just cause to be most angry with her, yet could I never find in my heart to hate her, imputing rather the fault to others than to herself. As for the title of my crown, for my time I think she will not attain it, nor make impediment to my issue, if any shall come of my body. For so long as I live, there shall be no other Queen in England but I.' As for the succession, that was a matter she would not meddle in. It was like the sacrament of the altar.

Some thought one thing, some another and 'whose judgement is best, God knows'. If Mary's right was good, Elizabeth would do nothing to prejudice it. 'I for my part,' she told Maitland, 'know none better, nor that myself would prefer to her.' Neither, in fact, could she think of any serious competitor.

At their next meeting, the Queen returned to the same thorny topic. 'I have always abhorred to draw in question the title of the crown,' she said feelingly, 'so many disputes have been already touching it in the mouths of men. Some that this marriage was unlawful, some that someone was a bastard, some other, to and fro, as they favour it or mislike it.' 'Howsoever it be,' declared Elizabeth Tudor, summing up the whole tangle in masterly fashion, 'so long as I live, I shall be Queen of England. When I am dead, they shall succeed that have most right.' If that person was Mary, well and good. If someone else could show a better right, then it was not reasonable to ask Elizabeth to do them 'a manifest injury'.

Maitland had urged that settling the succession on Mary would cement the friendship between them. Elizabeth did not agree. 'Think you that I could love my winding sheet?' she enquired brutally. There was another consideration – the most weighty of all. 'I know the inconstancy of the people of England,' remarked their Queen, 'how they ever mislike the present government and have their eyes fixed upon the person that is next to succeed, and naturally men be so disposed. *Plures adorant solem orientem quam occidentem.*' Many a politician to his sorrow has since learnt the truth of that piece of Elizabethan wisdom.

The Queen went on to illustrate her point by favouring Maitland with one of her infrequent references to her own early days. 'I have good experience of myself in my sister's time,' she said, 'how desirous men were that I should be in [her] place and earnest to set me up. And if I would have consented, I know what enterprises would have been attempted to bring it to pass, and now perhaps the affections of some are altered. As children dream in their sleep of apples, and in the morning when as they wake and find not the apples they weep; so every man that bore me good will when I was Lady Elizabeth ... imagineth with himself that immediately after my coming to the crown every man should be rewarded according to his own fantasy, and now finding the event answer not their expectation it may be that some could be content of new change, in hope to be then in better case.'

At the age of twenty-eight Elizabeth saw things clearly and saw them whole, without bitterness but without illusion, either about herself or her fellow men. 'No princes' revenues be so great that they are able to satisfy the insatiable cupidity of men,' she observed. 'And if we, either for not giving to men at their discretion or yet for any other cause, should miscontent any [of] our subjects, it is to be feared that if they knew a certain successor of our crown they would have recourse thither; and what danger it were, she being a puissant princess and so near our neighbour, ye may judge. I deal plainly with you, albeit my subjects I think love me as becomes them, yet is nowhere so great perfection that all are content.'

Maitland did his best to persuade her to change her mind. He was sure, he said, that Mary would be only too pleased to agree to whatever safeguards Elizabeth liked to name. Elizabeth was unimpressed. She 'still harped on that string: saying "It is hard to bind princes by any security where hope is offered of a kingdom"'. In private conversation she would admit that she considered Mary to be her natural and lawful successor. She was fully prepared to be friendly and would like to meet her 'good sister and cousin' as soon as it could be arranged. She was ready to have the Treaty of Edinburgh reviewed and to modify the clause which bound Mary to abstain from using and bearing the English royal arms and title 'at all times coming'. She would be quite content if Mary would agree not to bear the arms of England or style herself Queen of England during Elizabeth's lifetime or that of her children. Further than this she would not go. She would not make the Queen of Scots her heir 'by order of Parliament' and nothing Maitland could say would budge her.

No one, of course, had the bad taste to say so aloud, but the possibility that once Mary had received public and Parliamentary recognition of her right to the reversion of the English crown, the temptation to hasten the processes of nature might be too much for her (or for those of her friends who could feel they would be serving the Church of Rome at the same time) must have been in Elizabeth's mind. Something of the sort had certainly been in William Cecil's mind when, in the spring of 1561, he had drawn up a memoranda of certain precautions he and his colleagues wished their mistress to observe: 'We think it very convenient,' wrote the Secretary of State, 'that your Majesty's apparel, and especially all manner of things that shall touch any part of your Majesty's body bare, be circumspectly looked unto; and that no person be permitted to come near it, but such as have the trust and charge thereof.

'Item: That no manner of perfume either in apparel, or sleeves, gloves or suchlike, or otherwise that shall be appointed for your Majesty's savour, be presented by any stranger or other person, but that the same be corrected by some other fume.

'Item: That no foreign meat or dishes being dressed out of your Majesty's Court be brought to your food, without assured knowledge from whom the same cometh; and that no use be had hereof....

'Item: It may please your Majesty to give order who shall take the charge of the back doors to your chamberer's chambers where laundresses, tailors, wardrobers and such use to come; and that the same doors may be duly attended upon as becometh and not to stand open but upon necessity....'

Cecil had his moments of disenchantment with Elizabeth – 'God send our mistress a husband and by time a son, that we may hope our posterity shall have a masculine succession' he wrote to his friend Nicholas Throckmorton at a time when she was being particularly trying – but he and a number of others closely associated with the new regime were only too acutely conscious of how much depended on the fragile thread of one woman's life. The Queen's near fatal attack of smallpox in the autumn of 1562 brought this danger home to the country at large for the first time and led to a determined but fruitless attempt by both Houses of Parliament to persuade Elizabeth to marry and to name her successor, although none of the members showed any enthusiasm for the claims of the Queen of Scots.

The Queen of Scots had by no means given up hope of cajoling the Queen of England into changing her mind, and throughout the early sixties she worked hard and by no means unsuccessfully to build up an atmosphere of trust and goodwill. Then, in February 1565, she first set eyes on another of her cousins, Henry Stuart, Lord Darnley, a handsome baby-faced youth of nineteen, and fell head over heels in love. Prudence, politics and statecraft alike were thrown to the winds. Mary in the grip of physical passion was no longer willing 'to be ruled by good counsel'. She quarrelled fatally with her illegitimate half-brother James Stewart, now Earl of Moray, and had apparently ceased to care if she offended Queen Elizabeth. Her old admirer Nicholas Throckmorton was shocked at the change in her and William Cecil feared the worst.

After Mary herself Darnley, by the accepted laws of primogeniture, stood closest to the English throne, and Cecil not unnaturally considered that an alliance between them could only comfort and encourage 'all such as be affected to the Queen of Scots either for herself or for the opinion of her pretence to this crown or for the desire to have a change of the form of religion in this realm'. 'The general scope and mark of all their designs,' he wrote, 'is, and always shall be, to bring the Queen of Scots to have the royal crown of this realm. And therefore, although the devices may vary amongst themselves for the compass hereof ... yet all their purposes, drifts, devices and practices shall wholly and only tend to make the Queen of Scots queen of this realm and to deprive our sovereign thereof.'

But there was no stopping Mary and by July she had embarked on her disastrous second marriage. From then on the home life of the Queen of Scotland became different indeed from the general run of well-regulated royal households. None of the professional Scotland-watchers stationed at Berwick and in Edinburgh itself were in the least surprised when the egregious Darnley met his spectacularly messy end at Kirk o'Field, but his widow's subsequent career, culminating in her marriage to the Earl of Bothwell, a divorced man, according to the rites of the Protestant church, was watched with horrified astonishment by the outside world.

Mary's friends abroad could scarcely believe their eyes. The Venetian ambassador in Paris was of the opinion that Catholicism had now no hope of ever raising its head in Scotland again. The King of France and his mother told Mary's ambassador she 'had behaved so ill and made herself so hateful to her subjects' that they were unable to give her either help or advice. The Pope decided to have nothing more to do with her, 'unless by and by he shall discover in her some sign of improvement in life and religion'. The Holy Father, in fact, was moved to remark that he found it difficult to say which of the two queens in Britain was the worst.

It has been suggested that Mary may have been subject to attacks of porphyria, the hereditary disorder which caused the intermittent madness of her descendant George III. Certainly this is the most charitable explanation. Mary's contemporaries, however, could only suppose that the Queen of Scotland had allowed her illicit passion to run away with her and 'by yielding to spite and appetite' had conclusively demonstrated, as one Venetian delicately put it, 'that statecraft is no business for ladies'. But it was not long before the reaction began to set in. Mary Stuart at large and defiantly flouting every convention in the book was one thing. Mary Stuart in adversity, insulted, imprisoned, threatened and forced to abdicate by her own subjects, was quite another.

'Although she have merited all the evil she now endures,' wrote Michel Surian reflecting on the misfortunes of the Queen of Scots, 'yet does she deserve some measure of pity, since all are apt to err, not to say a lady, and a young lady, and meet for pleasure as she was.' Mary's escape from Lochleven helped to hasten the process of rehabilitation. 'With regard to her flight,' reported Giovanni Correr from Paris, 'it is judged here, by those who know the site and how strictly she was guarded, that her escape was most miraculous.'

Mary had also written to her uncle the Cardinal of Lorraine 'a letter . . . which should move every hard heart to have compassion upon her. The first lines express that she begs pardon of God, and of the world, for the past errors of her youth, which she promises to amend for the future. Then she acknowledges her release solely from His Divine Majesty, and returns him most humble thanks for having given her so much strength in these her afflictions; and she declares that she has never swerved in the least from her firm purpose to live and die a Catholic, as she now intends to do more than ever.' Thus by the time the Queen of Scots landed on the Queen of England's doorstep the romantic legend of the misprized heroine had already begun to flourish. With the Queen of Scots nothing succeeded like failure.

There can be no doubt of Mary's courage, her resourcefulness, her invincibly optimistic outlook, her personal charm and her ruthless egotism – all qualities which were to make her infinitely more dangerous as a homeless fugitive in her cousin's realm than she had ever been as a neighbouring sovereign.

CHAPTER FOUR

All the north is ready

'All the north is ready and only awaits the release of the Queen of Scotland.'

Guerau de Spes, London, 17 September 1569

FIFTEEN hundred and sixty-nine was a year of crisis for the Queen of England – a year when, in the words of John Strype, the clouds began to gather over her head and her peace seemed 'to be much threatened by Popish combinations'. Certainly the outlook was unsettled, both at home and abroad. In France religious civil war still raged intermittently. Elizabeth made no attempt to intervene – she had burnt her fingers at that game six years before – but the embattled Huguenots were receiving a good deal of unofficial aid from sympathisers across the Channel. In present circumstances the regime of Charles IX and Catherine de Medici was not looking for trouble but in the general turmoil there was always a danger that it might be overthrown by the ultra-Catholic Guises, who had a considerable popular following, especially in Paris. The Guise faction, led by Mary Stuart's influential relations, was dedicated to the extermination of heresy in general and to the promotion of the Queen of Scots' cause in particular. It represented an obvious menace to Elizabeth and rumours of plots were always coming out of France. In the summer of 1568 Captain François, an Italian secret agent otherwise known as Franchiotto, sent a warning to Cecil that these rumours should not be taken too lightly and advising the Queen to look well to her food, bedding and other furniture, in case an attempt was made to poison her.

There was trouble of a more immediate nature brewing across the North Sea where the Low Countries, England's old allies and trading partners, were in revolt against their Spanish sovereign. Unlike his father the Emperor, King Philip had never taken much interest in his Dutch and Flemish territories – legacy of that strange, long-ago marriage of his grandmother Juana of Castile to Philip of Burgundy – regarding them chiefly as a useful source of revenue. The nobility of the seventeen provinces resented the loss of their ancient liberties under his increasingly heavy-handed rule; the merchants and burghers resented his taxation. But the conflict had been sparked off by the spread of a militant form of Protestantism in the north and east and in Antwerp, commercial capital of Northern Europe. Philip might be obliged to tolerate heresy in other countries for reasons of political expediency; in no circumstances whatever would he tolerate it in his own dominions, and in 1567 he despatched the notorious Duke of Alva and an army of 10,000 'blackbeards' to carry out a policy of blood and iron in the disobedient provinces.

The thought of this kind of force no more than a day's sail from its own coastline was not a comforting one for the English government, especially as Anglo-Spanish relations began to deteriorate rapidly at the end of the sixties. There had been a good deal of unpleasantness over the expulsion by King Philip of Elizabeth's ambassador Dr John Man who, among other things, had been ill-mannered enough to refer to the Pope as 'a canting little monk' at a Madrid dinner party. The new Spanish ambassador who arrived in London late in 1568 was also singularly unfitted for his task. It was unfortunate, therefore, that Don Guerau de Spes at once had to deal with an incident which called for diplomatic skill and tact of a high order.

Some time in November four small coasters laden with bullion for Alva's army were driven by bad weather and French pirates to take shelter in Plymouth. The temptation thus offered to a queen perennially short of ready cash was hardly to be resisted. Elizabeth made no attempt to resist it – not when she discovered that the money could still technically be regarded as the property of the Genoese bankers who were lending it to Philip. The Genoese had no objection to transferring their business to another client. Philip and the Duke of Alva were predictably annoyed. When Alva, egged on by hysterical reports from de Spes, retaliated by placing an embargo on English trade in the Low Countries, he was even more annoyed to find that this hurt him more than Elizabeth. It also provided him with an illuminating demonstration of how completely an unfriendly England, assisted by Dutch and Huguenot privateers, could disrupt his communications with Spain, and the Duke, cursing de Spes, was obliged to open time-consuming negotiations with a blandly impenitent Elizabeth.

On paper, the King of Spain should have had no difficulty in dealing with the Queen of England as she deserved. In practice, the affair of the treasure ships was a classic and not unfamiliar example of the way in which a small nation, lucky enough to occupy a strategic position on the map, is able to tie tin cans on the tail of a giant.

All the same, some conservative members of the English Council looked askance at this form of brinkmanship and while England continued to harbour a Trojan horse in the shape of Mary Queen of Scots, it might well prove an expensive luxury. As early as July 1568 the then Spanish ambassador, Guzman de Silva, had reported, 'the Queen of Scots certainly has many friends, and they will increase hourly, as the accusations of complicity in the murder of her husband are being forgotten and her marriage with Bothwell is now being attributed to compulsion and fear. This view is being spread,' added de Silva, 'and friends easily persuade themselves of the truth of what they believe.' How right he was!

Guerau de Spes, writing to Philip in January 1569, described Mary as 'a lady of great spirit', gaining so many friends where she was that 'with little help she would be able to get this kingdom into her hands'. Later in the same despatch he wrote gleefully: 'the Queen of Scotland told my servant to convey to me the following message – "Tell the ambassador that if his master will help me, I shall be queen of England in three months and mass shall be said all over the country"'.

William Cecil, reviewing the state of the realm about this time in a memorandum divided into the headings Perils and Remedies, saw the general situation in thoroughly gloomy terms. At the top of his list of perils came 'a conspiration of the Pope, King Philip, the French king and sundry potentates of Italy to employ all their forces for the subversion of the professors of the gospel'. It was always Cecil's nightmare that sooner or later the Catholic powers would combine against Elizabeth. The fact that they had not already done so was, in his opinion, sheer good luck and Cecil did not believe in trusting to luck. The French Huguenots did occasionally win a battle or a temporary measure of toleration, but their destruction looked like being only a matter of time. It was hardly probable that the Calvinists in the Low Countries could

survive Alva's calculated reign of terror and already the pressure
on Philip's other flank by the Turks in the Mediterranean was
diminishing. As soon as France and Spain were free of internal
problems, they would turn their joint attention to England – where
Mary Stuart was waiting for them.

Cecil's remedies included a more vigorous application of the
law governing religious uniformity, a programme of aid for the
rebels in both France and the Low Countries, and the establishment of a defensive Protestant alliance with Denmark, Sweden
and the German Lutheran princes. He also recommended that the
country's defences should be strengthened, especially along the
south and east coasts, and that the navy should be put on a war
footing.

The English Secretary of State was never one for looking on
the bright side but he was unquestionably a highly experienced,
highly intelligent observer of the international political scene and
clearly he placed no reliance whatever on the possibility of peaceful
co-existence between the two ideologies. Cecil was no warmonger,
but by the end of the sixties he saw Western Europe in terms of
two armed camps with a final confrontation of might against right
as inevitable and perhaps not long delayed.

In fact, the troubles of 1569 came from within rather than
without and before the year's end they had culminated in the
first and, as it turned out, the only serious armed rebellion of
Elizabeth's reign. The Rising in the North or the Rising of the
Northern Earls, as it is variously known, was not primarily an
affair of Catholics versus Protestants, but it rapidly became an
affair of old versus new and its success could only have benefited
the Catholic cause. It had its origins in a suggestion that the
Queen of Scots might be married to the Duke of Norfolk, first put
forward in the autumn of 1568 by a well-meaning body of opinion
which was not happy about keeping Mary in England, to all
intents and purposes a State prisoner. Elizabeth was not happy
about keeping Mary in England either – she found it both expensive and embarrassing – but unless and until some formula could
be hammered out by which the Queen of Scots could be restored
to her throne without prejudicing the Earl of Moray's government,
there seemed no alternative.

Running parallel with the unofficial plan for Mary's future, but
soon to become inextricably involved with it, was a Cecil-Must-Go

movement gathering strength among the nobility, nominally headed by Norfolk. The conservative peers could see the same dangers from abroad that Cecil did, but they favoured a policy of appeasement – the return of Alva's bullion and all Spanish merchandise currently being detained in English ports, the cutting off of all aid to the French rebels, the release of the Queen of Scots and recognition of her status as heir presumptive. They were also, of course, jealous of the Secretary's power and influence. The reason why Cecil escaped the fate of Thomas Cromwell lay in the fact that the present Duke of Norfolk was not the man his grandfather had been and Queen Elizabeth was emphatically not the kind of monarch her father had been. She might drive her loyal servants to the verge of nervous breakdown, but she was not in the habit of throwing them to the wolves.

Nevertheless, it was an uneasy summer for the Queen and her Secretary of State. The Norfolk marriage scheme may, at its inception, have been an honest if somewhat naïve attempt to find a solution to the problem of Mary by subjecting her to a trustworthy and suitably high-ranking English husband; but it is noticeable that none of its promoters – least of all the bridegroom elect – could quite bring themselves to mention it to Elizabeth. Elizabeth soon got to hear about it, though, and was under no illusions as to who would be the dominant partner in such a union, or of what its consequences would be to herself. She told the Earl of Leicester in September that if it took place she would be in the Tower within four months and ordered Norfolk on his allegiance to deal no more in the matter. 'But,' wrote Guerau de Spes hopefully, 'I do not believe the Duke will desist from his enterprise in consequence. A stronger guard has been placed around the Queen of Scotland,' he went on, 'although I have understood that she will nevertheless soon find herself at liberty, and this country itself greatly disturbed. All the north is ready and only awaits the release of the Queen of Scotland.'

Vague but disquieting rumours had been coming in from the north for some weeks and when, at the end of September, the Duke of Norfolk suddenly bolted to his East Anglian estates, Elizabeth not unnaturally took alarm. 'I do not know what will happen' de Spes told King Philip on the 30th; 'but I understand, considering the number of the Duke's friends in England, he cannot be ruined, except by pusillanimity, and the Queen of Scot-

land has sent to urge him to behave valiantly and not to fear
for his life which God would protect'. In fact, the shifty Norfolk
who, without exactly meaning to, had become deeply involved with
Mary and the dubious activities of such right-wing Catholics as
the Earls of Northumberland and Westmorland, had lost his
nerve. Elizabeth ordered him back to Court. He sent excuses,
pleading illness. The Queen told him to come anyway, by litter
if necessary, and a few days later he obeyed.

De Spes, who had been busy stirring the pot all summer, reported
that 'the earls of Northumberland, Westmorland, Cumberland,
Derby and many others, all Catholics, are much grieved at this
cowardice, if such it can be called, of the Duke of Norfolk, and
they have sent Northumberland's servant, who spoke to me before
on the matter, to say that they will by armed force release the
Queen [of Scots] and take possession of all the north country,
restoring the Catholic religion in this country'.

Norfolk had sent a message to the northern earls warning them
not to go ahead with these enterprising plans and, for all their
large talk, both Northumberland and Westmorland would have
been glad enough of an excuse to back down. But Elizabeth, now
thoroughly roused, summoned them to Court to give an account
of themselves. The Earl of Sussex, President of the Council of the
North and more than doubtful about the loyalty of his local levies
should it come to a fight, advised against positive action. As the
man on the spot he wanted to be allowed to 'nourish quiet' until
the winter, when dark nights, wet weather and bad roads could
be trusted to take the heat out of the situation. Sussex may well
have been right. Unfortunately, though, Elizabeth had her doubts
– unfairly as it turned out – about *his* loyalty and in any case she
was in no mood to leave sedition to breed unchecked.

When the royal command reached Northumberland and Westmorland they were driven into a corner. Both had everything to
lose and the example of Norfolk, now in the Tower, was scarcely
encouraging; but they had gone too far to be able to refuse the
Queen's challenge without forfeiting every shred of credibility.
Northumberland's friends and servants, says William Camden,
'being now prepared for rebellion, seeing him thus wavering and
fearful, called upon him at unawares in the dead of the night,
crying that ... his enemies were at hand with an armed power
to carry him away prisoner.' They urged him not to betray the

religion of his fathers at a moment when the Catholics were ready to rise all over England. The Countess of Westmorland wept and exclaimed dramatically, 'We and our country were shamed for ever, that now in the end we should seek holes to creep into.'

Neither of the earls was proof against this form of blackmail, and to the sound of church bells being rung backwards 'to stir up the multitude' they issued proclamations declaring themselves 'the Queen's true and faithful subjects', but: 'Forasmuch as divers disordered and evil disposed persons about the Queen's majesty have, by their subtle and crafty dealing to advance themselves, overcome in this our realm the true and Catholic religion towards God; and by the same abused the Queen, disordered the realm and now, lastly, seek and procure the destruction of the nobility: we therefore have gathered ourselves together to resist by force ... to see redress of these things amiss, with restoring of all ancient customs and liberties to God's church and this noble realm; lest, if we should not do it ourselves, we might be reformed by strangers, to the great hazard of the state of this our country.'

The rebel forces went first to Durham, 'where they rent and trampled underfoot the English bibles and books of Common Prayer which they found in the churches. From thence they went small journeys, celebrating Mass in all places where they came, trooping together under their colours (wherein were painted in some the Five Wounds of Christ, in others the chalice), Richard Norton an old gentleman with a reverend gray head, bearing a Cross with a streamer before them.' These activities, faintly echoing the long-ago Pilgrimage of Grace, were no doubt a comfort to all those honest Catholics who had flocked to the banner of the Five Wounds. They were not, however, the most effective method of exploiting the rebels' brief initial advantage for, until reinforcements could be rushed from the Midlands and the South, the Earl of Sussex dared not risk an open engagement.

'There be not in all this country ten gentlemen that do favour and allow of her Majesty's proceedings in the cause of religion', wrote Sir Ralph Sadler to Cecil from York on 6 December, 'and the common people be ignorant, full of superstition and altogether blinded with the old popish doctrine, and therefore do so much favour the cause which the rebels make the colour of their rebellion, that though their persons be here with us, I assure you their hearts, for the most part, be with the rebels. ... If the father be on this side, the son is on the other, and one brother with us, the other with the rebels.'

The situation could easily have turned ugly but, in the event, the prophecy of that hard-faced realist the Duke of Alva was fulfilled and the business did all end in smoke. There was no general rising of the English Catholics – even local support proved disappointing, the rebel forces mustering no more than about 5,000 horse and foot – and as the royal army advanced inexorably northward the rebels wavered, broke and fled. Apart from a shortlived flare-up under the leadership of Leonard Dacres the following February, stamped out in the only pitched battle of the whole campaign, the rising was over by the end of the year and the painful process of retribution had begun.

If the Northern rebels had been better led and better equipped, if they had been able to release Mary Stuart, if help had come from abroad, above all if they had received more popular support, the story might have had a different ending. As it was, the failure of the Rising in the North only served to emphasise the fact that the old, turbulent, baronial England was dead and that the future belonged to the new men – the lawyers and businessmen, the sober civil servants and bureaucrats – denizens of an increasingly urbanised, increasingly settled and commercialised society. The long arm of the central government could now reach at will into the remotest corners of the realm and make itself obeyed; the putrefying corpses hanging 'for a terror' in every town and village which had sent men to join the rebel army drove this depressing point home with grim finality.

The Northern Earls themselves sought refuge across the border, traditional sanctuary of English dissidents. But here, too, thanks largely to Elizabeth's careful cultivation of the Earl of Moray, times were changing. The Scots caught the Earl of Northumberland and presently handed him over, for a consideration. Westmorland 'at length escaped with some Englishmen into the Netherlands, where he led a very poor life, even to his old age, living upon a very slender pension from the Spaniard.' No longer would Neville or Percy or Dacres rule their territories like petty kings – the day of the over-mighty subject was done at last.

Although the underlying causes of the rebellion lay in a complex web of personal and economic jealousies, the two earls had naturally chosen to present their cause in the light of a disinterested bid for a return to religious orthodoxy. Government propaganda, equally naturally, presented them as ungrateful traitors to their sovereign and disturbers of 'the public and blessed peace of the realm'. 'As to the reformation of any great matters,' observed the royal proclamation issued on 24 November, 'they were as ill chosen two persons, if their qualities were considered, to have credit, as could be in the whole realm. For they were both in poverty; one having but a very small portion of that which his ancestors had left; and the other having wasted almost all his patrimony. The Queen therefore saw in what sort they went about to satisfy their private lack and ambition, through the persuasion of the number of desperate persons associated as parasites with them.'

A statement put out by the Earl of Sussex four days later had been equally scathing about the 'popish holiness' assumed to give false colour to manifest treason and to mislead the Queen's subjects. In fact, the most heartening conclusion which the government was able to draw from the events of 1569 was the manifest reluctance of the Queen's subjects to be misled. Out of a possible total of at least 60,000 men of fighting age in the Northern counties, the rebels had never been able to raise more than 7,000 at most. The remainder, with true native caution, had waited to see which way the cat would jump. It was ironic, therefore, that this resounding display of inertia by the English Catholics should have provided the occasion for the launching of the long-delayed thunderbolts from Rome.

During the first half-dozen years of Elizabeth's reign, while hopes of her marriage and conversion were still being entertained, the Vatican had leaned over backwards to be conciliatory and a campaign conducted by the English exiles during the early sixties for her immediate excommunication met with little support. But after the death of the genial Pius IV in 1565, the beginnings of a hard line papal policy became discernible. Pius V, a former Dominican friar nicknamed Brother Woodenshoe, was an ascetic, a theologian and a man of strict moral principles who disapproved of playing politics with the Word of God just as strongly as any left-wing member of the House of Commons.

The distressing antics of Mary Stuart during the first years of his pontificate had caused Pius to hesitate to smooth her path to the English throne, but by 1569 Elizabeth's excommunication was

once more a live issue. The Pope sent a secret emissary to England
that summer to sound the feelings of the native Catholics and he
apparently brought back an encouraging report. Then, early in
November, the first rumours that the nobility were preparing to
rise against their heretic sovereign reached Rome. According to
various garbled 'newsletters' coming in from the Netherlands and
Germany, the Duke of Norfolk (curiously transmogrified into the
Earl of Suffolk) was already married to the Queen of Scots; an
insurgent army numbering 18,000 foot and 4,000 horse, all desperate
men vowed to live and die for the Church of God, was in the field;
there were disturbances in Wales and Ireland and 'opinion prevailed that the people would soon with one accord declare themselves for the Catholic faith and unite with the rest'. In February
1570 the Pope received an appeal for support from the Earls of
Westmorland and Northumberland which had been despatched the
previous November, and Nicholas Sander in Louvain assured him
that if the papacy would only make a bold gesture, England would
shortly be restored to the fold. Pius hesitated no longer and before
the end of the month he had signed the bull *Regnans in Excelsis*.
It was an uncompromising document.

'He that reigneth on high,' it ran, 'to whom is given all power
in Heaven and in Earth, hath committed his One, Holy, Catholick
and Apostolick Church, out of which there is no Salvation, to one
alone upon Earth, namely to Peter, the chief of the Apostles, and
to Peter's successor the Bishop of Rome, to be by him governed
with plenary Authority. Him alone hath he made Prince over all
People and all Kingdoms, to pluck up, destroy, scatter, consume,
plant and build; that he may preserve his faithful people ... in the
Unity of the Spirit and present them spotless and unblamable to
their Saviour. In Discharge of which Function, We, who are by
God's goodness called to the government of the aforesaid Church,
do spare no Pains, labouring with all earnestness, that Unity and
the Catholick Religion ... might be preserved sincere. But the
number of the Ungodly hath gotten such Power, that there is now
no place in the whole World left which they have not assayed to
corrupt with their utmost Doctrines; and amongst others, Elizabeth, the pretended Queen of England, the Servant of Wickedness,
lendeth thereunto her helping hand, with whom, as in a Sanctuary,
the most pernicious persons have found a Refuge. This very
Woman, having seized on the Kingdom, and monstrously usurped

the place of Supreme Head of the Church in all England, and the chief Authority and Jurisdiction thereof, hath again reduced the said Kingdom into a miserable and ruinous Condition, which was so lately reclaimed to the Catholick Faith and a thriving condition.

'... We, seeing that Impieties and Wicked actions are multiplied one upon another, as also that the Persecution of the Faithful and Affliction for Religion groweth every day heavier and heavier through the Instigation and by means of the said Elizabeth, and since We understand her heart to be so hardened and obdurate that she hath not only contemned the godly Request and Admonitions of Catholick Princes concerning her Cure and Conversion, but also hath not so much as suffered the Nuncios of this See to cross the Seas for this purpose into England, are constrained of necessity to betake ourselves to the Weapons of Justice against her. ...

'Being therefore supported with His authority whose pleasure it was to place Us (though unable for so great a Burthen) in this Supreme Throne of Justice, We do out of the fullness of our Apostolick Power, declare the aforesaid Elizabeth as being an Heretick and a Favourer of Hereticks, and her Adherents in the matters aforesaid, to have incurred the Sentence of Excommunication, and to be cut off from the Unity of the Body of Christ. And moreover We do declare her to be deprived of her pretended Title to the Kingdom aforesaid, and of all Dominion, Dignity and Privilege whatsoever; and also the Nobility, Subjects and People of the said Kingdom, and all others who have in any sort sworn unto her, to be for ever absolved from any such Oath, and all manner of Duty of Dominion, Allegiance and Obedience: and We also do by Authority of these Presents absolve them, and do deprive the said Elizabeth of her pretended Title to the Kingdom and all other things before named. And We do command and charge all and every the Noblemen, Subjects, People and others aforesaid, that they presume not to obey her, or her Orders, Mandates and Laws: and those which shall do the contrary, We do include them in the like Sentence of Anathema.'

For an organisation not normally noted for the speed of its reactions, the Vatican had on this occasion moved with commendable despatch – the whole process being completed within a period of three weeks. Even so, by the time copies of the bull could be circulated, the only visible signs of the Rising of the Northern

Earls were the gallows disfiguring the countryside, and if Pius had seriously expected to release an upsurge of Catholic militancy in England, he was disappointed. Nor did the Catholic princes of Europe display any particular enthusiasm for the papal initiative. In fact, it caused the most Catholic prince of them all to take serious umbrage.

'His Holiness has taken this step without communicating with me in any way,' wrote Philip of Spain to Guerau de Spes, 'which certainly has greatly surprised me, because my knowledge of English affairs is such that I believe I could give a better opinion upon them and the course that ought to have been adopted under the circumstances than anyone else. Since, however, His Holiness allowed himself to be carried away by his zeal, he no doubt thought that what he did was the only thing requisite for all to turn out as he wished, and if such were the case, I, of all the faithful sons of the Holy See, would rejoice the most. But I fear that not only will this not be the case, but that this sudden and unexpected step will exacerbate feeling there and drive the Queen and her friends the more to oppress and persecute the few good Catholics still remaining in England.'

There were obvious difficulties in the way of telling the English people about their Queen's altered status and this unenviable task was finally undertaken by John Felton, a well-to-do Catholic living in Southwark, who in the early hours of 15 May 1570 nailed a smuggled copy of *Regnans in Excelsis* to the Bishop of London's door. Popular reaction was predictable. Patriotic ballads, broadsheets and pamphlets flooded the market. A particularly glutinous form of mud, compounded of personal insult and biblical quotation in about equal parts, was flung enthusiastically in the direction of Rome, much opportunity for merry sport being afforded by the convenient double meaning of the word 'bull'. *A disclosing of the great Bull and certain calves that he hath gotten and specially the Monster Bull that roared at my Lord Bishop's Gate* was an example of this genre.

The Bishop of Salisbury, in his rather more sonorously phrased *View of a Seditious Bull,* likened it to Pandora's box 'full of hurtful and unwholesome evils'. He found it to be 'a matter of great blasphemy against God and a practice to work much unquietness, sedition and treason'. 'For,' he went on, 'it deposeth the Queen's majesty from her royal seat and teareth the crown from her head: it dischargeth all us her natural subjects from all due obedience: it armeth one side of us against another: it emboldeneth us to burn, to spoil, to rob, to kill, and to cut one another's throat.' After making an attack on the institution of the papacy in general ('Where did Christ make this commission to Peter only? where be the words? in what scripture? in what gospel or epistle? Where did Christ ever say to Peter, I commit the government of the church to thee alone?'), John Jewel addressed himself to matters of more immediate importance. How dared the Pope, that 'wilful and unlearned friar', how dared he say that Queen Elizabeth was no lawful Queen? Elizabeth, the right inheritor of the houses of York and Lancaster, accepted by the nobility and joyfully acknowledged by all the commons of the realm; Elizabeth who was to her people 'as a comfortable water in a dry place, as a refuge for the tempest, and as the shadow of a great rock in a weary land'. The bishop felt it unnecessary to remind his public of the blessings of peace, but he did so all the same. They had only to look at neighbouring lands such as France and Flanders to see the ruined homes, the burning cities, the bloodshed, the widows and the fatherless children. 'But God, even our God, gave us Queen Elizabeth; and with her gave us peace, and so long a peace as England hath seldom seen.'

The bull was not merely an unwarrantable interference in the affairs of another nation; by its call for civil disobedience it struck at the very roots of society. 'What shall we do then for laws of common peace,' demanded Jewel, 'and of holding our possessions and goods to our private use, and so maintaining the good estate of our neighbours; for paying our rents to landlords, and custom and tribute where custom and tribute are due?' The Pope had said, 'Let not any obey these laws.' Was this fatherly counsel? Or was it the road to anarchy and misery? Had Christ ever set himself up against the temporal ruler? Had not Peter said, 'It is the will of God that you obey your prince'? Had not Paul required the Roman to obey Nero, 'the most wicked ruler that ever reigned'? Had not the prophets willed the children of Israel to pray for the life of Nebuchadnezzar, even though he 'fired and rased their city, sacked their sanctuary and spoiled their temple'?

Bishop Jewel was in no doubt as to the answers to all these questions. 'Remember,' he thundered in his peroration, 'if thou obey thy prince as God hath commanded thee, thou art accursed

by the Pope; or, if thou disobey thy prince as the Pope requireth
thee, thou art condemned by the judgement of God. Remember
that the Pope hath conference with traitors in all countries, that
he raiseth subjects against their princes, that he causeth princes to
plague their subjects ... that he suffereth Jews and harlots to live
in wealth and peace with him at Rome, and yet will not suffer a
christian and lawful prince to live in the peace of her own country
at home; that he is the procurer of theft and murder, of rebellion
and dissension in the land; that he hath sent in a bull to show
his meaning, and to work our disquiet, so bold and vain and
impudent a bull, and so full fraught with blasphemy and untruth
as never before him did any. Let these things never be forgotten:
let your children remember them for ever.' And remember them
they did – for centuries.

At the time, condemnation of the Pope's action was pretty well
universal. In England 'the most part of the moderate sort of
Papists secretly misliked this Bull, because there had been no
Admonition preceded according to Law, and foreseeing also that
thereby a great heap of mischiefs hung over their heads.' Informed
Catholic opinion abroad regretted not so much the excommunication
itself as the fact that the bull had been published without adequate
arrangements – indeed without any arrangements at all – for putting it into effect. As the Bishop of Padua presently remarked to
the Cardinal of Como, there was not much point in turning the
key of Peter with one hand unless the other wielded the sword
of Paul. By resorting to sanctions which he was powerless to
enforce Pius appeared to have committed a political blunder of
unusual proportions; he had done nothing to improve the already
parlous state of Catholicism in England and, at the same time, had
seriously damaged the prestige of the papacy. This leads rather
naturally to the question – why on earth did he do it?

It seems to be generally accepted that the Pope acted in good
faith on the basis of inaccurate and out of date information; that
he genuinely believed the English Catholics were both able and
eager to throw off the heretic yoke and only hesitated to act lest,
by taking the law into their own hands, they might endanger their
souls. Clearly Pius was convinced that speed was of the essence –
the bull itself bears every evidence of hasty drafting and certain
formalities normally required by canon law were omitted from the
proceedings. Clearly, too, his intelligence service left much to be

desired. This in itself is surely a little odd. True, sixteenth-century international communications were slow and not infrequently impeded, but institutions like the great Italian banking houses and city states such as Venice were usually extremely well informed – they went to considerable trouble and expense to ensure that they were. Nor was England at this time in any sense an iron curtain country. Apart from little local difficulties like that with the Duke of Alva, trade and diplomatic relations with Catholic Europe went on uninterrupted and traffic moved freely in and out of English ports.

One is led to the conclusion that the Pope, impatient for an excuse to assert himself, preferred to listen to unconfirmed and prejudiced reports. In other words, he believed what he wanted to believe – a not uncommon human foible but perhaps an unfortunate one in the spiritual leader of Western Christendom. But although it is easy enough to condemn him for being precipitate, bigoted and stupid, it is also quite possible to see his predicament. For twelve years the papacy had patiently pursued a policy of wait and see towards the Queen of England with no visible results save a steady deterioration of its cause. By failing to seize an apparently golden opportunity when it was offered, Pius might lay himself open to the charge of having allowed some four million souls to go to eternal damnation without lifting a finger to save them. Even if the expected rising failed, a gesture would at least have been made; the surviving Catholics could feel they had not after all been abandoned by Rome. They might be emboldened to try again and succeed. The Catholic Powers might yet be shamed into assisting them.

So Pius appears to have reasoned, but the English government naturally found it hard to credit that he would have taken such a step without the prior knowledge and at any rate tacit approval of France and Spain. *Regnans in Excelsis* might be dismissed in London as 'a vain crack of words that made a noise only'; its implications nevertheless remained profoundly disturbing and suspicions that 'some monster was a-breeding' were inevitably heightened.

By his unequivocal declaration that orthodox Catholicism and allegiance to the Queen of England were no longer compatible, the Pope had given Elizabeth every excuse for treating all her Catholic subjects as potential traitors. But apart from a certain stepping-up in the number of prosecutions, due largely to the aftermath of the Northern Rising, there were few tangible signs of any further hardening of official attitudes during the summer of 1570, and in June the Queen issued a reassuring public statement, read on her behalf by Lord Keeper Bacon in the Star Chamber.

'Whereas certain rumours are carried and spread abroad among sundry her Majesty's subjects that her Majesty hath caused, or will hereafter cause, inquisition and examination to be had of men's consciences in matters of religion; her Majesty would have it known that such reports are utterly untrue, and grounded either of malice, or of some fear more than there is cause. For although certain persons have been lately convented before her Majesty's council upon just causes, and that some of them have been treated withal upon some matter of religion; yet the cause thereof hath grown merely of themselves, in that they have first manifestly broken the laws established for religion in not coming at all to the church, to common prayer and divine service. . . .

'Wherefore her Majesty would have all her loving subjects to understand that, as long as they shall openly continue in the observation of her laws and shall not wilfully and manifestly break them by their open actions, her Majesty's meaning is not to have any of them molested by an inquisition or examination of their consciences in causes of religion; but will accept and entreat them as her good and obedient subjects. And if any shall otherwise by their open deeds and facts declare themselves wilfully disobedient to break her laws; then she cannot but use them according to their deserts, and will not forbear to inquire of their demeanours and of what mind and disposition they are, as by her laws her Majesty shall find it necessary.

'Of all which, her Majesty would have her subjects in all parts of her realm discreetly warned and admonished not to be abused by such untrue reports, to bring them any wise to doubt of her Majesty's honourable intention towards them . . . being also very loath to be provoked by the overmuch boldness and wilfulness of her subjects to alter her natural clemency into a princely severity.'

By offering her Catholic subjects what amounted to a bargain—freedom to practise their religion in private in exchange for public observance of the Anglican rite—Elizabeth was merely restating her personal attitude to the whole religious controversy: an attitude which can be stigmatised as displaying cynical disregard for Christian belief or admired for its humanity and good sense. To restate it so openly in the political climate of 1570 remains an act of courage and faith. But then Elizabeth always valued national unity at a much higher price than theological purity and never really believed that any significant number of her people would rise against her on the orders of a foreign bishop. Whether she would be able to maintain her liberal stand in the face of a nervous Council and a belligerent House of Commons was another matter. In time of ideological war humanity and good sense are usually the first qualities to fly out of the window.

Elizabeth's experience of Parliament to date had not caused her to feel any particular affection for that institution and it was only with reluctance that she agreed to summon it again in the spring of 1571. This was the first occasion on which every member had to take the Oath of Supremacy before taking his seat. It was the first occasion, therefore, when not a single committed Catholic was present at Westminster and the Commons soon revealed itself to be in a singularly unecumenical frame of mind. The left-wing Protestants, or Puritans as they were beginning to be labelled, backed by the younger, more radical clergy, had grown in strength and self-confidence and were becoming increasingly difficult to control.

Their loyalty and patriotism could hardly be faulted but their attempts to interfere in matters which the Queen considered none of their business infuriated her. Apart from her personal predilection for a bit of decent ceremony, she regarded demands for further Church reform – curtailment of the powers of the episcopacy, the abolishing of copes and surplices, doing away with wedding rings and kneeling at communion – to be a direct attack on her prerogative, an attack she would resist to the uttermost. The left-wingers were also pressing for more stringent enforcement of the Uniformity laws, but a bill which would have made it compulsory for everyone to come to communion and receive the sacrament at least once a year, although it had the support of the bishops and the Privy Council, was vetoed by the Queen.

There was no trouble over a government measure to make it a treasonable offence to bring papal bulls or similar documents into the country. By the same act, anyone who imported or received Agnus Dei, rosaries 'or such like vain and superstitious things', became liable to lose his life and property. Another bill was passed making it high treason to write or signify that Elizabeth was not the lawful Queen, or that she was a heretic, schismatic, tyrant, infidel or usurper. This was the other half of the government's answer to *Regnans in Excelsis*. It was given its first reading in the Commons on 9 April and one Thomas Norton, 'a man wise, bold and eloquent', was quickly on his feet to remind the House 'that her Majesty was and is the only pillar and stay of all our safety'. The 'care, prayer and chief endeavour' of Parliament must therefore be for the preservation of her life and estate. He liked the bill but thought it did not go far enough. He wanted, in fact, to extend its provisions to exclude from the succession anyone who 'hath [made] or hereafter shall make claim to the crown of England during her Majesty's life, or shall say she hath not lawful right, or shall refuse to acknowledge her to be undoubted Queen'.

Norton's 'addition' was clearly aimed at the Queen of Scots and he had a good deal of support in both Houses, but Elizabeth rejected it. 'This being brought unto us,' she told the assembled Lords and Commons at the end of the session, 'we misliked it very much; being not of the mind to offer extremity or injury to any person. For as we mind no harm to others, so we hope none will mind [it] unto us. And therefore, reserving to every his right, we thought it not good to deal so hardly with anybody as by that bill was meant.'

Parliament was dissolved on 29 May, not without a few pointed remarks from the Queen about the arrogance and presumption of certain members who had wasted everyone's time with 'frivolous and superfluous speech' and by 'meddling with matters neither pertaining unto them nor within the capacity of their understanding'. Nevertheless, she had succeeded for the time being in preserving a measure of indulgence for loyal conservatives and in restraining left-wing exuberance. If the Commons had known what she and William Cecil already knew – or guessed – about the activities of a certain Roberto Ridolfi, her task would have been more difficult.

Although labyrinthine in its ramifications, the objectives of the so-called Ridolfi Plot were straightforward enough – to take Elizabeth alive or dead, to free the Queen of Scots and set her on the throne with the Duke of Norfolk as her consort and, of course, to restore the Catholic religion; three remarkable feats which were to be accomplished by the native Catholics led by Norfolk and assisted by a Spanish army from the Netherlands. It is hardly surprising that a scheme so unrealistic in conception and based on almost total ignorance of actual political and geographical conditions should be regarded with a certain amount of scepticism today. Indeed, one Catholic historian has made out a detailed case to show that Ridolfi may have been acting as an *agent provocateur* in the pay of William Cecil – a case which, however, remains and is likely to remain 'not proven'. It is tempting now either to laugh off Ridolfi's machinations or to try and find some hidden meaning beneath such an apparently incredible set of circumstances. But at a time when England faced a potentially hostile Europe (since the assassination of the Regent Moray in January 1570 not even Scotland was assured) and when the government was suffering from that uncomfortably itchy feeling between the shoulder blades which afflicts those who fear a stab in the back from potential traitors within, the situation would have had a very different flavour.

Ridolfi himself was a member of an influential Florentine banking family with longstanding English connections and had been living and working in London for the past ten years. Lately, though, he had begun to find plotting a more stimulating occupation than banking. He had certainly had a finger in the pie of the Northern Rising and in October 1569 he had been arrested and confined for a time in the house of no less a person than Francis Walsingham. Ridolfi succeeded in convincing Walsingham of his innocence – an achievement which is regarded as highly suspicious in some circles – and was let off with a caution. There may have been no more to it than that. Rather than antagonise important Italian banking interests, the authorities may have preferred to give him the benefit of the doubt. They may have hoped that given enough rope he would hang himself and others. Ridolfi may have come to a mutually advantageous arrangement with his captors. Whatever the truth of the matter, he at once returned with unabated zest to performing the functions of unofficial papal nuncio and conspirator-in-chief – for which his legitimate business activities provided excellent cover.

In March 1571, his work in England completed, Ridolfi left for Rome, taking with him letters of credence and detailed 'Instructions' from the Queen of Scots and the Duke of Norfolk. On the way, he called at Brussels to see the Duke of Alva, who was notably unimpressed by the talkative Italian and his impracticable schemes. But in Rome and later in Madrid, Ridolfi had nothing to complain of in the welcome he received. He brought the Pope just the sort of news that Pius wanted to hear and when he continued his journey to Spain at the end of May, Ridolfi carried a letter from the Holy Father charging and imploring the Catholic King 'to repose in him unhesitating faith'.

Philip's co-operation was all-important. The Pope could provide blessings, absolutions and moral support for the invasion of England. He might even provide some cash. But no soldiers would embark at the ports of Flanders without the King of Spain's word. The King of Spain, therefore, was worthy of Ridolfi's best persuasive efforts, and Ridolfi's best efforts were very persuasive. Seldom or never, he told Philip, did such an opportunity befall a Christian prince to store up treasure in heaven by doing God's work on earth at so little cost to himself. Vast numbers of Englishmen were not yet abandoned by the grace of God and loathed the life they were being forced to lead. They could no longer endure the unjust laws, the perfidy, the welter of schism and heresies which prevailed in their country. The self-styled Queen was already distraught and suspicious, a prey to terror and vacillation. It would all be so easy. The English ports were open and undefended. The Queen of Scots' party was great and powerful. The insurgent nobility were the greatest and most powerful in the land and were ready to lead the way. They were only asking for a supporting force – a few men, a few arms, a little money. The Queen of Scots would be grateful for ever and would use her influence to prevent any future trouble with France. She would also be willing to send her son to Spain to be brought up a Catholic under Philip's eye. In any case, quite apart from all the material benefits which would accrue, what work could be more just and acceptable to God than to defend a widow, aid a child and succour the oppressed?

Philip, cautious at first, became steadily more enthusiastic and soon Ridolfi was writing letters to Mary and Norfolk to tell them that the business was as good as settled. The only spoilsport in the game of let's pretend as played in Rome and Madrid that summer was the Duke of Alva, who placed no reliance whatever on the English Catholics and could see himself with horrid clarity being forced to take part in a disastrous fiasco – a sixteenth-century

Bay of Pigs. As for Ridolfi – 'A man like this,' wrote the Duke scornfully, 'who is no soldier, who has never witnessed a campaign in his life, thinks that armies can be poured out of the air, or kept up one's sleeve, and he will do with them whatever fancy suggests.' Alva seems also to have been the only person to spell out the undoubted fact that the first consequence of failure would be the permanent destruction of Mary Stuart – the best, indeed the only hope for the future of Catholicism in the British Isles.

But Ridolfi's triumphal progress round Europe had not passed unnoticed in London, and to Alva's unspeakable relief before the point of no return had been reached the inevitable happened. In April Charles Bailly, a servant of Mary's ambassador the Bishop of Ross, was arrested as he landed at Dover and found to be in possession of prohibited books. Bailly carried something more incriminating than books, but the official in charge at the port – he was Lord Cobham – was sympathetic towards the English refugees in Flanders and allowed a packet of letters to be sent on to their recipient. All the same, the Council had its suspicions and subsequently discovered, by means of a stool-pigeon that Bailly was corresponding with his master in code. Pressure was applied and 'after much ado' Bailly revealed the key, but still the identities of the principles referred to remained a mystery. Then, about the end of August, the fortunate curiosity of a Welsh draper conveying a parcel to Shrewsbury provided the vital clue – the Duke of Norfolk had been caught in the act of sending money and letters to the Queen of Scots' partisans. Now at last the government was able to move in for the kill.

Norfolk himself, who had been released from the Tower and allowed to live under surveillance in his own house, was re-arrested on 7 September. His servants were rounded up for questioning and the whole sorry affair began to come into the open. Letters were found under mats and the 'alphabets' of codes hidden under the roof tiles at Howard House. The Council's representatives heard about 'writings' smuggled in and out in bottles of drink with specially marked corks and of other messages wrapped in black paper and thrown into 'a little dark privy-house' to be retrieved when the coast was clear. In the light of these new developments, the Bishop of Ross was re-examined and, after it had been forcibly pointed out to him that neither his cloth nor his ambassadorial status would protect him in a crisis of this nature, his lordship in a cold sweat told all he knew. It turned out to be a good deal.

Although Norfolk had retained just enough sense not to sign letters for Ridolfi, there can be no reasonable doubt that he had fallen in with at least part of that enterprising individual's suggestions. There is no doubt at all that, despite his solemn undertaking to the Queen, he had continued to correspond with Mary, to lend her money and to advise her not only about her plans for escape but on the terms of the treaty she was negotiating with Elizabeth. The Duke, in fact, had been riding a tiger for the past three years and was lucky to have lasted so long. By the end of November the case against him was complete and on 16 January 1572 he was brought to trial, convicted and condemned.

As for Mary, her own ambassador had not hesitated to implicate her in the plot. Mary herself naturally denied all charges of conspiracy but, while it has to be remembered that the Bishop of Ross was almost indecently anxious to save his skin and that some of the documentary evidence is not above suspicion, it is a little hard to believe in the Queen of Scots' lilywhite innocence. After all, why should she have been innocent? Mary was a fighter and an inveterate optimist. She considered herself to be unjustly imprisoned. As a Catholic she now had moral justification for regarding Elizabeth as an usurper to be deposed by force, and Ridolfi's schemes were exactly calculated to appeal to her gambling instincts. 'Ah, the poor fool will never cease until she lose her head,' exclaimed the King of France after reading the report of his ambassador in London.

Nevertheless, there seemed no immediate prospect of this happening. Elizabeth was angry. She abandoned her policy of negotiation with Mary and significantly allowed the Earl of Moray's version of the Darnley affair, together with the much disputed Casket Letters, to be published for the first time. Mary's household was cut down and her confinement became more rigorous, at least temporarily. But this was apparently as far as the Queen of England meant to go. Even Norfolk was still alive. Three times the warrant for his execution had been signed. Three times Elizabeth had revoked it at the last moment. Her well-wishers were in despair at this display of feminine weakness. 'The Queen's majesty hath been always a merciful lady and by mercy she hath taken more harm than by justice' wrote Cecil, or Lord Burghley as he now was, to Francis Walsingham after the first of these postponements.

'God's will be fulfilled and aid her Majesty to do herself good'
he wrote after the second one.

Lord Burghley's nervous system was not improved when Elizabeth succumbed to a short but violent attack of food poisoning
towards the end of March. He and the Earl of Leicester spent
three nights at her bedside and it is not difficult to imagine the
kind of thoughts passing through their heads during this vigil.
Thomas Smith put the general feeling into words when he wrote
from the embassy in Paris to thank Burghley for his bulletins
and for 'calling to our remembrance and laying before our eyes
the trouble, the uncertainty, the disorder, the peril and danger
which had been like to follow if at that time God had taken
from us that stay of the Commonwealth and hope of our repose,
that lantern of our light next God'.

No doubt this scare stiffened the Council in their resolve to
call another Parliament. Strong pressure must have been brought
to bear on the Queen to get her to agree and certainly it was an
unusual step to summon the members to Westminster so late in
the year. It was May before they could be assembled and summer
was not a healthy time to be in the plague-ridden capital. However,
'the cause was so necessary and so weighty as it could not otherwise be'. A committee of both Houses immediately met to discuss
this weighty cause – the future of the Queen of Scots – and after
listening to its report the Commons proceeded to make it crystal
clear what they wanted done about Mary. In the words of Richard
Gallys, member for New Windsor, they wanted to 'cut off her head
and make no more ado about her'. With scarcely a dissenting voice
the clamour grew for a final solution to the problem of that sower
of sedition and disturber of the peace, that notorious whore, adul-
teress and murderess, that monstrous and huge dragon.

It is easy now to condemn this baying for blood as vindictive
and hysterical but the Parliament of 1572 did not see it in that
light. The sober knights and burgesses gathered in the Palace of
Westminster could see their whole way of life, their peace and
prosperity, the future peace and prosperity of their children and
grandchildren being put at risk for the sake of a scruple. They
knew what was happening in France and the Low Countries.
Enough people living in the south and east had heard enough first-
hand atrocity stories from Flemish, Dutch and Huguenot refugees
to make their blood boil and their flesh creep – and such stories lost

nothing in the re-telling. Fears of Popish plots, of the invading armies of anti-Christ breathing fire and slaughter may have been exaggerated, but they were very understandable. The vast majority of Englishmen knew that everything they held dear depended, quite literally, on Elizabeth's life, and every Elizabethan knew that in the midst of life they were in death.

The Queen knew this too, but she was unmoved by all the urgent and piteous pleas being addressed to her. She was grateful for so much concern for her safety but she was unmoved. Even the numerous precedents for the putting to death of wicked kings cited from the Old Testament failed to impress her. 'Partly for honour, partly for conscience, for causes to herself known' she would not consent to a Bill of Attainder against the Queen of Scots. To the consternation and near despair of her faithful Lords, Commons and Council, she would not even agree to a bill excluding Mary from the succession. Norfolk had to be sacrificed, Parliament would not be baulked entirely of its prey, but Mary survived.

For the second time Elizabeth, by her deliberate, personal intervention, had saved the life of her mortal enemy. From a distance of four hundred years one can only wonder at the astonishing force emanating from this woman, isolated in a world of men, who was prepared to back her own instinct, intuition and judgement against the will of the nation as expressed by both Houses of Parliament, against the combined weight of her Council, against every reasonable argument of expediency, prudence and ordinary common sense. But Elizabeth Tudor intended to play the game of statecraft by her rules or not at all. In her way she was as great a gambler as Mary Stuart. The size of the stakes did not appear to dismay her in the least.

CHAPTER FIVE

God is daily glorified

'God is daily glorified and served in our country with great increase of the Catholic faith.'

William Allen, Cambrai, 10 August 1577

T H E public image of Catholicism had suffered serious damage as a result of *Regnans in Excelsis* and the disclosures of the Ridolfi Plot. Both had provided the Protestant cause with first-rate propaganda material and sober Protestant citizens shuddered at the thought of their narrow escape from Alva's blackbeards. Mary Stuart ceased to be regarded as a somewhat forlorn figure, a queen torn from her throne, a mother torn from her child, a prisoner to be secretly pitied, and became instead the ungrateful 'bosom serpent' of Francis Walsingham's telling phrase, a snake in the grass who had been ready to welcome an invading army into the country – a crime no Englishman would readily forgive. The Queen of Scots in particular and the Catholic religion in general were now firmly associated in the popular imagination with subversion, treachery and foreign interference. Then, at the end of August 1572, came news from France which confirmed every Protestant fear and prejudice.

The Massacre of St Bartholomew's Day is one of history's more spectacular horror stories and provides a depressingly familiar example of mob savagery. Ironically enough the occasion of this particular demonstration was an apparent *rapprochement* between Charles IX and his Huguenot subjects, sealed on 18 August by the marriage of the King's sister and the Huguenot prince, Henri of Navarre. Both *rapprochement* and marriage had been engineered by the King's mother, that optimistic politique Catherine de Medici, who needed allies to play off against the predatory Guise family. But Catherine had become seriously alarmed by the influence which the veteran Huguenot leader, Admiral Coligny, was establishing over her neurotic and unstable son, and feared that he was about to involve Charles in a Huguenot relief expedition to the Netherlands.

The Italian Queen would go to any lengths to protect her position as the power behind the throne and decided with devastating practicality that Coligny must go, confidently entrusting the Guises with the actual task of disposal. This should have been carried out on 22 August, but at the crucial moment the Admiral stooped to adjust a slipping overshoe and the assassin's bullet missed its mark, shattering the victim's arm. Charles sent his own physicians to attend Coligny, came personally to enquire, and promised a full investigation into the outrage. His mother, realising that her own complicity would be bound to emerge, hastily counter-attacked. She persuaded Charles that his own life was in grave danger from a Huguenot conspiracy and that his only recourse was to sanction the immediate and wholesale murder of the Huguenot notables so conveniently assembled for the Navarre wedding.

Catherine anticipated no difficulty in putting a policy of over-kill into action. The Parisians were predominantly and hot-temperedly Catholic and the presence of several thousand angry and suspicious Protestants was doing nothing to lower the tempera-ture in the capital. Although the wedding festivities had ended, the streets remained unusually full of people showing an odd reluct-ance to go back to work and numbers of armed men could be observed mingling with the crowds.

Across the river in the Faubourg St Germain, Queen Elizabeth's ambassador, that dour Kentish gentleman and devout Protestant, Francis Walsingham, his wife and daughter and their guest Philip Sidney waited nervously for news. In the small hours of 24 August the distant sound of church bells may have disturbed a wakeful member of the Walsingham family and during the morning rumours of a disturbance of some kind near the Louvre began to trickle through; but it was not until groups of terrified Pro-testants, both English and foreign, began to seek sanctuary at the embassy that they learnt the full horror of the situation. Those church bells had been a signal for Catholic to fall upon Huguenot. Paris was like a sacked city, the streets littered with corpses, the very gutters, according to some accounts, running with blood.

That night the beleaguered occupants of the English embassy huddled together in fear, praying for deliverance and expecting an unpleasant form of death at any moment. They were, in fact, lucky to escape. A mob which has tasted blood is no respecter of diplomatic immunity and the French government had quickly lost control of the monster it had unleashed. The slaughter spread to the provinces and altogether it is estimated that about ten thousand Huguenots or suspected Huguenots – men, women and children – lost their lives. Until now the atrocity score in the struggle between idolatry and heresy taking place in France had been roughly equal, but after St Bartholomew the Catholics gained an undeniably winning lead.

Reaction from abroad varied. Te Deums were sung in Rome which was illuminated as for a great victory. The Pope ordered commemorative medals to be struck and the King of Spain sent his personal congratulations to the King of France. The Dutch insurgent leader William of Orange, on the other hand, declared that Charles would never be able to cleanse himself of the bloody deed and even Ivan the Terrible was moved to enter a protest.

The first news of the massacre reached England on 27 August from Huguenot refugees pouring across the Channel into Rye and other ports in the south-east. The French ambassador was astonished at the depth of feeling it aroused. The English, he reported, were expressing 'extreme indignation and a marvellous hatred against the French, reproaching loudly broken faith, with great execration of excesses and so many kinds of outrages, mixed with words of defiance by those who bear arms'. Even after the matter had been explained to them La Mothe Fénelon was pained to see that the islanders showed no signs of moderating their opinions, 'holding that it was the Pope and the King of Spain who kindled the fire in France ... and that there is something evil afoot from all three of them against England'. The Bishop of London put a widespread fear into words when he wrote to Lord Burghley on 5 September, 'These evil times trouble all good men's heads and make their hearts ache, fearing that this barbarous treachery will not cease in France but will reach over unto us. Neither fear we the mangling of our body, but we sore dread the hurt of our head, for therein consisteth our life and safety.'

News of the death of Admiral Coligny in the general holocaust on St Bartholomew's Day brought a special sense of foreboding to England. It was not merely that Coligny had been a wounded man trusting to the protection of the French King which made his murder so shocking. He was the second Protestant leader to die by assassination in less than three years. In the autumn of 1572 the writing on the wall looked plain enough and one immediate repercussion was a renewed outcry against Mary Stuart. No one suggested that Mary had been in any way responsible for events in Paris, although it was being remembered that Mary's relations had led the killer pack (Henri of Guise had personally supervised the despatch of Coligny). Mary's intentions, innocent or otherwise, were becoming less and less relevant. It was the mere fact of her existence within the Protestant state which was becoming more and more intolerable, 'as nothing presently is more necessary than that the realm might be delivered of her'. 'If the sore be not salved,' wrote Francis Walsingham ominously, 'I fear we shall have a Bartholomew breakfast or a Florence banquet.' The Bishop of London recommended that the Scottish Queen's head should be cut off forthwith and even gentle Archbishop Parker offered much the same advice.

Top-secret contingency plans were, in fact, being made to send Mary back to Scotland where, it was hoped, the Regent Mar and his party might be 'by some good means wrought ... so they would without fail proceed with her by way of justice, so as neither that realm nor this should be dangered by her hereafter'. As it turned out the Scots demanded too high a price for doing the Queen of England's dirty work and, no doubt fortunately for Elizabeth's reputation at the hands of latter-day moralists, this somewhat sinister plan came to nothing. That it was seriously considered is an indication of the near-panic created in government circles by the events in France.

England and France had recently signed a defensive treaty, but to those not privileged to read the minds of Catherine de Medici and her son, the attempted extermination of the Huguenots and the re-emergence of the Guises looked at first very much like the beginning of a concerted Catholic attack on Protestantism everywhere. Certainly it revived that perennial nightmare of a hostile league of Catholic powers which was to recur in a more or less acute form throughout Elizabeth's reign. This nightmare has been ridiculed by modern Catholic historians as a mere propaganda bogey, invented and nurtured by Protestant leaders to frighten their followers and keep their ardour alive. We know now that it was indeed a chimera, that no such Papal League ever existed, even on paper. But anyone who has lived through the years since the Second World War also knows just how powerfully fear and suspicion can work on the minds of governments and peoples when the passions aroused by rival ideologies are poisoning international relations. In such conditions threats of encirclement and aggression do not need to be actual to be real.

In view of the various political crises of the late 1560s and early 1570s, it might have been expected that the lot of the English Catholics would have altered dramatically for the worse, but there seems no evidence that this was so. Had the Catholic minority showed any signs of responding to the call of *Regnans in Excelsis* no doubt the story would have been different. No such signs were forthcoming. The bull itself contained enough legal flaws to offer loopholes to all but the most tender consciences and it could plausibly be argued that as long as Elizabeth remained the *de facto* queen, her Catholic subjects could safely go on obeying her laws – or at any rate most of them.

Pockets of resistance remained. In July 1574 Lancashire was being described as 'the very sincke of Poperie', and despite periodic drives by the Earl of Derby and the Bishop of Chester, the region was to continue to present the authorities with an especially intractable problem. East Anglia, where families such as the Huddlestons, Walpoles and Bedingfields kept the flame alight, was another trouble spot. In December 1571 the Bishop of Norwich received orders from London to carry out a purge of recusants in his diocese and the following February addressed a letter to a certain Mr Townsend of Braken Ashe.

'I have been often advertised,' wrote his lordship, 'that you, and my lady your wife, do absent yourselves from church and hearing divine service and the receiving of the sacrament. I have hoped still that my favourable forbearing, together with your duties in this behalf, would have moved you to have conformed yourselves. And yet I hear, and thank God for it, that for your own part you come on very well and shall by God's grace increase daily. But touching my lady, I hear she is wilfully bent, and little hope as yet of her reformation, to the displeasure of Almighty God, the breach of the Queen's majesty's laws, my danger and peril to suffer so long, and an evil example and encouragement to many others.' The bishop had been very patient with the Townsends, but now, he went on, 'My duty and place of calling, together with my conscience to Godward, cannot suffer me to know such disorder and to suffer the same any longer. And therefore I desire you both from henceforth to frequent the church and the receiving of the sacrament as becometh Christians: so as I may be certified forthwith both of the one and the other; which I look for. Otherwise, this is most assured, I will not fail to complain of you both to her Majesty's Council.'

Although the headmasterish tone of the bishop's letter concealed a real enough threat, it was still not precisely comparable to persecution as understood by his French and Spanish counterparts. Queen Elizabeth's government sensibly preferred to use mental rather than physical pressure wherever possible. One Catholic who could be persuaded to attend the Protestant service – even one like Sir Thomas Cornwallis who ostentatiously read 'some Lady psalter or portasse' throughout the proceedings – was worth fifty martyrs from a propaganda point of view. The Queen herself certainly thought so, although her well-wishers often felt she carried her low-profile policy too far.

The Bishop of London had long suspected that the Portuguese ambassador was abusing his diplomatic privilege by admitting the general public to his private family mass and on 1 March 1572 Edwin Sandys ordered the sheriff, Mr Pipe, to raid the embassy in Tower Street and arrest any of the Queen's subjects found 'committing idolatry'. The ambassador appears to have put up a spirited resistance, offering 'to shoot dags' at the intruders. During the general uproar, the congregation was able to melt away and the sheriff's officers only succeeded in bagging four Irish law students. The aftermath of this affair was even more disappointing, for the ambassador rushed off to Court to complain, getting his story in first so that the Queen took his part and 'was somewhat offended with these proceedings'. The bishop, much aggrieved, wrote to Lord Burghley, 'Truly, my lord, such an example is not to be suffered. God will be mighty angry with it. It is too offensive. If her Majesty should grant it, or tolerate it, she can never answer God for it. God's cause must be carefully considered of. God willeth that his ministers purge the church of idolatry and superstition. To wink at it is to be partaker of it.'

In the opinion of such sturdy left-wingers as Edwin Sandys, the Catholic envoys were no more than spies lurking in the realm to practise mischief and the sooner they were all packed off 'to serve their god Baal at home' the better it would be. But it was

not only in embassy chapels that mass was said in London. On
Palm Sunday 1574, fifty-three people, 'whereof the most part were
ladies, gentlewomen and gentlemen', were rounded-up at illegal
Catholic services in various parts of the city – in Lady Morley's
chamber at Aldgate, at the Lady Guildford's in Trinity Lane,
Queenhithe, at 'Mr. Carus his house beside Limehouse'. According
to Dr Gardiner, Dean of Norwich, writing to his bishop from the
Court: 'The priests gloried in their doings, and affirmed that
there were five hundred masses in England said that day.' The
dean went on to utter a warning against complacency. 'The days
be dangerous. The Devil is busy to lull men asleep in security,
and to be negligent in their offices that require vigilant pastors, to
such time as he may by policy plant ignorance and idolatry to be
commended with cruelty. The greatest diligence is too little and
the least spark of careless negligence is too much.'

Just as it is impossible to say with any degree of accuracy how
many Catholics in the early seventies were still practising their
religion in defiance of the law, it is impossible to compute how
many priests ordained before 1559 were still at work among them.
Apart from those who had so horrified William Allen and Edward
Rishton by partaking on the same day of the chalice of the Lord
and the chalice of devils and the 'stragling doctors' who had found
shelter in the houses of sympathisers, there were others going from
place to place 'disguised in apparel, either after the manner of
servingmen or of some other artificers' maintaining the Queen's
subjects in 'superstition and error'. Dr Humphrey Ely of St John's
College and a close friend of William Allen knew of 'many ancient
priests of Queen Marie's days that stood firm and stable in their
faith, and drew daily some out of the mire of schism by preaching
and teaching'. William Allen himself paid tribute to the labours
of the Marian priests who had 'by the secret administration of the
sacraments and by their exhortations confirmed many in the faith
and brought back some who had gone wrong'. But the numbers
of these ageing men, which can never have been more than a
few hundred, were being steadily eroded by natural wastage, and
as long as no replacements were forthcoming, a religion like
Catholicism which depended so heavily on its priests must eventually wither and die. This was the logic on which the Elizabethan
government had based its policy, and it goes some way towards
explaining the intense official vexation when replacements did start

to filter through from abroad and when it began to look as though the fruits of fifteen years of patience had been wasted.

The activities of the exiles in Flanders had not gone unnoticed. The Parliament of 1571 had passed an Act Against Fugitives over the Sea, which laid down that anyone who had gone abroad without permission since the beginning of the reign and who did not return in a contrite spirit within six months was to forfeit his goods and chattels and the profits of his estates. In a scrupulous attempt to avoid the appearance of religious persecution, the Act included a provision for the relief of the 'desolate wife and children' of any man who had gone into exile 'by reason of blind zeal and conscience only' and who was not accused of being involved in treason. The steady trickle of Catholic books and propaganda tracts which, despite the efforts of the customs authorities, was still finding its way into the country continued to be a source of annoyance, but in 1574 the government felt confident enough to release conditionally several prominent Catholics who had been in prison since the early sixties. By a curious irony this was the very year in which the first Douai-trained missionaries arrived in England.

Contrary to many people's expectations, the college at Douai had not only survived, it had prospered. By the mid-seventies, less than ten years after its foundation, there were eighty students at the seminary and their numbers increased steadily. The chief problems continued to be financial ones, especially after 1571 when the wealthier exiles could no longer draw on their English revenues and as it became more and more difficult for Catholics at home to send money overseas. But William Allen was not a man to let anything so paltry as lack of funds interfere with his work for souls or to allow it to discourage anyone 'whom Christ had touched with the thought of taking holy orders'. 'None were rejected,' wrote Dr Ely, 'had they money or had they none, brought they commendations or brought they none. After they had been tried there awhile, such as were not found fit (which God knoweth were but few) were graciously and courteously dismissed with money in their purses.'

The fame of Douai was spreading and it was becoming, just as Allen had always hoped it would, a powerhouse for the revival and refreshment of English Catholicism in general. Some of those who passed through its ever open doors were gentlemen's sons, 'who were studying humanities, philosophy or jurisprudence, and who either of their own accord or through the exhortations of Catholic relations and friends, had been moved by the fame of the seminary to seek here a Catholic education'. These lay students paid for their board and lodging and remained 'until, according to their age and condition, they had been duly catechised and reconciled to the Church by penance for their previous life and schism'. 'There came at the same time,' records William Allen, 'not a few who were simply heretics, and even heretical ministers and preachers, all of whom being moved to penance through our instructions and conversation were not only sincerely reconciled to the Church, but after a year or two spent under the college discipline desired to become priests, and when they had obtained their wish zealously devoted themselves to the English harvest.'

A steady stream of visitors was also soon penetrating to Douai. As well as those who had business with the students, travellers on their way to France or Italy would come to see a friend at the seminary or simply out of curiosity to have a look at a place 'about which there was already much talk'. The majority of these callers were, by Douai standards, either 'devoid of all religion' or at the least serious backsliders, but all would be welcomed and pressed to stay for a few days. Those without means would be offered a month's free board and instruction in 'the chief heads of the Catholic religion'. Allen lost no chance, however slight, of reconciling a soul to God, no opportunity of publicising the aims and work of his foundation. This policy played havoc with his budget but it paid dividends in other ways. Many who came to stare or to scoff, returned home deeply impressed by what they had seen, and, wrote Allen, 'persuaded many others to leave all and come to us at Douai, or at least to come once to hear and see us, as some heretics had done'.

As part of its publicity campaign, the college issued invitations to 'the more learned heretics' in England who had been misled by bad education, 'praying them to make for once a trial of our mode of life and teaching, and promising them, so long as they remained with us, such courteous entertainment as befitted their dignity'. There is no record of any response to these hopeful offers, but some contact was established between Douai and the remnants of the Catholic priesthood at home. Allen was anxious that these weary labourers in the Lord's vineyard should come over to the college for a refresher course and specialised instruction suitable for 'the necessities of the present time' such as his own students were receiving. This was a good deal easier said than done but one Marian priest, Father John Peel, did make the pilgrimage in 1576 and there may have been others. At any rate, the knowledge that someone somewhere was interested in keeping the flame alight must have encouraged those members of the older generation still active in the field.

It was four and a half years before William Allen saw the first tangible results of his hard work when he presented four of his students at the Easter ordination held in Brussels. Another six were ordained in 1574 and it was in that year that the first pioneers left for England. They were Louis Barlow, Henry Shaw, Martin Nelson and Thomas Metham. Seven more crossed over in 1575, eighteen in 1576, fifteen in 1577 and by the end of the decade a hundred priests had been sent out from Douai. Very little seems to be known about these earliest missionaries or how they set about their task but, at least according to their own accounts, their success was immediate and spectacular.

'The number of Catholics increases so abundantly on all sides,' wrote Henry Shaw to Allen in 1575, 'that he who almost alone holds the rudder of the state [presumably Lord Burghley] has privately admitted to one of his friends that for one staunch Catholic at the beginning of the reign there were now, he knew for certain, ten.' John Payne, writing the following summer, declared that the numbers of those being reconciled to the Church increased daily and he added: 'the heretics are as much troubled at the name of the Anglo-Douai priests, which is now famous throughout England, as all the Catholics are consoled thereby'. Early in 1577, Allen heard from people coming over to France that 'the numbers of those who were daily restored to the Catholic Church almost surpassed belief' and that 'one of the younger priests lately sent on the mission had reconciled no fewer than eighty persons in one day'.

Some allowance should be made for wishful-thinking in these reports and it has to be remembered that the missionaries were to a certain extent preaching to the converted, in the sense that they naturally gravitated to Catholic houses and Catholic neighbourhoods, finding shelter among sympathisers. But these young men were a different breed of priest to the old ignorant 'mass-monger', 'the popish Sir John Mumblemattins' who all too often had done little more than gabble his unintelligible Latin prayers over a largely uncomprehending and indifferent congregation. The Douai priests, highly trained, highly educated and burning with the thirst for souls, were both able and willing to answer awkward questions, discuss and resolve problems and expound points of doctrine. Most important of all, they were manifestly ready to practise what they preached, to accept hardship and death 'for the deliverance of the Church and their brethren'. They came too late and too few to reverse the Protestant tide, but they did succeed in breathing new life into the dying embers of English Catholicism.

By no means all the Catholic hierarchy approved of the initiative taken by William Allen and in 1577 he found himself defending his ex-students to Father Maurice Chauncy, Prior of the English Carthusians at Bruges, who, with a remarkable failure to grasp the realities of the current situation, had apparently objected to the secular disguises adopted by the Douai priests in their battle 'to win the souls of their dearest countrymen'. Allen had no illusions about the dangers, spiritual as well as physical, to which the missionaries were exposed. Once they arrived in England they were on their own and would certainly need 'to pray instantly and fast much and watch and ward themselves well, lest the needful use of sundry enticements to sin and necessary dissimulation in things of themselves indifferent, to be fit for every company, bring them to offend God, and so while they labour to save others themselves become reprobate'.

Allen fully realised the vulnerability of those 'who had taken upon them to be guides of other men's lives and belief' – especially those whose declared aim was to persuade other men to abandon a comfortable compromise and deliberately invite trouble on themselves for the sake of a principle. He knew the Douai priests would be watched lynx-eyed for the slightest lapse. He had no illusions, but he clearly found it difficult to be patient when armchair critics like Father Chauncy carped at his *protégés*. 'Most men mark their misses,' he wrote, 'and few consider in what fears and dangers they be in, and what unspeakable pains they take to serve good men's turns to their least peril. I could reckon unto you the miseries they suffer in night journeys in the worst weather that can be picked, peril of thieves, of waters, of watches, of false brethren; their close abode in chambers as in prison or dungeon without fire and candle lest they give token to the enemy where they be; their often and sudden rising from their beds at midnight to avoid the diligent searches of heretics; all which and divers other discontentments, disgraces and reproaches they willingly suffer.' These 'pains' Allen considered were surely penance enough for the 'feathers' of their secular dress and pains which, he added tartly, few men pitied or rewarded as they should.

Another of the criticisms being levelled at the missionaries was that they were too young and too inexperienced for the responsibilities they were being called upon to carry. Allen might have pointed out that the 'English harvest' was essentially an undertaking for younger men, who would not only have the necessary physical stamina but who would know how to appeal to the all-important younger generation. He was, however, intensely conscious that it was an undertaking for handpicked men. None of the candidates he had presented for ordination had been under twenty-five, he told Father Chauncy. All the priests he had sent to England had been 'thirty years old or not far under and many of them much more'. All of them, it went without saying, were 'of irreprovable life and conversation and of very good testimony'.

In fact, the consistently high reputation of the Douai priests was a tribute to Allen's judgement and the quality of the training he provided. In 1577 he could thank God that he had not yet heard of any 'enormous crimes or notorious offences by any of them all, nor that any is so ill and inconstant to fall, by fear or force, to deny their faith or to schism or heresy'. It was true that some had 'unadvisedly uttered in their sudden fear some places and persons of their resort and catholic exercise'. Allen was sorry about this, but then the missionaries were only human. There were bound to be those who would crack under interrogation or nervous strain and betray the names of their contacts. In the circumstances, he could only be grateful that no one had fallen any further from grace. He admitted that his students, being not all 'of settled age, experience and discretion', might be more likely to make mistakes but he had had to work with the material available to him. 'And though they were never so old,' he went on, 'would there be no faults spied among them, think you? Would all such live and teach and deal in those matters without all offence, trow you? It were to be wished, but it is not to be hoped. The busy enemy to all good intentions, the devil, can cast impediments enough among the oldest that be, to make their labour less profitable and less grateful to the people.'

It was easy enough, Allen implied, to wring one's hands about the state of England from a safe distance. His venture might be inadequate. He did not pretend for a moment that it was perfect, but at least as a result of the travails of the Douai priests 'God is daily glorified and served in our country with great increase of the Catholic faith'. Many of those secret Catholics, the so-called Church papists who had hitherto conformed 'for worldly fear', were now being emboldened to confess their faith openly and 'abhor all communion and participation with the sectaries in their service and sacraments'. As well as this, wrote Allen, 'there is daily such joyful resort of many to this side the seas to learn their belief and to take experience of the Church's discipline by our said priests' special exhortation, that it is wonderful to strangers and comfortable to us to behold'. For his part, he would have considered his 'poor pains and desires' well rewarded if every one of his missionaries had succeeded in saving only one soul from perdition but, he concluded with a touch of pardonable smugness, 'I have assured intelligence every one gaineth full many.'

A few months after William Allen had despatched this broad-side in the direction of Father Chauncy, Douai gained added respectability in the eyes of the Catholic world by acquiring its first martyr – the distinction falling to one of those wandering heretical sheep whose painful search for truth had led them into Allen's fold. Cuthbert Mayne was a West Countryman, born in the parish of Sherwell near Barnstaple in 1544. Brought up as a Protestant by a parson uncle, who wanted his nephew to follow in his footsteps and inherit his own fat benefice, the boy was educated at Barnstaple Grammar School and then Oxford, where he was ordained and appointed chaplain to St John's College at a time when, as he later lamented, 'he knew neither what ministry nor religion meant'. Mayne, an attractive and intelligent young man, soon became influenced by the prevailing pro-Catholic atmosphere of Oxford.

Just as Cambridge in the thirties and forties had been a hotbed of advanced Protestant ideas, so Oxford in the sixties and seventies was flirting dangerously with Rome. This was not really surprising. The Church of England as set up in 1559 had been essentially a political compromise and therefore could scarcely be expected to appeal to earnest, high-minded youth, sheltered from and impatient of political realities. The fact that Catholicism was anti-establishment added to its appeal among undergraduates, while William Allen's success in improving its intellectual image had attracted many of the younger Fellows – Cuthbert Mayne must certainly have spent some of his time sitting at the feet of Edmund Campion, the brilliant tutor at St John's.

Sooner or later all these restless spirits had to face the decision of whether or not they were going to settle down and accept the law of the land. In the end most did accept it. It was one thing to attend an occasional illicit Mass in a 'safe house' near Oxford and indulge in the stimulating luxury of theological dissent in the cosy common room of one's own college – quite another deliberately to abandon family, career, livelihood and possessions and go out into the cold for conscience sake. But by the beginning of the seventies Edmund Campion had chosen the hard way. So had Gregory Martin, also a St John's man, and Thomas Ford, another member of the circle and a close friend of Cuthbert Mayne. Mayne himself still hesitated, unhappy but apparently not yet able to summon the courage to make the break, and there is no doubt that it needed courage as well as conviction. While he hovered on the brink, he continued to correspond with his friends overseas and before long the inevitable had happened.

Mayne was away from Oxford, probably visiting his uncle, when he received a warning that some of these letters had been intercepted and that the Bishop of London was about to take an unfriendly interest in him. His decision had been made for him, and early in 1573 he 'took shipping on the coast of Cornwall' and found his way to Douai. Two years later he was ordained for the second time and in April 1576 joined the ranks of the missionaries, crossing to England in the company of John Payne. The two priests separated on the night of their arrival and Mayne set off for the West. He had apparently brought letters of introduction to Francis Tregian of Wolveden or Golden in Cornwall. At any rate he found sanctuary in the household, being passed off as the steward.

The Tregians were a comparatively new family but wealthy and well-connected. Francis Tregian's father had married a daughter of the Arundells of Lanherne, aristocratic, influential and obstinately Catholic. Tregian himself was married to a daughter of Lord

Stourton whose widow had married an Arundell. The Tregian estates extended widely between Truro and Launceston and his position as 'steward' gave Mayne excellent cover for his journeys about the countryside, saying Mass and reconciling the lapsed. He was later to admit that he had often been with his master to Sir John Arundell's at Lanherne, sometimes staying for as much as a week or a fortnight.

In this small, closed community it must soon have been common knowledge that there was a priest at work among the Catholics, but Mayne was able to carry on his ministry undisturbed for over a year. This state of affairs was probably not unconnected with the fact that the sheriff of Cornwall in 1576 was an easy-going old gentleman, unwilling to cause unpleasantness among his neigh-bours – an illustration of how difficult it could be to enforce the law at local level when the local justices were too idle, too timorous or too sympathetic to take action. In November, however, came an ominous change for Cuthbert Mayne and his hosts when Richard Grenville of Stowe took over as sheriff. Grenville, of Revenge fame, was a tough, thrusting, vigorous character with no inhibitions about causing unpleasantness, and determined to deal with the active Catholic cell within his territory. All the same, it was not until the following summer that he was in a position to take action.

In June 1577 the Bishop of Exeter was holding a visitation at Truro and Grenville took the opportunity of asking his help in smoking out the seminary at Golden. A force of nearly a hundred men – the sheriff himself, several justices of the peace and their servants, and the bishop's chancellor, who was to lend ecclesiastical authority to a search party proceeding without a warrant – accord-ingly set out on 8 June. It seems odd that no advance warning of this formidable little army riding the dusty lanes from Truro should have reached Golden, but Francis Tregian's security arrange-ments appear to have been lax to the point of non-existence. Just before the sheriff's posse arrived, Mayne had been in the garden, where, says the account later prepared by William Allen, 'he might have gone from them'. Instead, he unwisely returned to his room and locked himself in.

Meanwhile, Francis Tregian had met Grenville on the threshold and an altercation developed about his right of entry. According to Allen's informant, who may well have been an eye-witness: 'As soon as they came to Mr. Tregian's house, the Sheriff first spake unto him saying that he and his company were come to search for one Bourne, which had committed a fault in London, and so fled to Cornwall and was in his house as he was informed. Mr. Tregian answering that he was not there, and swearing by his faith that he did not know where he was, further telling him that to have his house searched he thought it a great discourtesy, for that he was a gentleman as he was, for that he did account his house as his castle: also stoutly denying them, for that they had no commission from the Prince.' But Francis Tregian was no match for Richard Grenville. 'The Sheriff being very bold, because he had a great company with him, sware by all the oaths he could devise that he would search his house or else he would kill or be killed, holding his hand upon his dagger as though he would have stabbed it into the gentleman. This violence being used, he had leave to search the house.'

As it turned out, not much searching took place. Evidently someone had already told Grenville all he needed to know about the domestic arrangements at Golden, for he made straight for Mayne's room and hammered on the door. 'As soon as the Sheriff came into the chamber, he took Mr. Mayne by the bosom and said unto him "What art thou?" and he answered "I am a man". Whereat the Sheriff, being very hot, asked whether he had a coat of mail under his doublet, and so unbuttoned it and found an Agnus Dei case about his neck, which he took from him and called him a traitor and rebel with many other opprobrious names.'

The sheriff now had all the justification he needed for his high-handed proceedings. To be in possession of an Agnus Dei (a small wax disc made from the Paschal candles, bearing the imprint of a lamb and blessed by the Pope) was a penal offence under the Act of 1571 and Mayne was certainly very foolish to have allowed himself to be caught wearing one. His books and papers were also seized and Richard Grenville added a chalice and vestments to the haul before bearing his prisoner off to the bishop at Truro. Mayne was later transferred to the gaol in Launceston Castle where 'he was confined to a filthy and dark underground prison, loaded with heavy irons, chained to his bedposts, allowed no books or writing materials ... and not permitted to see anyone except in the presence of a gaoler'. Francis Tregian, as befitted a gentleman of substance, was granted bail.

Cuthbert Mayne came up for trial at the Michaelmas Sessions

before Judges Manwood and Jefferys. He was indicted on five counts: traitorously obtaining from the See of Rome a certain printed instrument containing a pretended matter of absolution of divers subjects of the realm; traitorously publishing a certain printed instrument obtained from the See of Rome; upholding, maintaining and setting forth the ecclesiastical power, authority and jurisdiction of a foreign prelate, the Bishop of Rome; bringing a certain vain sign and superstitious thing called an Agnus Dei into the realm and giving it to Francis Tregian; and, finally, saying a certain public and open prayer called a private Mass and ministering the Sacrament of the Lord's Supper after a papistical manner. Mayne was convicted on all five counts and condemned to death – the first two charges automatically carrying the penalty for high treason.

Among the papers found at Golden had been a Bull of Absolution issued by Pope Gregory for the Jubilee Year of 1575 and which had now expired. Mayne's defence was that he had bought a copy in a printer's shop at Douai and must have packed it up accidentally with his other belongings before coming to England. He pointed out that anyway it was now merely a void paper 'of no force and out of all use'. He denied ever 'publishing' it. Since the Bull was now out of date, there was some doubt in the judges' minds as to whether it did actually come within the meaning of the Act, and sentence was respited while further advice was sought. Although, as a result of his own extraordinary carelessness, Mayne could technically be regarded as a traitor, in normal circumstances he might have expected to receive the benefit of the doubt on a tricky point of law. Circumstances, however, were far from normal. The government was irritated and alarmed by the arrival of the new priests, and determined to make an example. On 12 November orders came from the Council that the execution was to proceed without further delay.

All the same, on the day before he died, a sustained attempt was made to persuade Cuthbert Mayne to recant – an apostate priest would be infinitely more valuable than a dead priest. But he was not to be tempted by offers of life and liberty. Whatever doubts and hesitations he may once have felt were long behind him now. Weakened by the rigorous conditions of his imprisonment, with nothing before him but a particularly unpleasant form of death, Mayne demonstrated the terrible, immovable strength that comes from utter conviction. His teachers at Douai had done their work well.

The Queen, he told his examiners, never was, nor is, nor ever shall be Head of the Church of England. No one who called himself a Catholic might 'in any wise receive the Sacrament, come to the Church or hear the schismatical service which is established in the same here in England'. He believed that the people of England might be won back to Roman Catholicism by the 'secret instructors' already in the country and those who would be coming in the future. He refused to give any information about these secret instructors but hoped they and others would 'use secret conference to withdraw the minds of the subjects of the realm from the religion established in the same'. He went on to affirm 'that if any Catholic prince took in hand to invade any realm to reform the same to the authority of the See of Rome, that then the Catholics in that realm invaded by foreigners should be ready to assist and help them'. Here was the heart of the matter. It was not for these opinions that Cuthbert Mayne had been condemned, but they were why he had been condemned.

The sentence on him – hanging, disembowelling and dismembering – was duly carried out in Launceston market-place and the remains of the first of the Douai martyrs were thoughtfully distributed over North Devon and Cornwall – to Barnstaple, Bodmin, Wadebridge and Tregony. As well as Mayne and Francis Tregian (who was subjected to the pains of praemunire for harbouring, aiding and abetting the priest and who was to remain in prison until 1601), a number of prominent Cornish recusants had been rounded up and fined and a potentially dangerous Catholic remnant rooted out. The Council was understandably pleased with the High Sheriff, and Richard Grenville received the accolade at Windsor that October at the end of an eventful year of office.

Less than three months after Mayne's death, a second missionary priest suffered at Tyburn. This was John Nelson, a Yorkshireman of good family who had gone over to Douai in 1573 at the unusually mature age of forty. He came back to England in November 1576 and like Mayne remained at liberty for just over a year. He was arrested in London late in the evening of Sunday, 1 December 1577 as he was saying Matins for the next day and was committed to Newgate on suspicion of papistry. The Oath of Supremacy was put to him in prison and was refused. Although suggestive, this in itself was not necessarily an offence, since it had not been proved that Nelson came within any of the categories who could be compelled to take it. When, however, he was questioned about his reasons for refusing, he replied that he had never heard or read that a lay prince could have that pre-eminence. When asked who then, in his opinion, was Head of the Church, his answer was unequivocal, 'the Roman Pontiff, as being Christ's Vicar and the lawful successor of St. Peter'. When asked his opinion of the religion now established in England there could, therefore, be only one reply, that it was schismatical and heretical. This line of questioning could lead to only one end: was the Queen, as Governor of the Church of England, herself a schismatic?

Nelson seems to have tried to evade the open trap by replying that he could not tell, not knowing her mind with regard to the support and promulgation of schism. His questioners had no intention of letting him off the hook. The Queen, they told him, was a wholehearted supporter of Protestantism. After this there could, again, be only one reply. 'If she be the setter forth and defender of this religion now practised in England, then is she a schismatic and a heretic.' Having thus brought himself within the scope of the Treasons Act of 1571, Nelson's fate became a foregone conclusion. At his trial the evidence was clear. Indeed he made no attempt to deny it and met his death on 3 February 1578 with constancy and courage.

The third victim of the government's new hard-line policy was a layman, Thomas Sherwood. A Londoner by birth and son of a pious, middle-class Catholic family (his mother, Elizabeth, was the sister of Francis Tregian), Thomas went into his father's drapery business on leaving school, but 'being more devoted to a religious course of life than to a worldly, he obtained from his parents leave to pass the seas and come to Douai'. He did not, however, enter the college at once but came back to London to settle his affairs and 'to procure some competent means to maintain him for some time at his study'.

This was to prove his undoing. He spent a good deal of his time in the house of Lady Tregony or Tregonwell and her son – either fearing that his mother would get into trouble as a result, or out of jealousy – denounced Sherwood as a Papist. He was arrested one morning in November 1577 while walking down Chancery Lane and brought before Thomas Fleetwood, the

Recorder of London, well known for his anti-Catholic zeal. During the course of his first examination Sherwood, like Nelson, denied the Royal Supremacy and went on to say that if the Pope had indeed excommunicated Elizabeth, he thought she could not be lawful Queen. This brought Sherwood, like Nelson, within the scope of the 1571 Act. Unlike Nelson though, Sherwood was presently handed over to the Lieutenant of the Tower and confined in an especially noisome dungeon 'amongst the rats'. His friends were not allowed the customary privilege of providing him with bedding and extra food and he was racked on several occasions in an attempt to discover the names of his associates and the houses where he had heard Mass. It was also hoped that he might perchance 'bolt out some other matters or persons worthy to be known'.

This appears to have been the first use of torture – later to become a highly controversial issue – to extort information from Catholics and Sherwood may well have been singled out for such treatment because of his close connection with the Tregians. But although an undersized young man (he was twenty-seven at the time of his death) and unsupported either by priestly vows or the thorough-going indoctrination supplied at Douai, Thomas Sherwood betrayed no 'matters or persons worthy to be known'. Indeed, he displayed all the desperate, pathetic gallantry of which the human spirit can be capable. The story goes that when he was warned by a sympathetic gaoler that he was to be racked again, he answered 'merrily and with a cheerful countenance . . . "I am very little and you are very tall. You may hide me in your great hose and so they shall not find me"'. According to the report which presently reached Douai, 'in all his torments his cry had been, "Lord Jesus, I am not worthy to suffer these things for Thee, much less receive those rewards which Thou hast promised to such as confess Thee",' and it was said that even the Recorder Fleetwood shed tears at the sight of his sufferings.

Sherwood was tried at Westminster on 3 February 1578 charged with upholding the authority of the Pope; denying the Royal Supremacy; declaring that Elizabeth was not lawful Queen; and diabolically, maliciously and traitorously affirming 'in the presence and hearing of divers faithful subjects of the said Lady our Queen . . . that our said Queen Elizabeth . . . is a schismatic and an heretic, to the very great scandal and derogation of the person of our said Lady the Queen and the subversion of the state of this realm of

England'. His conviction followed speedily and he was condemned to the dreadful traitor's death: 'that the aforesaid Thomas Sherwood be led by the aforesaid Lieutenant unto the Tower of London, and thence be dragged through the midst of the city of London, directly unto the gallows at Tyburn, and upon the gallows there be hanged, and thrown living to the earth, and that his bowels be taken from his belly, and whilst he is alive be burnt, and that his head be cut off, and that his body be divided into four parts, and that his head and quarters be placed where our Lady the Queen shall please to assign them'.

Catholic historians and hagiographers have naturally made the most of the sufferings inflicted on the missionary priests and unfortunates like Thomas Sherwood, but when one remembers the sort of fate normally reserved for heretics and other religious deviants in Catholic countries at the time, they are perhaps not in the best position to throw stones. Hanging, drawing and quartering – to us an unimaginably obscene form of death – was nothing new. It had been the accepted end for traitors in England since mediaeval times and was to continue, at least in theory, until the eighteenth century. In practice, the victim was frequently allowed to hang until he was dead, unless his crime was considered to be extra heinous or unless the authorities wanted to make an example. The thought of any living, breathing creature being subjected to these and other horrors for whatever reason must arouse extreme revulsion now among all civilised people – it aroused revulsion among the tenderhearted then. But in an age without the benefit of anaesthetics or pain-killing drugs, physical discomfort and physical pain of an acute kind were commonplaces of daily life. It followed, therefore, that physical punishments had to be drastic to be effective and that something rather special had to be devised as a deterrent for traitors – generally regarded as society's most dangerous enemies.

No one ever suggested that Cuthbert Mayne, John Nelson or Thomas Sherwood were traitors in any but a technical sense – it was their connection with Douai and thence with Rome which made them politically dangerous. By the calculated ferocity of its reaction, the government showed just how seriously it took the threat of a Catholic revival at home, at a time when the international situation was steadily approaching crisis point.

CHAPTER SIX

If these fellows stand thus immovable

'If these fellows stand thus immovable before such Princes in
Rome, what will they do in England before the heretics?'
Robert Parsons, Rome, March 1579

F OR the English government the 1570s was a decade of intense
diplomatic activity, labyrinthine in its complexity. In the
conduct of her foreign policy, the Queen of England has frequently
been accused of tergiversation, indecision and plain bloodyminded-
ness – both by her contemporaries and by historians trying to grope
their way through the baffling palisade she erected to conceal her
intentions. While Elizabeth must surely have been a most infuriat-
ing female to serve and to negotiate with, it is now possible to see
that her underlying purpose was paradoxically not only extremely
simple but unwavering in its aim – to keep her people, her kingdom
and her throne peaceful, prosperous and secure. In order to achieve
that aim and to stay dryshod in the quicksand of European politics,
Elizabeth was prepared to shift her ground as often as seemed
necessary. In fact, the more confusion and uncertainty she could
create in the minds of others, the more freedom of action she
retained for herself. Flexibility was the keynote of her policy.
Among its cardinal principles were always to leave open as many
options as possible, never to be manoeuvred into some exclusive
commitment and, above all, to keep out of other people's bloody
and self-destructive faction fights.

The diplomatic poker game as played by Elizabeth Tudor
demanded strong nerves and unremitting concentration. The fact
that it also demanded subtlety, subterfuge and histrionic ability of
a high order only added to its zest. There can be no doubt that Elizabeth enjoyed the game for its own sake – certainly her skill as a
player has never been equalled. Its justification is that it paid off.
While the Spanish Empire went slowly bankrupt, France tore
herself to pieces and the Low Countries became a desert, England

remained solvent, united and increasingly powerful. When war did come it affected only a tiny minority of the population and provided a not uncongenial outlet for the energies of those who might well have got into mischief at home. No foot of English countryside was laid waste. No English farmstead was burnt down, no English town looted or put to the sword, no Englishman, woman or child slaughtered by an invading army.

This was Elizabeth's achievement, and if it has laid her open to accusations of selfishness and deceit she would have thought the price cheap. She had started, of course, with several built-in advantages. Still 'the best match in her parish', she unblushingly employed the weapon of courtship twice during the seventies and early eighties. She was unhampered by any masculine urge to prove virility by conquest. Most important of all, she was unhampered by those rigid ideological convictions which caused such untold misery throughout her century.

The Queen's cold-bloodedly secular approach to politics was often a source of sorrow to her well-wishers. Francis Walsingham, who had succeeded Lord Burghley as Principal Secretary in 1573, believed there could be no coexistence with the Catholic powers, for 'Christ and Belial can hardly agree'. To Walsingham and others of his way of thinking, the only safe and moral method of dealing with Philip of Spain was to recognise him as an enemy and treat him as such. 'What juster cause can a Prince that maketh profession of the Gospel have to enter into wars,' wrote Walsingham, 'than when he seeth confederacies made for the rooting out of the Gospel and religion he professeth?' But Elizabeth was not interested in wars, just or otherwise. Her only interest in confrontations, whether between Christ and Belial or between herself and Spain, lay in seeking the surest way of avoiding them. Slowly but inexorably the position of Protestant champion was to be forced upon her, but Elizabeth, who undertook foreign adventures only with extreme reluctance, never accepted the role of crusader.

The issue which dominated her diplomacy throughout the 1570s was the future of the Netherlands – a matter of immense importance to England from a strategic as well as a commercial point of view. The prospect of a Spanish victory leaving a Spanish army in undisputed possession of the invasion ports of Flanders represented a threat to English security which no English government could be expected to accept. It was true that at the beginning of the decade there seemed no immediate danger of this particular nightmare coming true. The forces of the revolted Dutch provinces under the leadership of William of Orange were frequently down but somehow never entirely out. William did have the advantage of sea-power which cushioned him to some extent from the effects of disaster on land. All the same, his position in general looked pretty desperate and very few people would have been prepared to bet on his future, unless he got outside help and got it quickly.

To the simple-minded it might have seemed that William of Orange would need to look no further than Elizabeth of England for assistance in embarrassing the King of Spain, but although a number of far from simple-minded persons were urging this very course upon her, Elizabeth was currently showing a more friendly face towards Spain than towards William. There were several cogent reasons for this apparently surprising attitude. Apart from her ineradicable dislike for the dangerous and unethical practice of lending official recognition to other sovereigns' rebels (unofficial aid was another matter altogether), Elizabeth had a low opinion of the Dutch in general, regarding them as grasping, quarrelsome, untrustworthy and Calvinist. She had no illusions about what it would cost to finance a foreign war, and no illusions about the limitations of her resources. She was also well aware that those who clamoured loudest for action against Anti-Christ would be the first to grumble when it came to paying the bills. By careful management and good housekeeping, she had just succeeded in freeing herself from debt and her credit was excellent. She had no intention of losing that priceless advantage if she could help it. Words were a great deal cheaper than armies and the thrifty Queen would continue to use them for as long as possible.

Elizabeth had no desire to see either a Spanish or an Orange triumph. Even less did she want to see France, that inveterate enemy of Spain, go on a fishing expedition in those troubled waters. What she wanted was a negotiated settlement by which all foreign troops would be evacuated from the Netherlands and the provinces restored to their traditional civil rights and liberties. In return, the Netherlanders would remain under Spanish suzerainty and Philip would have the right to impose Catholicism as the state religion. It was, after all, generally accepted that a prince should impose one form of belief on his subjects in the interests of national unity and was a right which Elizabeth exercised herself. Such a settlement could only benefit Europe at large and England in particular, removing the threat to her south-eastern coastline and allowing trade and commerce to function normally again. To one of Elizabeth's essentially pragmatic nature, this was the obvious solution to an irritating and unnecessary problem and one which she pursued with astonishing pertinacity.

She was undeterred by repeated failure, unmoved by all appeals to sentiment on behalf of the embattled Dutch Protestants, by the openly-voiced disapproval of an influential section of public opinion at home, and by the near despair of councillors who were convinced that the enemy's only interest in peace talks lay in keeping England off guard. She was still doggedly pursuing it when her own troops were fighting in Flanders, when the Spanish invasion fleet was preparing to weigh anchor in Lisbon harbour. Nothing and nobody, in fact, could shake her faith in the axiom that 'to jaw jaw is better than war war'. From every commonsense point of view, of course, she was right, but by her stubborn insistence on regarding the problem in purely political terms she failed to take enough account of the depth and bitterness of Dutch hatred and distrust of Spain, or the inflexibility of Philip's resolve not to yield one inch of ground to his rebel subjects. As a sensible woman and practical sovereign, Elizabeth naturally found it hard to take seriously the King of Spain's pronouncement that he would rather rule over a desert than a nation of heretics. It would have made little difference if she had and perhaps it was just as well that she didn't, for by refusing to be discouraged so long as any spark of hope remained she both postponed and minimised England's involvement in this sixteenth-century Vietnam war.

The Queen began to mend her fences with Spain in the aftermath of the St Bartholomew massacre, when it looked as though the French alliance would have to be written off. In April 1573 she reached an agreement with the Duke of Alva by which trade with the Netherlands, suspended since the crisis of 1568, was restored for a period of two years and negotiations were started on the claims of both sides for compensation over the seizures of property. Other negotiations followed, and in March 1575 a further agreement was concluded with Alva's successor, Don Luis Requesens. This confirmed, under certain conditions, the privileges of English merchants in Antwerp and also conceded that Requesens would expel the English Catholic exiles from their refuge in the Netherlands, for some time a sore point with Elizabeth. In return, Elizabeth closed her ports to William of Orange and forbade her subjects, officially at any rate, to succour the Dutch rebels until they returned to their natural obedience.

This looked a promising beginning and in 1576 events in the Netherlands seemed to offer an opening for just the sort of settlement Elizabeth had in mind. A mutinous Spanish army, unpaid and temporarily leaderless, went on the rampage, and the resultant reign of terror in Flanders produced such intensity of anti-Spanish feeling that the Flemings and Brabanters temporarily joined with the Dutch and Zeelanders in demanding the expulsion of Spain. The new Spanish Governor, Don John of Austria, faced by a united and hostile front was forced (in the intervals of planning the invasion of England and offering himself as a bridegroom to the Queen of Scots) to adopt a conciliatory attitude. For a time things looked really hopeful. Don John set himself out to charm; while from the side-lines the Queen of England urged the States General for God's sake not to lose any occasion for obtaining peace and threatened Don John that if he attempted to renew the conflict she would help the provinces with all the might and power she could.

In the end, the victor of Lepanto had to come to terms, promising to evacuate the Spanish garrisons and to respect the provinces' civil liberties. As a result he was received in Brussels in May 1577 amid scenes of much rejoicing. Only William of Orange held aloof – implacably hostile, immovably suspicious. As it turned out, his distrust of Spanish fair words proved fully justified. In July, Don John threw off the irksome restraints that had been imposed upon him and, on the not improbable pretext that his life was in danger, seized Namur with a company of Walloons, making such unconciliatory declarations as swearing to avenge his honour by bathing in the blood of traitors. The war was on again, the newborn settlement drowned in Flanders mud.

Don John died of plague the following year and was succeeded by Alexander Farnese, Duke of Parma, by far the ablest of Philip's generals but hamstrung like all his predecessors by shortage of cash and poor communications with Spain. Meanwhile, the affairs of William of Orange went from bad to worse and back again to bad. In 1579 the Catholic Walloon provinces made a separate peace with Spain, but in the north William – assisted by grudging subsidies from England and some not very helpful forays by France

– grimly carried on the struggle. And so it went on, and on, and famine, pestilence and atrocity stalked the land.

Although Artois in the south had not been directly affected by the war, it was inevitable that the political upheavals in the Netherlands would sooner or later have repercussions on the seminary at Douai. Until the mid-seventies the English college continued to flourish, with recruits flowing in as fast or faster than they could be accommodated. In August 1575 Pope Gregory had conferred extensive discretionary powers of absolution and dispensation on William Allen, authorising him to delegate these faculties to such of his missionaries as he thought fit. Also in 1575 the Pope granted the college an official allowance of one hundred gold crowns a month which went some way towards alleviating its chronic financial problems, and by Michaelmas 1576 there were a hundred and twenty students in the college.

Trouble, however, was already brewing. After the 'Spanish Fury' in November of that year, the anti-Spanish fury in the Netherlands began to spill over on to any foreigners who could be suspected of pro-Spanish sympathies. So sensitive was the situation that, it was said, even a cheerful expression on the face of an English exile was liable to be interpreted as a sign of rejoicing over local misfortunes. The college itself was subjected to a campaign of harassment by the municipal authorities and the inmates had to submit to the indignity of having their rooms searched for arms. They had to give their names to the magistrates at frequent intervals and every member of the college was called on to renew his oath of allegiance to the university and town of Douai. On top of these irritations, rumours began to circulate that English government agents, men of 'sinister aspect and well-mounted', had been seen loitering in the vicinity with intent to kidnap or assassinate William Allen.

In the circumstances it was hardly surprising that many of the students felt it would be prudent to remove themselves for a while, and within three months their numbers had fallen dramatically. Allen himself went on a trip to Paris, partly as a precaution for his own safety and partly to explore the possibilities of finding a French sanctuary for his flock should the climate at Douai deteriorate still further. In the spring of 1577, after Don John had made his peace with the Netherlanders under the terms of the unfortunately named Perpetual Edict, conditions improved for a time.

Allen returned from France and the numbers in residence at the college rose again to a hundred and fifteen. By mid-summer, though, the situation had taken another turn for the worse. The students were warned to be especially careful not to give the townspeople any excuse for taking offence or exciting murmurs against them. Even so, the atmosphere once more became acutely uncomfortable. Professors and students were liable to insult when they ventured into the town – Dr Humphrey Ely was called a traitor to his face – and one morning in August a visiting Englishman was greeted with some surprise by a passing local and asked if all the English had not been killed the previous night.

William Allen reviewed his evacuation plans and he and the senior members of his staff made several reconnaissance trips to the city of Rheims, where the French government had offered them hospitality. Allen was reluctant to leave the dominions of the King of Spain, whom he regarded as the natural protector of the English Catholics, but if a move became unavoidable Rheims had obvious advantages. It contained a famous university and was within reasonable travelling distance of Douai. It was also ruled by the ultra-Catholic Guise family who, as relations of the Queen of Scots, could hardly fail to be friendly towards the exiles. Mary herself had written to Allen that summer, warmly praising his work and telling him not to hesitate to use her name if it would help him in any way.

Matters came to a head early in 1578. The Duke of Parma's victory over the states at Gembloux at the end of January caused a resurgence of patriotic nationalism. A new governor and new magistrates appointed by William of Orange took office at Douai, and it was freely predicted that the English would soon be expelled bag and baggage. On 11 February the governor paid a visit to the college asking searching questions about the number and ages of the students and how they were supported. On 22 March, the day before Palm Sunday, a proclamation was issued commanding all the English residents except the old men, women and children and university professors to leave the town within twenty-four hours. The expulsion order, in fact, only applied to the students at the seminary, young and able-bodied men capable of bearing arms, but students and staff migrated in a body.

Thanks to Allen's foresight and careful staffwork the seminary was able to settle down in its new quarters at Rheims with the minimum of disruption, and on 27 May there were fifty-five students on the roll – forty-four living in college and the remainder in the town. They had received a flattering welcome from the Cardinal Archbishop, Louis of Guise, as well as from the university and municipal authorities, but even here there was a good deal of ill-feeling among the local people. At Douai the English had become unpopular because they were regarded as pensioners and partisans of Spain. At Rheims they were unpopular because they were English.

Gregory Martin, writing to Edmund Campion in August, observed, 'It is most uncertain whether we shall remain here in quiet and permanently, though the family of Guise is very favour-able to us, because the name itself of Englishman begets suspicion in the French.' Allen also had second thoughts about the wisdom of their move, and in September he made enquiries about the chance of some other home in Belgium. Louvain was suggested, but Louvain, not for the last time in its history, had been devas-tated by war. Plague was rife in the town, the university had virtually disappeared and horses were being stabled in the burnt-out colleges. Clearly the Netherlands were out of the question until the political and military situation had quietened down. The English would have to stick it out where they were and put up with the widely held belief that they crept out at night to make plans of the fortifications. As it turned out, they were to stay for nearly twenty years.

Although the unsettled conditions of the past two years had not been exactly conducive to a programme of concentrated study, the work of the college suffered only temporary interruption and was in fact soon to be extended by the establishment of another English college in Rome itself. In common with most other European countries, pre-Reformation England had maintained a hostel for its pilgrims in the Holy City and as early as 1559 or 1560 there had been some talk of converting this institution into a seminary for English priests. The proposal, however, had languished in the Vatican's pending tray until the success and reputation being gained by William Allen at Douai stirred certain individuals, in parti-cular Dr Owen Lewis, one of the Welsh exiles, to emulatory zeal. When Allen visited Rome in 1575, the setting up of another factory of labourers for the English vineyard was among the subjects discussed and certainly it had become a matter of some urgency –

with numbers now topping the hundred mark, Douai was bursting at the seams.

It was therefore agreed that Allen should send his overflow to be accommodated at the hostel and during the next three years several batches of recruits arrived from Douai and Rheims. As a result of intensive lobbying by Owen Lewis, Cardinal Moroni, official 'protector' of the English nation, advised the Pope to appoint the warden of the old hospice, another Welshman, Dr Maurice Clenock, to be rector of the new foundation. Two Jesuit fathers moved in to help him and the *Venerabile Collegium Anglorum de Urbe* was formally inaugurated at Christmas 1578.

The early history of the English college in Rome clearly shows how much Douai had owed to the personality of William Allen. Dr Clenock was an elderly man and quite unequal to the task of running a college of forty students. He also appears to have been unfortunately lacking in both tact and commonsense, 'so there arose many complaints and many suspicions of a lack of right and fair administration and various accusations of more indulgent treatment being meted out to Welshmen than to Englishmen in the distribution of the things of the house'. Encouraged by Archdeacon Lewis and his nephew Hugh Griffin (a natural trouble-maker by the sound of him), the Welsh seem to have taken the view that the new seminary had been founded 'for the peculiar benefit of their race'. National feelings were soon running high and the English, who formed the great majority of the student body, became so irritated that they petitioned Cardinal Moroni for the removal of Dr Clenock and for the management of the college to be made over entirely to the Jesuits.

Cardinal Moroni was not accustomed to being told his business by students, Drs Clenock and Lewis were long-established and respected members of the Roman community and in any case the Cardinal could hardly be expected to appreciate the finer points of Celtic and Anglo-Saxon hostility. He attempted to dismiss the petitioners without more ado, 'making a sharp reprehension unto them for their stir' and threatening them with expulsion 'except they admitted quietly the government appointed'. But the English students, penniless exiles though they might be, were not going to put up with that sort of treatment. His Eminence was therefore treated to some plain North Country speaking by their representatives, much to the surprise of the standers-by who 'did wonder to see such liberty of speech before so great a personage'. It seems to have surprised the Cardinal as well, for he changed his tune, promising the students 'to consider better their matter' and asking them 'to give him in writing both the defects of Mr Maurice in particular and the manner of government which they desired'.

The affair was soon the talk of Rome. The apparent fearlessness of the English in demanding their rights gave rise to much admiring comment. 'If these fellows stand thus immovable before such Princes in Rome,' it was asked, 'what will they do in England before the heretics?' Some people declared that although they had previously doubted reports of the bold answers made by priests captured in England, now they could believe anything of them. But while public sympathy was largely on the side of the dissidents, a first-class row was brewing over the future of the English college, with the Welsh faction supported by Cardinal Moroni accusing the Jesuits of trying to make a take-over bid. On the other side it was being said that Dr Clenock was trying to increase his party by inviting Welshmen, however unsuitable, from all over Europe to enter the college. Hints were also dropped that the Welsh students had no intention of ever making the journey to England.

The battle was still raging when four of the students, led by Richard Haydock, William Allen's nephew, went on their own initiative to lay their troubles before the Pope. But, so the story goes, Cardinal Moroni 'showed his anger and aversion, and persuaded Pope Gregory, who seemed inclined to give way to the scholars' petitions, to reject the frequent memorials which they presented'. In any event, Clenock was confirmed in his office, whereupon the Welsh became so overweening that knives were flourished in the refectory and open brawling was only averted by the two Jesuits on the staff – at least according to a Jesuit account. Something clearly had to be done about a situation rapidly getting out of hand and the authorities ordered the four ringleaders of the revolt to leave the college, presumably in the hope that this would intimidate the rest. The English, however, accepted the challenge with enthusiasm and in the best trade union tradition they marched out in a body – an event which caused Hugh Griffin to give a leap in the college hall saying 'Who now but a Welshman?' The homeless students spent that night in the house of a sympathetic compatriot and next morning appeared on the streets to beg alms for their journey back to Rheims.

It was the beginning of Lent – Ash Wednesday in fact – and the streets were full of pious citizens on their way to church. 'When the news spread that so many young men of great expectations, some of them even being priests, were purposing and proposing to return to England, there to risk their lives for the Catholic faith, braving the fury of the heretics, there was a great stir in men's minds'. The Lenten preachers took up the students' cause and from pulpit after pulpit 'the necessities of these scholars were commended to the charity of the faithful'. The warm-hearted, sentimental Italians responded eagerly and it was soon obvious that there would be no lack of charity. It was also obvious that the Pope would have to take action. That afternoon, therefore, when the students went to take their leave of him, the Holy Father greeted them with tears and smiles, and after an affecting scene of reconciliation sent them back to the college escorted by a papal chamberlain, promising to meet their demands in full. The rebels had conducted their campaign with considerable tactical skill and won a notable victory over the Roman establishment. The long-term consequences, however, were not so happy, for the seeds of a bitter quarrel which was to react disastrously on English Catholicism had been sown in fertile ground.

The Society or Company of Jesus, which took over responsibility for the English college on 23 April 1579 and which now for the first time became actively associated with the English mission, had started life in 1534 as a small group of priests dedicated to practical social work among the poor, the heathen and the illiterate. Their founder, the crippled Spanish ex-soldier turned soldier of Christ, also dreamed of restoring the Catholic Church to the position of pre-eminence it had occupied in the Middle Ages. Ignatius Loyola believed in the military virtues of discipline, efficiency and obedience, and although his ultimate aim may have been to put the clock back, he was not afraid to use modern methods, to adapt the old monastic ideal to meet the needs of the times. Loyola's new society was in no sense enclosed – in fact he dispensed altogether with the normal obligation of a religious order to recite the office in choir. The Society of Jesus was to provide front line troops for the Church and therefore its members must be free at all times to go about in the world, fighting the Church's battles wherever they were to be found. Loyola had passed through a phase of extreme religious asceticism, but he was to prove himself a born leader, a hard-working, intelligent administrator, and when he died in 1556 his army had become a highly-trained, well-organised body of men over a thousand strong.

Jesuit missionaries had followed the *Conquistadores* to America and had penetrated as far as China and Japan in the east. Jesuit schools were already deservedly famous. Jesuit fathers held key positions in the Catholic universities of Europe and on the councils of many European rulers. They kept representatives at the Imperial Diet in Germany; they were said to have the ear of Philip of Spain, to be whispering advice to Catherine de Medici in France. It was as palace politicians that the Jesuits made enemies, both inside and outside the Church, but it was on their proficiency as schoolmasters that their real power was based. From teaching the children of the illiterate poor, they had progressed to teaching the children of the aristocracy, to the all-important task of forming the minds of each successive generation of the international Catholic establishment.

Although the Superiors of the Order had, in fact, been somewhat reluctant to add yet another commitment to an already long list, training candidates for the English mission was to provide the Society of Jesus with an opportunity to exercise their skill on some of the finest material available. As one contemporary writer pointed out, even in Catholic countries there were many who entered the priesthood only for honour and gain, but the pupils at the English seminaries, 'among whom are noblemen and eldest sons not a few', had already accepted the loss not only of their natural heritage but of any other earthly reward. When, after a period of probation, the young men at the college in Rome took an oath to be ready and willing to receive holy orders in God's good time and to return to England for the salvation of souls 'whenever it shall seem good to the superior of this college to order me to do so', they were, in nine cases out of ten, consciously and cheerfully signing their own death warrants.

Human nature being what it is, not quite everyone who came to Rome did so from the highest motives. There were those who made the pilgrimage out of restlessness, curiosity, or simply to see if there was anything to be got out of it. Among these 'tourists' was one Anthony Munday, an enterprising stationer's apprentice who, in 1578, broke his indentures and left England with a friend named Thomas Nowell. Although Munday declared that he had been moved only by an urge for self-improvement, a 'desire to see strange countries, as also affection to learn the languages', he was later in a position to provide the government with valuable information about the inmates of the English college. He became, in fact, a useful witness for the Crown at the trials of Edmund Campion and of other priests he had known at Rome. It was after this, when certain unsympathetic people began to show signs of doubting his word and to hint that he had never been out of England, that Munday first published the graphic account of his adventures.

He and Nowell had crossed the Channel to Boulogne, but on the road to Amiens were robbed of their money and most of their possessions by 'despoiling soldiers'. In the town they were befriended by an old English priest who gave them a night's lodging and provided them with letters of introduction to William Allen at Rheims. The travellers sold their cloaks for two French crowns and set out on their journey. Three or four miles from Amiens, however, they sat down 'on the side of a hill' to consider the situation. Munday, who always represented himself as a staunch Protestant, had decided it would be a waste of time to go to Rheims, and brushing aside his companion's feeble expostulations about their destitute state and the dangers they were likely to encounter, persuaded Nowell to come with him to Paris instead. In Paris they first paid a visit to the English ambassador, who 'bestowed his honourable liberality' on them and sensibly advised them to go home. But on leaving the embassy and walking into the city, Munday and Nowell fell in with some English gentlemen who showed themselves 'very courteous' in offering them money, lodging and other necessaries.

Through these new friends, Munday records, 'we became acquainted with a number of Englishmen more who lay in the city, some in Colleges and some at their own houses: where using daily company among them, sometime at dinner and sometime at supper, we heard many girds and nips against our country of England, her Majesty very unreverently handled in words and certain of her honourable Council undutifully termed'. The visitors heard a lot of talk about a projected invasion of Ireland by an army of Spaniards; how the famous Dr Sander 'under the Pope's standard, would give such an attempt there as soon after should make all England to quake'; and how other Englishmen had gone to the Pope for more aid 'at whose return, certain noblemen Englishmen, then being in those parts ... would prosecute the matter with as much speed as might be'. This agreed in almost every point with the gossip they had picked up from the priest at Amiens, which made Munday 'to doubt, because in every man's mouth her Majesty's style was aimed at, in such manner as I tremble and shake to think on their words'.

He and Nowell were being 'very earnestly persuaded' to join the ranks of expatriates and to travel on to Rome where, they were assured, they would be entertained in style. 'We were soon entreated to take the journey on us,' wrote Munday, 'because we thought if we could go to Rome and return safely again into England we should accomplish a great matter, the place being so far off and the voyage so dangerous.' If nothing else, it would give them a story to dine out on for the rest of their lives. Being now accepted as members of the club, the travellers were showered with money and with letters of introduction to Owen Lewis and Maurice Clenock, 'then the Rector of the English Hospital or College in Rome'. They left Paris some time in the autumn and made the dangerous voyage without mishap. According to Munday there were friendly Englishmen 'almost in every city by the way', an illuminating comment on the extent of the network of Catholic exiles now established in Europe.

Munday and Nowell reached Rome at the beginning of February 1579. They were given a kind welcome by Dr Clenock and besieged by the students with so many questions 'that we knew not which to answer first'. Munday, however, was soon buttonholed by one of the priests and carried off into the garden for a private conversation. In Paris he had been mistaken for the son of a Catholic gentleman, whom he discreetly omits to name, and had turned this fortunate accident to good account. Now it transpired that the priest knew his supposed 'father' well and a sweating Munday began to find the situation distinctly uncomfortable. He knew none of the people he was being asked about and 'was put to so hard a shift that I knew not well what to say'. Fear of exposure sharpened his wits and he managed to extricate himself by explaining that it was a long time since he had been at home, as he had been sent to London and Paris to study. All the same, when the bell rang, he remarked that 'the priest was not so ready to go to his supper as I was glad for that time to break off company'.

Munday was in Rome while the Anglo-Welsh quarrel was at its height, but the most interesting part of his narrative is the detailed account he gives of daily life at the English college. The students slept four or six to a room, but 'every man hath his bed proper to himself, which is two little trestles with four or five boards laid along over them, and thereon a quilted mattress as we call it in England, which every morning after they are risen, they fold up their sheets handsomely, laying them in the midst of the bed and so roll it up to one end, covering it with the quilt that is their coverlet all the night time'. The students' day was governed by the sound of the bell. After the rising bell came a bell for private prayer, 'when as every one presently kneeling on his knees, prayeth for the space of half an hour: at which time, the bell being tolled again, they arise and bestow a certain time in study, every one having his desk, table and chair to himself very orderly, and all the time of study silence is used of every one in the chamber, not one offering molestation in speech to another'. After the study period came breakfast, which consisted of a glass of wine and a quarter of a manchet loaf. After breakfast, signalled by another bell, the students walked two by two to the Roman college or Gymnasium Societatis Jesu, where they spent the morning attending lectures in divinity, logic and rhetoric; then back to their own college to walk up and down in the garden talking, until the bell called them to dinner.

'The custom is' wrote Munday, 'that daily two of the students take it by turns to serve all the others at the table, who to help them have the butler, the porter and a poor Jesuit that looketh to all the scholars' necessaries.... As to their fare, trust me it is very fine and delicate, for every man hath his own trencher, his manchet, knife, spoon and fork laid by it, and then a fair white napkin covering it, with his glass and pot of wine set by him.' The meal consisted of four courses – an 'antepast' which might be Spanish anchovies or stewed prunes and raisins, followed by 'a certain mess of potage of that country manner' made of 'divers things' whose names Munday could not remember but which he considered to be 'both good and wholesome'. Then came two meat courses, one boiled, the other stewed, roasted or baked, and dinner – which was accompanied by readings from the Bible and martyrology – ended with cheese and some 'preserved conceits', figs, almonds, raisins, a lemon and sugar, a pomegranate 'or some such sweet gear, for they know that Englishmen loveth sweetmeats'. After an hour's recreation came more study and more lectures and then a collation of bread and wine as at breakfast (Munday had no complaints about the food).

In the early evening there were exercises in disputation and then the students were free again until supper time. 'After supper, if it be winter time, they go with the Jesuits and sit about a great fire talking, and in all their talk they strive who shall speak worst of her Majesty, of some of her Council, of some bishop here, or such like: so that the Jesuits themselves will often take up their hands and bless themselves to hear what abominable tales they will tell them. After they have talked a good while, the bell calleth them to their chambers, the porter going from chamber to chamber and lighteth a lamp in every one: so when the scholars come, they light their lamps, lay down their beds and go sit at their desks and study a little till the bell rings, when every one falls on his knees to prayers. Then one of the priests in the chamber, as in every chamber there is some, beginneth the Latin litany, all the scholars in the chamber answering him, and so they spend the time till the bell rings again, which is for every one to go to bed.'

Discipline in the college was strictly enforced. The student who failed to 'turn up his bed handsomely', was late on his knees for prayers, missed the daily Mass or forgot to put a peg against his name on the board 'to give knowledge who is abroad and who remaineth within', had to perform public penance at dinner time. 'Either to kneel in the midst of the hall on his bare knees and there to say his beads over; or to say certain Pater Nosters and Ave Marias; or to stand upright and have a dish of potage before him on the ground and so to bring up every spoonful to his mouth; or to lose either one or two or three of his dishes appointed for his dinner; or to stand there all dinner time and eat no meat.' Munday observed ruefully that he had been forced to do all these penances during his stay at the college, 'for that I was always apt to break one order or other'.

Heavier penances were meted out in the confessional and for the more spectacular of these the penitent appeared, either at dinner or supper, 'clothed in a canvas vesture down to the ground, a hood of the same on his head, with two holes where through he hath sight, and a good big round place bare against the midst of his back. In this order he goeth up and down the hall, whipping himself at that bare place, insomuch that the blood doth trickle on the ground after him.' Munday would have nothing to do with this practice, which he considered to be unscriptural, but he was not the only one to disapprove. 'When a man doth it at the first,' wrote Dr Humphrey Ely, 'he is so far ordinarily from amendment that in his heart he doth grutch and repine at his superiors for the giving of it. But when he is used three or four times to do it, then he maketh a very scoff and mocking or may game of it. So far is it from a true penance as it engendreth ... both hatred and mockery.'

Anthony Munday did not stay the course at the college for long. It was no part of his intention to be drawn into regular membership, besides which the climate of Rome could at any time have turned unhealthy. He left after a few months in an odour of goodwill, being entrusted with messages and holy pictures to be delivered to Catholics at home. But the numbers of young Englishmen between the ages of eighteen and twenty-five, physically sound and of blameless reputation who had forsaken families, friends, even in some cases brides, to seek the road to Calvary showed no signs of decreasing. As the Jesuits tightened their hold, supervision of every aspect of the students' lives and thoughts became closer. Contact with the outside world was reduced to a minimum. Private reading was limited to devotional books and lives of the saints, correspondence was censored, personal friendships restricted and discouraged. On the practical level every last detail of the college rule was directed to total sublimation of the ego into a conscious and deliberate preparation for self-immolation. Even the walls of the house were covered with pictures of the scaffold and torture-chamber and the college itself earned the respectful sobriquet of *Seminarium Martyrum*. Every normal emotion of human love, ambition and patriotism was harnessed to this end.

The students were taught in all seriousness that they alone had been chosen by Divine mercy – an elect and sacrificial few – to save their countrymen from the pains of eternal damnation by the example of their teaching; their example and their suffering. In this context physical martyrdom became unimportant, except insofar that it must be willingly and cheerfully embraced. To drive this lesson home, the Spiritual Exercises, originally formulated by Ignatius Loyola, were used to help the initiate to exercise his will by contemplation to the extreme point where fantasy and reality became indistinguishable. 'To see in imagination the length, breadth and depth of hell.... To beg for a deep sense of the pain which the lost suffer.... To see the vast fires and the souls enclosed, as it were, in bodies of fire. To hear the wailing, the howling, cries and blasphemies against Christ our Lord.... With the sense of smell to perceive the smoke, the sulphur, the filth and corruption. To taste the bitterness of tears, sadness and remorse of conscience. With the sense of touch to feel the flames which envelop and burn the souls.'

Whatever may be thought of this system of training – or brain-washing – as applied to impressionable, idealistic youth, it was certainly efficient in producing the required result. Not surprisingly though, in that highly-charged emotional atmosphere the English college at Rome continued to be subject to bitter internal feuds and jealousies. In order to extend their control over their charges' private thoughts and opinions, the Jesuits unwisely resorted to the time-honoured but questionable practice of introducing *Angeli custodes*, or to put it more bluntly, spies among the students. These 'guardian angels' would 'speak liberally' against the college authorities and lead their companions on 'to complain of their government and usage towards them, of their apparel, meat and drink, and against the straight keeping of them in, and against whatsoever they think is not well done in the college'. Having accumulated enough evidence, the informers would then 'carry the whole discourse straight to the Rector'. 'If such spies were at Oxford,' commented Humphrey Ely, 'they would be plucked in pieces.' Another cause of ill-feeling was the fact that the Society of Jesus not unnaturally sought recruits for the Order from the ranks of the English students. This soon led to complaints that these novices were given favoured treatment and helped to fan the flames of the smouldering quarrel between secular and Jesuit factions – a quarrel which was eventually to divide the college once again into 'two hostile camps'.

From Rheims, William Allen had followed the progress of the early troubles at Rome with close attention. He was naturally anxious that the new foundation should be a success and also that nothing should happen to alienate the Pope's support – both moral and financial. Allen was acutely aware of the danger of internal dissension and of the 'marvellous scandal and inconvenience' it could so easily breed. 'My first care was that it should take no hold in our company,' he told Owen Lewis in 1579, 'where I thank God at this day they live as sweetly together without all differences or respect of nations or other distraction as ever I knew any such number in my life. And yet so to hold it, because we well perceived the common inclinations of Adam to like and whisper underhand for their own against others of other countries, great moderation and dexterity was necessary I assure you.' In view of the rapidly disintegrating situation, Allen's relief when the Jesuits took over was understandable and made 'a double Easter' at Rheims. Whether or not he foresaw future difficulties, he could only be glad that the continuation of the second English college was now assured. The community at Douai and later at Rheims had flourished without oaths and statutes, stringent rules and regulations or degrading physical punishments because there had been no need for them. These were men drawn together by a common ideal, sustained by the vision and determination of a single, much-loved leader. But Allen knew that this was not enough. If the English mission was ever to make a lasting and significant contribution to the survival of English Catholicism, it must expand. Its amateur days were over. It was time for the professionals to move in.

Allen had another, more specific, reason for being pleased at the new turn of events. As an intellectual *élite*, the Society of Jesus was naturally attracting some of the best minds among the younger generation. As a first-rank corps in the battle for the counter-reformation it was also attracting some of the most fervent souls. Allen had seen a number of his own pupils, perhaps most notably the outstanding Edmund Campion, join the Society. He would not stand in their way, but until now a recruit won by the Jesuits had meant a labourer lost by the English harvest. William Allen hoped that this need no longer be so – it certainly seemed a pity to be sending English members of the Society as missionaries to the Indies when there was work for them so much nearer home, and this was a point which soon occurred to the English students at Rome.

Father Robert Parsons, the English Jesuit who had had a good deal to do with stage-managing the students' revolt, had his ear to the ground (he usually did) and quickly picked up 'a certain murmur' which, according to Humphrey Ely, would in time have grown into open sedition, if by Father Parsons' wisdom and industry it had not been prevented. 'The cause was this', wrote Ely. 'Our scholars, having obtained their desire and falling to their studies, used very zealously all the godly exercises of mortification, in such sort as some one or two of them became so contemplative that they would needs be Jesuits. Which when their companions understood, they began to mislike of those spirits, alleging that the College was founded for the education of virtuous and learned priests to help their country and not to bring up men to enter into religion and leave the harvest at home. Whereupon Father Parsons procured Dr. Allen's coming up to Rome, who obtained of the Pope to command the General of the Jesuits to send of his religious into England, the which appeased all this murmur. For (quoth the scholars) let as many now enter the Society as will, for when they have been sufficiently brought up therein they shall be sent into England. And thus each party was pleased; the fathers for that they might receive of the scholars into their Society without grudge or mislike, and the scholars because such as entered, most of all (if not all) should be in time employed for their country.'

Allen's third visit to Rome in the summer of 1579 turned into something of a personal triumph. The Pope treated him as an honoured guest and when Allen remarked how he had longed to see the students of His Holiness at Rome, Gregory replied 'They are thine, Allen, not mine'. All this was very gratifying and the ostensible purpose of his visit – to act as peace-maker and heal by his presence any lingering resentment between the factions at the college – was duly carried out in a moving address to the assembled students. But even more important, negotiations with the Superiors of the Society of Jesus were brought to a successful conclusion and it was agreed that Robert Parsons and Edmund Campion should be the pioneers of the Order in the English mission field. When Allen returned to France in February 1580 he had reason to feel a modest degree of optimism. In the eleven years which had passed since the renting of that house in Douai, he had himself sent a hundred labourers into the vineyard. Now he not only had the very human satisfaction of knowing that his work was being supported and appreciated but also that it would be carried on.

CHAPTER SEVEN

The enterprise is begun

'The expense is reckoned, the enterprise is begun. It is of God, it cannot be withstood.'

Edmund Campion, Hoxton, 19 July 1580

I T has been said that the first Jesuit mission or, to be more precise, the first batch of missionaries to include Jesuit fathers in their number, marked the beginning of the 'heroic' period of the English Mission. Certainly it marked the beginning of a new, more bitterly contested phase of the ideological struggle. If the image of the Jesuit priest flitting through the corridors of power aroused complicated emotions of jealousy and suspicion among the members of longer established, less enterprising Catholic orders, the feelings it evoked in Protestant circles were not in the least complicated. To the English government, perennially (some would say morbidly) preoccupied with the dangers of subversion from within and encirclement from without, the Society of Jesus embodied everything they feared and hated most about Roman Catholicism. By the early 1580s the bogeyman of the 'pollyticke Jesuit' had become ineradicably established in the official mind as public enemy number one of the Protestant state. Official reaction to the news that Jesuits were actually planning to set their cloven hooves on English soil was therefore excitable.

In spite of their highly-coloured reputation, the Superiors of the Order had been far from eager to involve themselves in the English harvest. The Society of Jesus was a closely-knit, highly organised body – therein lay its strength, and its weakness. The Jesuit General and his advisers knew that under present conditions in England it would be virtually impossible to maintain either organisation or discipline. They hesitated to send their members into such outer darkness and, according to Robert Parsons, 'found divers difficulties in the matter in respect of the novelty thereof, especially about their manner of living there in secular men's houses in secular apparel ... as how also their rules and orders for conservation of religious spirit might there be observed'. Apart from the spiritual dangers to be overcome, England was a political hot potato which would need the most delicate handling if the missionaries were not to lay themselves open to charges of plotting and intrigue – thus damaging both the Society and the cause it served.

However, having once committed themselves, the Jesuits began preparing for the task which lay ahead with their usual efficiency and attention to detail. Full instructions were drawn up for the guidance of the pioneers, who were to keep to the rules of the Society as far as circumstances would permit and 'so behave that all may see that the only gain they covet is that of souls'. They were to be very careful about the company they kept, associating only with Catholics and preferably reconciled Catholics of high rank. It was emphasised that the principle aim of the mission was 'the preservation and augmentation of the Faith of the Catholics of England' and the fathers were to avoid any temptation to dispute with heretics. In fact, they were to avoid contact with heretics altogether. They must not carry about anything forbidden by English law – no amateurish mistakes such as Cuthbert Mayne had made – or letters which might compromise them. Most important of all, 'they must not entangle themselves in affairs of State' or write to Rome about political matters. They were not to speak against the Queen, or allow others to do so in their presence, 'except perhaps in the company of those whose fidelity has been long and steadfast and even then not without strong reasons'. In a later version of the instructions, issued the following year, this proviso was omitted and the official prohibition on talking politics became absolute.

Before the missionaries actually set out on their journey, there was one thing which the Jesuits wanted settled – the debatable question of the continued force of *Regnans in Excelsis*. Were pious Catholics in England really obliged to consider themselves under interdict if they recognised and obeyed (in civil matters at least) their deposed and schismatic Queen? During the eleven years which had passed since Pius V loosed the papal thunderbolts in Elizabeth's direction, none of William Allen's pupils had apparently thought it necessary to seek a ruling on this point. In typically English fashion the problem had been quietly swept under the carpet and left there. Such a solution was not acceptable to the logical Latin minds which ruled the Society of Jesus and they accordingly extracted an *Explanatio* from Pope Gregory, laying down that although the provisions of the bull still applied in full to Queen Elizabeth and her heretical supporters, while things remained as they were it in no way bound the English Catholics, 'except when public execution of the said bull shall become possible'. In other words, it seemed that the Queen's Catholic subjects might continue to accept her as their *de facto* sovereign unless and until means could be found to overthrow her. The Jesuits would have been wiser to have left well alone, for when in due course this interesting piece of information found its way into the hands of the English government, they showed no signs of gratitude for the respite thus thoughtfully granted.

Edmund Campion who, with Robert Parsons, was to form the spearhead of the Jesuit advance, reached Rome from Prague on 5 April 1580 and on the 18th, after an audience with the Pope, the party was ready to set out. It was, in fact, quite a large party. In addition to Parsons, Campion and Ralph Emerson, a Jesuit 'coadjutor' or lay-brother, five young graduates of the English college (including Ralph Sherwin, one of the leaders of the student revolt) were making the journey. There were also four elderly English priests dating from the Marian era who had been chaplains at the hospice, and such notable names among the first generation of exiles as Laurence Vaux, Edward Rishton and Dr Nicholas Morton. The most senior of the travellers, however, was Thomas Goldwell, once Bishop of St Asaph and almost the last survivor of the Marian hierarchy.

On 18 April a Welsh friend of Humphrey Ely living in Rome wrote to him at Rheims with the news that 'my lord of St. Asaph and Mr Dr Morton are gone hence, some say to Venice, some to Flanders, and so further, which if it be true you shall know sooner than we here. God send them well to do whithersoever they go, and specially if they be gone to the harvest.... This day depart hence many of our countrymen thitherward, and withal good Father Campion.' This letter was intercepted by an English spy who promptly forwarded it to Francis Walsingham, but it would not have greatly taxed the powers of any spy to send advance warning to London. The departure of the missionaries was about as secret as that of a hopeful Cup Final team. The whole of the

English colony in Rome came to see them off, and scenes of solemn and affectionate farewell took place at the Ponte Molle.

The first destination was Rheims, which Campion and Parsons reached at the end of May and where they heard for the first time that theirs was not the only expedition which had been despatched against the heretics with a papal blessing. There had for some time been talk of armed intervention in Ireland, Anthony Munday had heard all about it in Paris in 1578, and in that year Sir Thomas Stukeley, Devonian, rogue, vagabond and soldier of fortune, had sailed from Civita Vecchia with a ship, six hundred men and a quantity of arms provided by the Pope at a cost, according to a wistful Cardinal of Como, of 'thousands and thousands of crowns'. But Stukeley, one of those comic opera characters who flourished in the sixteenth century, got no nearer to Ireland than Lisbon. There he and his men were diverted to North Africa by the King of Portugal, and Sir Thomas was killed at the Battle of Alcazar.

But Pope Gregory, who was the spiritual heir of Pius V in more ways than one, did not abandon the idea of stirring up trouble in Ireland – that at least never presented any difficulty – and presently found another candidate in the person of James Fitz-maurice, first cousin of the Earl of Desmond. Irish internal politics, then as now, were a quagmire into which outsiders ventured at their own risk, but to anyone looking for an opportunity to embarrass the English government the temptation was understand-able. A full-scale rebellion would divert English forces and English money from assisting continental Protestants. It would leave Eng-land open to attack along her south-eastern approaches. Ireland might also serve as a springboard for invasion from the west.

Fitzmaurice was a native Irishman, an ardent Catholic, an ardent enemy of England, and could command the support of the Desmond clan. He seemed to have a fighting chance and in the opinion of Nicholas Sander – the most articulate and irreconcilable of the English exiles – it was a chance well worth taking. When Fitz-maurice with a handful of men landed at Dingle Bay on 17 July 1579 he was accompanied by Sander in the capacity of papal nuncio If any further confirmation of the Vatican's involvement was needed, Fitzmaurice provided it in proclamations declaring that the Pope had deprived Elizabeth of her unjust possession of her king-dom and that he – Fitzmaurice – was the Pope's captain come to unseat a tyrant 'which refuseth to hear Christ, speaking by his vicar'. In the event, the landing was a failure. Fitzmaurice was killed quite early on and although Sander kept the insurrection alive for a time, the English had no particular difficulty in dealing with it. Sander himself ended as a hunted fugitive, dying in 1581 of exhaustion and exposure.

The Irish *débâcle* was the Vatican's second major tactical blunder in its campaign against Elizabeth. By a futile demonstration of hostility, Gregory had only succeeded in irritating his opponents. More seriously – since the English government could hardly be expected to appreciate the distinction between the Pope wearing his temporal hat and his spiritual one – he had gone a long way towards destroying the credibility of the missionary priests as a non-political force. None realised this more clearly than the missionary priests themselves. 'Though it belonged not to us to mislike this journey of Dr. Sander, because it was made by order of his superiors,' wrote Robert Parsons, 'yet were we heartily sorry, partly because we feared that which really happened, the destruction of so rare and worthy a man, and partly because we plainly foresaw that this would be laid against us and other priests, if we should be taken in England, as though we had been privy or partakers thereof, as in very truth we were not, nor ever heard or suspected the same to this day. But as we could not remedy the matters, and as our consciences were clear, we resolved through evil report or good report to go on with the purely spiritual action we had in hand; and if God destined any of us to suffer under a wrong title, it was only what he had done, and would be no loss, but rather gain, in his eyes who knew the truth, and for whose sake alone we had undertaken the enterprise.'

In spite of these brave words, both Parsons and Campion felt some very natural doubt as to whether there was now any point in going on, especially since they had been told that their arrival was expected and the ports being watched for them. But after discussing the matter with William Allen and the Jesuit fathers at St Omer, they decided it was too late to turn back and that further delay would probably only increase the danger. One of the travellers who did decide to turn back was old Thomas Goldwell, whose nerve had understandably failed. Allen was disappointed, because he was becoming increasingly aware of the need for someone on the spot to exercise overall control of the priests at work in England. But it was obviously unrealistic to expect a man of

Goldwell's age (he was in his eightieth year) to withstand the rigours of life underground and certainly it was better that the bishop 'should yield to fear now than later on, at the other side'. The remaining members of the party, which had been reinforced by more priests from Rheims, now split up to find their way across the Channel in twos and threes by separate routes. Nearly all were to end in prison or on the gallows but after the defection of Thomas Goldwell, public interest focused exclusively on Edmund Campion and Robert Parsons. Both were men of outstanding ability but circumstances and history were to deal with them very differently.

Edmund Campion, born in 1540, was the son of a London bookseller. His father had planned to apprentice him to a merchant, but one of the London companies – most probably the Grocers – took an interest in the clever boy and he was sent instead to the new foundation of Christ's Hospital. Campion achieved his first public distinction at the age of thirteen, when he was chosen to speak a Latin oration on behalf of the London grammar schoolchildren on the occasion of Queen Mary's triumphant progress through the City. Still sponsored by the Grocers' Company, he went on to St John's College, Oxford. Unlike Allen, he was not a committed Catholic at this stage of his career and took the Oath of Supremacy when it was required of him in 1564 apparently without serious misgiving. He was soon making a name for himself as a tutor and lecturer. Like William Allen, Campion was a born teacher and attracted a devoted following among the undergraduates, known as the 'Campionists'. He was appointed proctor and public orator, and in the latter capacity scored a notable success when the Queen visited Oxford in 1566. Elizabeth praised his eloquence and recommended him to the patronage of the Earl of Leicester, Chancellor of the University. Leicester is said to have sent for Campion to ask what he could do for him and to have urged him not to be too modest, for it was not only the Queen's command but his own inclination to befriend him. 'Ask what you like for the present,' declared the chancellor expansively. 'The Queen and I will provide for the future.' Lord Burghley (or William Cecil as he then was) also made a favourable note of the promising young Fellow of St John's.

At the age of twenty-six, therefore, Edmund Campion had the world at his feet. In addition to his persuasive intellectual gifts, he was blessed with the sort of sweetness of nature which disarms jealousy – at any rate no one at Oxford seems to have grudged him his triumphs. Tragically, though, Campion's conscience was beginning to stir. He had made friends with Richard Cheney, Bishop of Gloucester, one of the more right-wing members of the Elizabethan hierarchy, and had allowed himself to be ordained as a deacon, but the further he progressed in the study of theology the more unsettled he became. Finally, in 1569, he left Oxford for Ireland to take a post as a private tutor, hoping in due course to find congenial employment at the reconstituted University of Dublin. This plan came to nothing and Campion filled in his time by writing a history of Ireland which he dedicated to the Earl of Leicester. He returned home early in 1571 and, so Robert Parsons says, was present at the trial of Dr Storey – one of the original exiles who had been kidnapped in somewhat dubious circumstances and brought back to England to be executed as a traitor.

Whether it was this episode which made up Campion's mind for him, or whether he had succumbed to the persuasion of his friend Gregory Martin who had gone over to Douai some years previously, he now left England for the second time. He spent two years under the tutelage of William Allen and then set off on foot to Rome where he joined the Society of Jesus. He was sent to the University of Prague by his superiors and occupied the position of Professor of Rhetoric – scarcely, it might be thought, the most rewarding fulfilment for a man who Lord Burghley himself had described as 'one of the diamonds of England'.

It is difficult for the twentieth-century mind to comprehend a man like Edmund Campion and it is tempting to try and explain him in terms of guilt complexes, death wishes, or plain inability to face the stresses and responsibilities of the career of public service which had undoubtedly been his for the asking. Robert Parsons makes a revealing remark in his biography of his friend. Speaking of the time when the Jesuits were competing for services of their new recruit, he says that Campion was 'incredibly comforted with this battle of the provincials for possession of his body, because he saw that he was no more his own man, but in the hands of others who, under God, would dispose of him better than he could do for himself'. But however one attempts to rationalise such a man he remains elusive and, in spite of his noble reputation, subtly unsympathetic. Robert Parsons, though he was harshly judged by his own contemporaries and has had a bad press from historians ever since, is paradoxically more likeable – perhaps because as a human being he is immediately recognisable.

Robert Parsons (or Persons) was a West Countryman born in 1546 in the village of Nether Stowey on the edge of the Quantock Hills. He says himself that his parents 'were of humble worldly condition but honourable and of somewhat better rank than their neighbours around'. It is thought that his father was a blacksmith and as such would have been a figure of importance in the rural community. Young Robert was one of a family of eleven and 'scarcely was he out of childhood when he was given over to an elder brother, a merchant, to learn business'. But, again according to Parsons' own account, 'it happened by the seeming providence of God that his brother lost nearly the whole of his fortune, and sent Robert back home to his parents'. The local vicar now took a hand. 'He was pleased with Robert's disposition, and also some-what moved by the consideration that this was the first child that he had baptized after his entry into the parish.' He therefore per-suaded Robert's father to send him to the grammar school at Stogursey, offering to pay part of the expenses. (The early careers of both Campion and Parsons provide an interesting illustration of the ways in which clever boys of comparatively humble birth were helped to rise in the world.)

Robert and another of his brothers spent a year at Stogursey and then went on to the larger free school at Taunton. Robert was unhappy there, and at the age of fifteen decided he had had more than enough of education. He wrote home complaining bitterly about his teacher's severity and offering a number of cogent reasons why he should be allowed 'to give over his book'. According to the recollections of yet another of the Parsons brothers, his father was ready to be persuaded by this 'fine and smooth letter', but his mother would not hear of it. She had set her heart on seeing Robert become a scholar and personally rode the seven miles to Taunton to ensure that he stayed. After the failure of this bid for freedom, Robert seems to have settled down. 'He fell to his book very heartily and became the best in the school, and so con-tinued as long as he was there.'

When he was eighteen he progressed to Oxford, studying logic at St Mary's Hall and becoming a Fellow of Balliol in 1568. Like so many of the younger Oxford men, he had begun to flirt with

Catholicism and Edmund Campion, who was proctor that year, offered to help him to evade the Oath of Supremacy. But his efforts were unsuccessful and, says Parsons in his autobiography, 'wicked and ambitious youth that I was, not to lose my degree, I twice pronounced with my lips that abominable oath, though at heart I detested it'. Like Campion he was a successful tutor, but his career at Oxford ended under a cloud, and in 1573 he was expelled from Balliol 'even with public ringing of bells'. Later, when Robert Parsons had become a target for official vilification, it was put about that he had been found to be illegitimate and therefore ineligible for his Fellowship; also that he was suspected of misappropriating college funds. Parsons himself claimed that he was the victim of a conspiracy and had resigned 'both freely and perforce'.

The most likely explanation seems to be that he had become generally disliked by his colleagues, who combined to get rid of him. Unlike Campion, Parsons was an abrasive personality of the kind which easily makes enemies – especially in the touchy atmosphere of a college common room. One of his fellow dons described him as 'a man wonderfully given to scoffing, and that with bitterness, which was the cause that none of the company loved him'. William Camden, who also knew him at Oxford, says he was 'fierce natured' and has left a felicitous picture of him in his student days 'much noted for his singular impudency and disorder in apparel, going in great barrel hose, as was the fashion of hacksters of those times, and drawing also deep in a barrel of ale'. It is all a very familiar pattern – the brilliant 'scholarship boy' with a chip on his shoulder, the lonely young man driven to use his bitter, sarcastic tongue to conceal the frightening insecurity within.

After his ignominious departure from Oxford, Parsons decided to go to Padua to study medicine. He had a little money from the sale of a piece of land given him by the father of one of his pupils and left England in the early summer of 1574. He was in no sense a religious refugee, but while he waited at Antwerp for company on the road through Germany, he was persuaded to visit Louvain where he made his first acquaintance with the Society of Jesus and spent several days going through the Spiritual Exercises. The experience moved him deeply and he might have stayed if he had not already sent his money on to Italy. In the end he travelled to Padua as planned and early the following year went on a trip to Rome, afterwards regretting that he 'had attended more to see profane monuments of Caesar, Cicero and other such like, than to places of devotion'. Back in Padua, he set up house with two English law students, bought a supply of medical books and some clothes from the wardrobe of an English nobleman who had recently died in Venice. But somehow the idea of becoming a doctor had lost its appeal and Parsons spent the next few months in an agony of indecision about his future.

'Many cogitations passed my mind,' he wrote, 'what course it were best for me to take, sometimes thinking to steal away out of Padua and to go to the Alps and there to put myself into some remote and solitary monastery or cell, never to converse more with men; some other times purposed to live a secular life, but yet retired and given to study'. Robert Parsons would certainly not have made a successful hermit. He needed the stimulus of the world, even if he sometimes found it difficult to get on with its inhabitants. In May 1575 he left Padua on foot for Rome – a self-imposed penance for, as he plaintively remarked, he was 'no good goer a-foot and the weather was hot'. However, he stuck it out and having at last made up his mind what he wanted to do with his life, entered the Jesuit novitiate on 25 June, the day after his twenty-ninth birthday.

The Society of Jesus seems to have quickly appreciated his executive as well as his intellectual abilities – at any rate there was never any question of sending him off to some distant corner of Europe. Given polish and self-confidence by Jesuit training, Parsons stayed in Rome, cutting his political teeth on the gritty problems of the English college and becoming a persuasive advocate of the English Mission. When it came to choosing the pioneers, he was an obvious candidate and, although junior to Campion both in age and religion, was put in charge of the party.

If even half the rumours flying round St Omer in June 1580 were true, it was obvious that the task of getting the three Jesuits safely into England was not going to be easy. Robert Parsons therefore consulted the leader of the English community, a Mr George Chamberlain, who had a reputation for being discreet and well-qualified to give advice. It was decided that Parsons should go on ahead by the short sea-route to Dover, 'under the habit and profession of a captain returned from the Low Countries'. If all went well, Campion would follow disguised as a merchant in precious stones with Ralph Emerson as his servant. Although there was no official expeditionary force in the Netherlands as yet, quite a number of the Queen's subjects – some from conviction but probably more out of a taste for rough games – were fighting with the Dutch rebels on a freelance basis. The mercenary captain on his way to or from the wars was therefore a familiar enough sight at the Channel ports and George Chamberlain undertook to provide a military coat of buff leather suitably embellished with gold lace and a hat with a feather.

Parsons adopted his new personality with enthusiasm. 'Such a peacock, such a swaggerer,' wrote Campion, 'that a man needs must have very sharp eyes to catch a glimpse of any holiness and modesty shrouded beneath such a garb, such a look, such a strut.' None of this was precisely in accordance with the instructions of the Superiors in Rome who, while recognising that the missionaries would be obliged to dress as laymen, had laid down that such dress 'ought to be of a modest and sober kind, and to give no appearance of levity and vanity'; but Parsons took a certain ironic pleasure in the appropriateness of the disguises chosen. Their mission was, after all, one of warfare, albeit spiritual warfare, and they were bringing with them the 'jewel' of the Faith.

Parsons sailed from Calais some time after midnight on 16 June and reached Dover without incident. Nor did he experience any difficulty with the immigration authorities, who 'found no cause of doubt in him, but let him pass with all favour, procuring him both horse and all other things necessary for his journey to Gravesend'. No one, it seemed, suspected the dark, rugged-featured, swaggering soldier and Parsons was quick to follow up his advantage. He asked a friendly official to look out for his friend Mr Edmunds, a merchant with urgent business in London, and left a letter to be forwarded to St Omer, telling Campion that if he made haste he could help him to sell his jewels. Parsons then went on his way to Gravesend which he reached late that night, just twenty-four hours after leaving Calais. He got himself a place on a boat taking a convivial party of musicians up river but, feeling it would be unwise to prolong the acquaintance, he hailed a passing wherry which landed him in Southwark about four o'clock in the morning of the 17th.

Parsons was now in the heart of enemy territory and soon discovered that 'the greatest danger of all seemed to be in London itself'. Innkeepers were suspicious of lone travellers on foot and his military appearance, which had occasioned no surprise at the seaports, was uncomfortably conspicuous in the capital. As Parsons trudged round Southwark looking for a lodging, he became conscious of curious glances cast in his direction and realised that he was courting disaster by staying on the streets. It seems odd that although it was now six years since the first missionaries had begun to work in England, there was still no sort of organisation for meeting and helping incoming priests. There were, however, places where a Catholic could be certain of finding friends, and after walking up and down for half the day Robert Parsons 'resolved to adventure into the prison of the Marshalsea and to ask for a gentleman prisoner there named Mr. Thomas Pound'. This was not quite such a desperate step as it sounds – though it provides an illuminating comment on the Elizabethan prison system. In general, the 'better sort' of Catholics in gaol for simple recusancy were able to live in reasonable comfort – that is, as long as they could pay for their comforts – and the Marshalsea was a five star prison. It was expensive but the wealthier inmates could receive visitors, send messages and even sometimes get out for a while. Mr Pound, however, was in residence and delighted to welcome Father Parsons.

After dinner he was able to introduce him to another visitor, Mr Edward Brooksby, who bore him off to a 'safe house' in the City. Here Parsons met again a young man he had known in Rome. This was George Gilbert who, although brought up a Protestant, had been converted to Catholicism while travelling abroad – Parsons had actually stood godfather to him. Gilbert at once attached himself to his sponsor and was to become the forerunner of a group of enthusiastic young gentlemen – all scions of well-to-do families – who took it on themselves to act as guides, couriers and bankers for the missionary priests. As news of Parsons' arrival spread along the grapevine, he was showered with invitations and, after making arrangements for the reception of Campion and Emerson, he left London to 'employ himself in the best manner he could to the comfort of Catholics' in the surrounding countryside.

Meanwhile, Campion and Emerson were preparing to leave St Omer. Unlike Parsons, Campion had little relish for the business of dressing-up. 'You may imagine the expense,' he wrote to the

Jesuit General on 20 June, 'especially as none of our old things can be henceforth used. As we want to disguise our persons, and to cheat the madness of this world, we are obliged to buy several little things which seem to us altogether absurd.' Campion had no illusions about the dangers which lay ahead. 'It is a venture which only the wisdom of God can bring to good,' he wrote, 'and to his wisdom we lovingly resign ourselves.' As soon as Parsons' letter arrived, Campion and Emerson set off for the coast and sailed from Calais on the evening of 24 June. At Dover they immediately ran into trouble – in fact it looked for a time as though their mission would be ended before it had begun. There was a security scare on at the port and the Customer had received orders to examine all incoming travellers with extra care 'for that it had been understood that certain priests had come that way into England of late days'. To make matters worse, the Council had been tipped off that William Allen's brother Gabriel was coming over and Campion apparently fitted his description. Both Campion and Emerson were brought before the Mayor of Dover as suspicious characters and were told they would be sent up to London under guard. Then, as they waited despondently in an antechamber, they were suddenly dismissed without explanation and told to be on their way. After this remarkable reprieve the two Jesuits reached London without further incident, travelling by river as Parsons had done, and as they stepped ashore were met by a Mr Thomas James who came up to Campion saying, 'Mr. Edmunds, give me your hand; I stay here for you to lead you to your friends.'

Parsons had left instructions that Campion should wait for his return to London and spend the time doing all he could for the comfort of the Catholics. Campion was at once surrounded by the young men of George Gilbert's circle who begged him to preach for them. Through the good offices of Lord Paget they were able to use the great hall of Lord Norreys' house at Smithfield and here, on 29 June, three days after his arrival, Campion addressed a considerable audience. He had not lost his gift of oratory and the congregation was profoundly moved, but although the doors were guarded by gentleman volunteers 'of worship and honour' such an event could hardly be kept secret. Campion was high on the wanted list and the government would have liked to catch him in the act of preaching. Agents were therefore sent out on the streets with orders to 'sigh after Catholic sermons and to show

great devotion and desire of the same, especially if any of the
Jesuits might be heard'. But Campion, though impatient of security
measures, had enough sense not to be trapped by quite such obvious
methods and when Parsons returned to London early in July, he
found his friend had 'retired for his more safety into a certain
poor man's house in Southwark'. Even so, the hunt was becoming
uncomfortably hot. Already several priests out of the recent larger
than usual draft from Rome and Rheims had been captured. 'The
searches,' wrote Parsons, 'grew to be so eager and frequent at
this time and the spies so many and diligent as every hour almost
we heard of some taken, either upon suspicion or detection against
them.'

Parsons needed no warning that the sooner he and Campion were
away the better, but before they left town he was anxious to hold
a conference with the more influential Catholic priests and laymen
in the capital; partly to remove any misconceptions about the nature
of their mission, and partly to ensure general conformity of teaching on such tricky matters of Church discipline as whether it could
ever be regarded as permissible for a Catholic to be present at an
Anglican service. The assembly, which met at St Mary Ovaries,
became known as the Synod of Southwark, and Parsons opened
the proceedings by making a solemn declaration on oath that
neither he nor Campion had had any prior knowledge of Sander's
Irish adventure. He went on to reaffirm that their purpose was
apostolic – 'to attend to the gaining of souls without knowledge
or intention in the world of matters of state'.

The question of church-going, a matter of close personal interest
to all the laymen present, was then discussed. The government's
requirements in this respect could scarcely be described as onerous,
for Parsons told the rector of the college in Rome of some Catholic
gentlemen then in prison who were offered their freedom 'if they
would attend the churches of the heretics once a year only, making
a declaration in advance that they came not for the sake of religion
or of approving the doctrine there, but merely to yield external
obedience to the Queen'. A lady of high birth had also apparently
been told she would be released from gaol if she would agree
'merely to pass through the middle of the church whilst the heretics
were holding service there, making no stay and giving no sign
of reverence'. These offers, Parsons noted with satisfaction, had
been virtuously refused and he went on to tell another story of the

kind which makes one despair for the human race. A boy of ten years old had been tricked into entering a church by walking in a bridal procession. When he realised he had fallen into schism he was inconsolable until a few days later 'he chanced to meet' Robert Parsons. 'Whereupon he ran to me and falling at my feet begged me with a flood of tears that he might make confession of his sins, promising that he would be racked with every kind of torment rather than again consent to so great a sin.'

Other Catholics of a more practical turn of mind were arguing that if it could be made clear that they attended an occasional service only from obedience to the law and to save themselves and their families from harassment, they could surely not be accused of schism. Unfortunately, it was not as simple as that. The Roman Church held that by the public act of appearing at the heretical service, Catholics were giving countenance to the Elizabethan Settlement which exalted a temporal sovereign at the expense of the Pope. Whether they took part in the service or not was beside the point. This was an issue on which there could be no compromise and the Synod of Southwark, like the Council of Trent before it, stood firm. It was agreed that the missionary priests would continue to 'teach and insinuate unto Catholics in all places' that even a token attendance at the parish church must be regarded as an act of the highest iniquity and impiety. This, plus the fact that attendance at the parish church was beginning more and more to represent an act of allegiance to the state, did nothing to make life easier for the great majority of English Catholics doing their best to be loyal to their Queen and their religion.

After going on to discuss such matters as the correct observation of fast days and in which parts of the country priests could most usefully be employed, the assembly broke up. It was none too soon, for two members of the circle – Henry Orton, Parsons' companion on his recent tour, and a priest named Johnson – had actually been denounced and arrested while on their way to Southwark. The traitor on both occasions was a man called Charles Sledd or Slade, once a hanger-on at Rome who was now turning his memory for faces to profitable account. 'I am not surprised at the Apostle complaining so bitterly of false brethren,' wrote Parsons; 'here they are most troublesome to us and more deadly than anything else.' Parsons and Campion had had at least two very narrow escapes in less than a month. It was high time to be away from the poisoned atmosphere of London and on 18 July they set off on their travels, going by night for greater security. They paused at the village of Hoxton on the eastern outskirts of the City and here they were followed by Thomas Pound, who had contrived to bribe his way temporarily out of the Marshalsea.

Thomas Pound had been visited by a brilliant idea. If, as seemed only too probable, either or both of the Fathers were captured, the government propaganda machine would certainly represent them as traitors and stirrers-up of rebellion and they would be given no opportunity of stating their side of the case. Let them, therefore, write declarations now, setting out the true meaning and purpose of their coming. Pound would keep the documents safe and would have them published only if necessity arose. It seemed a sensible suggestion and Campion is said to have written his statement, addressed to the Lords of the Council, in less than half an hour. It was duly handed over to Pound but, either from carelessness or trustfulness, Campion had omitted to seal it. Pound, who has been described as very fervent 'but somewhat abounding in singularities', could not resist the temptation to read it and was at once thrown into such transports that he was obliged to show it to several close friends. Manuscript copies were made and passed from one 'safe' man to another so that, of course, it was not long before it reached some very unsafe men indeed.

'My charge is, of free cost to preach the Gospel,' Campion had written, 'to minister the Sacraments, to instruct the simple, to reform sinners, to confute errors – in brief, to cry alarm spiritual against foul vice and proud ignorance wherewith many my dear countrymen are abused.' He reiterated that he was expressly forbidden to meddle 'with matters of state or policy' and went on to ask 'with all humility, and under your correction, three sorts of indifferent and quiet audience. The first before your honours; wherein I shall discourse of religion so far as it toucheth the commonwealth and your nobilities. The second, whereof I make most account, before the doctors and masters and chosen men of both universities; wherein I undertake to avow the faith of our Catholic Church by proofs invincible, scriptures, councils, fathers, histories, natural and moral reason. The third, before the lawyers spiritual and temporal; wherein I will justify the said faith by the common wisdom of the laws standing yet in force and practice.'

Campion would be loth, he declared, to say anything which might sound like 'an insolent brag or challenge', especially as he considered himself 'being now as a dead man to this world'. He was, however, perfectly confident of victory, because he knew 'that none of the Protestants, nor all the Protestants living, nor any sect of our adversaries ... can maintain their cause in disputation'. In fact, 'the better furnished' his opponents, the more welcome they would be, and Campion was ready to cast his bait for the biggest fish of all. 'Because it hath pleased God to enrich the Queen my sovereign lady with noble gifts of nature, learning and princely education, I do verily trust, that if her highness would vouchsafe her royal person and good attention to such a conference ... or to a few sermons which in her or your hearing I am to utter, such a manifest and fair light, by good method and plain dealing, may be cast upon those controversies, that possibly her zeal of truth and love of her people shall incline her noble grace to disfavour some proceedings hurtful to the realm, and procure towards us oppressed more equity.'

Whatever happened the fight would be carried on 'by those English students whose posterity shall not die, which, beyond the seas, gathering virtue and sufficient knowledge for the purpose, are determined never to give you over, but either to win you to Heaven or to die upon your pikes. And touching our Society,' wrote Campion, 'be it known unto you, that we have made a league – all the Jesuits in the world, whose succession and multitude must overreach all the practices of England – cheerfully to carry the cross that you shall lay upon us, and never to despair your recovery while we have a man left to enjoy your Tyburn, or to be racked with your torments, or to be consumed with your prisons. The expense is reckoned, the enterprise is begun. It is of God, it cannot be withstood. So the faith was planted, so it must be restored.'

Looked at dispassionately, Campion's Bragge as it quickly became known, is a quite astonishing mixture of naivety and arrogance. It is not difficult to imagine the sort of reception a similar threat of conversion made by a Protestant divine at large in his dominions would have been given by King Philip of Spain. The first reaction of Queen Elizabeth's government was one of studied but heavy breathing calm. In mid-July an official proclamation was issued in the Queen's name restating her determination 'to main-

tain her honour and glory by retaining her people in the true
profession of the Gospel and free from the bondage of Roman
tyranny'. Any who harboured 'unnatural affections' were warned
'not to irritate her Majesty to use the rod or sword of justice against
them ... from which, of her own natural goodness, she hath a
long time abstained'. Her Majesty was aware of the danger
threatened by rebels and traitors overseas, not to mention their
sympathisers at home, who were seeking foreign aid to overthrow
her. She was also aware that these same rebels and traitors were
spreading tales about how the Pope and the King of Spain meant
to invade England to 'dispose of the Crown and of the possessions
of the subjects of the realm at pleasure', with the result that some
were 'emboldened to persist in their undutifulness, some to be
afraid to continue dutiful'.

But the Queen thanked God that she had 'such a strength as,
in comparison, never any king of the realm hath had the like, to
overcome all foreign malice to her and to the state of true Christian
religion'. She therefore urged all her good people to 'continue in
the true and dutiful service of Almighty God ... and also to
remain constant in courage with their bodies and substance to
withstand any enterprise that may be offered to this realm'. They
should not be influenced by any 'false rumours' and do their best
to help the authorities to round up 'all such spreading like rumours'.

The proclamation carefully avoided any specific mention of the
Jesuits. Lord Burghley, who had been responsible for drafting
this somewhat long-winded document, saw no reason to advertise
the fact that they had slipped through his defensive outworks, but
there was a noticeable tightening-up of security that summer as the
newly arrived Spanish ambassador, Bernardino de Mendoza,
reported to King Philip in July. 'All the Catholics in London,' he
wrote, 'and the whole of the country, who had been released on
bail, or had given sureties to appear when summoned, have been
ordered to surrender themselves in the London prisons within
twenty days, under pain of death. A great number of them have
already done so, and it is a subject of heartfelt gratitude to God
that they bear with joy and confidence this travail and persecution,
such as they have never been afflicted with before.' Whether Mendoza's last statement is strictly accurate or not may be doubtful,
but the time of tacit toleration for the Catholic minority was now
fast running out. No one could any longer pretend that Catholicism

was withering away of its own accord. In the words of one London preacher who believed in calling a spade a spade, 'the Papists and Jesuites, with other the riffe raffe and scumme of this Realme are nowe seen to appeare, who before this tyme have beene hidden in the dytches and channelles of England'.

It was a nervous summer, made more nervous by rumours of Spanish reinforcements on their way to Ireland and a fresh spate of highly circumstantial reports from abroad about the dreaded Papal League. A letter was sent to the Earl of Huntingdon, President of the Council of the North (always a black spot), authorising him to pursue a more stringent policy. Plans were drawn up for the stricter segregation of Catholic prisoners, especially 'the principal persons of most mark', and preparatory steps were taken towards strengthening the anti-recusancy laws. The twelve pence fine for non-attendance at church had remained unchanged since the beginning of the reign and a committee of judges, Queen's Counsel, 'together with some well-learned civilians', was set up to consider 'how by canon and common law a greater penalty might lawfully be set upon wilful and usual recusants that come not to the church at all'. In the autumn of 1580, however, the government was concentrating its efforts on the most effective counter-measure of all – that of catching the missionary priests.

And Christ their capitaine

'...It is that noble traine,
That fight with word and not with sword,
And Christ their capitaine.'
The complaint of a Catholic for the death of M. Edmund Campion

---

AFTER a brief stay at Hoxton, Parsons and Campion separated, arranging to meet again in London at the end of September. Parsons then set off on a circuit of the Midlands and part of the West Country, while Campion went on a less ambitious trip into Berkshire and Oxfordshire. The idea of these missionary tours was a new one and reflects the increased efficiency of organisation and method which the Jesuits brought to the English harvest, as well as the energy and foresight of Robert Parsons. The Douai priests, operating individually, had for the most part returned to their own part of the country, or at any rate had stayed in one place or one district where their labours, however devoted, affected only a comparatively small circle. Parsons saw that to achieve maximum results, every missionary must reach as many people as he could in the probably all too short time at his disposal, and to do that he must travel. In order to make such travel on any useful scale a feasible proposition, it would be essential for the priests to have the support of a network of reliable helpers with a wide range of contacts among Catholics and Catholic sympathisers, and Parsons had already taken the opportunity of channelling the fervour of the newly converted George Gilbert into the task of recruiting the nucleus of an underground army. The prospect of acting as aides to the heroic fathers and sharing something of the danger and excitement of their work naturally appealed strongly to idealistic Catholic youth, and by the time Parsons and Campion landed in England Gilbert had collected a number of volunteers from among his own friends – all with plenty of spare time and spare cash to devote to the cause.

While they were inevitably accused of aiding and abetting the priests in subversive activities, there is no evidence that these lay assistants, or 'sub-seminaries' as they became known, ever formed a political group in the accepted sense – although the names of some of them, such as Francis Throckmorton, Anthony Babington and Chideock Tichborne, were later to recur in a rather less innocent context. All these young men came of good family – indeed it was during Elizabeth's reign that native English Catholicism first acquired its close connection with the upper classes or, to put it more crudely, the specialised snob appeal which it has not entirely lost to this day. There was undoubtedly an element of class-consciousness – a feeling that Calvinism was no religion for a gentleman – in the missionaries' somewhat obsessive concern with the high rank of their supporters, and Campion's contemptuous dismissal of the Marian martyrs as 'a few apostates and cobblers' has a somewhat distasteful ring about it today.

At the same time, this apparent snobbism was based on sound practical considerations. The priests were in no position to make direct contact with the general public and the mission was only possible with the assistance – active or passive – of the gentry. The newer nobility, whose fortunes had been made out of the loot of the Reformation, were naturally predominantly Protestant, as were the bourgeoisie, merchants and artisans to whom the Elizabethan Settlement had brought peace, stability and freedom to get on with their lives with the minimum of clerical interference. It was among the remnants of the ancient nobility and to an even greater extent the older gentry families, often untitled, who owed neither their lands nor their position to an upstart royal house that the missionaries found shelter. These families, who had been part of the local scene for centuries, commanded an influence over their neighbours out of all proportion to the size of their estates or fortunes and their patronage was therefore the most valuable. It was, in fact, the constancy and clannishness of a handful of squires and small landowners which kept the faith alive, and in their houses that Parsons and Campion were welcomed as they travelled through England that faraway summer on their gallant but hopeless attempt to put the clock back.

'I ride about some piece of the country every day,' wrote Campion. 'The harvest is wonderful great. On horseback I meditate my sermon; when I come to the house, I polish it. Then I talk with such as come to speak with me, or hear their confessions. In the morning, after Mass, I preach; they hear with exceeding greediness and very often receive the sacrament, for the ministration whereof we are ever well assisted by priests, whom we find in every place, whereby both the people is well served, and we much eased in our charge.... I cannot long escape the hands of the heretics; the enemies have so many eyes, so many tongues, so many scouts and crafts. I am in apparel to myself very ridiculous; I often change it, and my name also. I read letters sometimes myself that in the first front tell news that Campion is taken, which, noised in every place where I come, so filleth my ears with the sound thereof, that fear itself hath taken away all fear. My soul is in mine own hands ever.' Neither Campion nor Parsons was under any illusion about the risks they and their hosts were running. According to Campion, 'at the very writing hereof, the persecution rages most cruelly. The house where I am is sad; no other talk but of death, flight, prison, or spoil of their friends; nevertheless they proceed with courage.' 'We never have a single day free from danger,' remarked Parsons but unlike Campion, who had considered himself as a dead man from the moment he left Rome, Parsons took a more optimistic view of their chances of survival, feeling that the dangers were not so great as to make capture unavoidable. Indeed, he hoped they might escape 'for many years, or at any rate months'.

Both men were united in begging their Superiors in Rome to send reinforcements as soon as possible and neither had any doubt about the worthwhile nature of their work. 'Very many, even at this present,' wrote Campion, '[are] being restored to the Church, new soldiers give up their names, while the old offer up their blood; by which holy hosts and oblations God will be pleased, and we shall no question by Him overcome.... There will never want in England men that will have care of their own salvation, nor such as shall advance other men's; neither shall this Church here ever fail so long as priests and pastors shall be found for their sheep, rage man or devil never so much.' 'The hope of a harvest is excellent,' wrote Parsons, 'for we are so spoilt by the Catholics and kept so busy that we have neither time nor strength sufficient. I am forced two or three times every day on this my tour to give discourses to men of rank, and they are touched by the spirit of God and are most ready for any distinguished service. More often than not they put at my disposal their persons and all their chattels, and their zeal and fervour is worthy of astonishment.' This letter, which was written on 5 August to the rector of the English college in Rome, ends with another appeal for reinforcements. 'I beg your Reverence to get for me from his Holiness and from our Father General the help of men of the Society, men of learning, not fewer than three or four.'

Meanwhile the journeys continued. 'We passed through the most part of the shires of England,' Parsons recorded, 'preaching and administering the sacraments in almost every gentleman and nobleman's house that we passed by, whether he himself were a Catholic or no, if he had any Catholics in the house'. The usual procedure in a doubtful place was to claim hospitality by posing as a friend or kinsman of some member of the household known to be a Catholic. When this was impracticable, the priest was introduced as the travelling companion of one of George Gilbert's young men. The Catholics would then arrange for him to be quartered 'in some part of the house retired from the rest', where a temporary chapel was set up. There he could change out of his lay disguise and there, when everybody else was in bed, as many of the local faithful who could manage it would gather to ask his blessing, lay their problems before him and make confession. In the early morning Mass would be celebrated and a sermon or exhortation delivered and then the priest, dressed once more in his sober riding clothes, took the road again. It seems likely that in most cases the master of the house must have been perfectly well aware of what was going on under his roof but, providing the visit was kept short and discreet, was prepared to be conveniently unobservant.

In houses where the whole family was Catholic, things became a little easier. The visiting father could stay longer, move about more freely and preach to a wider audience. But neither the priest nor his hosts could ever relax completely, for there was danger as well as protection to be found in the large, hospitable establishments kept up by the average landed gentleman. While the arrival of a couple of additional house-guests would not necessarily attract any particular attention, in places where too many people were in the secret there was always a very real risk that careless talk might rouse the suspicions of an inquisitive neighbour, or that some disgruntled servant or dependant might seize the opportunity to pay off an old grudge and make a bit of extra money by laying information to the authorities.

Robert Parsons has left us an unforgettable description of what it felt like to be part of such a household when a priest was being entertained. 'Sometimes,' he wrote, 'when we are sitting at table quite cheerfully, conversing familiarly about matters of faith or piety (for this is the most frequent subject of conversation), it happens that someone knocks on the front door a little more insistently than usual, so that he can be put down as an official. Immediately, like deer that have heard the huntsman and prick up their ears, all stand to attention, stop eating and commend themselves to God in the briefest of prayers. No word or sound of any sort is heard until the servants come to report what the matter is. If it turns out that there is no danger, we laugh at our fright.'

Many Catholic families had already taken the precaution of providing secret places where a wanted man could be hidden in case of emergency. As time went on the construction of such hides became a highly skilled and specialised craft – Nicholas Owen, son of an Oxford carpenter, being its most noted practitioner. But in the early days the hiding places were often amateurish affairs and known to too many people, so that the priests would prefer to take refuge in woods and thickets, lying in ditches or even holes in the ground. The atmosphere, as Parsons noted, was reminiscent of the primitive church. Services were held in attics and cellars, in barns and caves and, not surprisingly in such circumstances, the emotional temperature was high. 'No one is found in these parts to complain that services last too long. If at any time Mass fails to last nearly an whole hour, this is not much to the taste of many of them.' Everywhere the missionaries and especially the Jesuits went they were greeted with rapture, importuned with requests for sermons, blessings and advice, begged to stay as long as possible and released only with great reluctance. Campion hardly liked to touch on the 'exceeding reverence all Catholics do unto us', while Parsons wrote that he would never come to an end if he began to talk about the zeal and fervour of the Catholics.

All this was highly gratifying from the point of view of the mission, but the unremitting physical and mental strain imposed on the individual priests was killing. No human being could have withstood it for long without a breakdown and after about two

and a half months on the road Parsons returned to London. He
had intended to look for a suitable lodging where Campion could
join him, but when he discovered that the 'Bragge' was still the
main topic of dinner-table conversation with its author heading
the government's wanted list, he realised that this plan would have
to be abandoned. He got off a hasty warning which reached
Campion at Uxbridge, fifteen miles away, in time for him to find
a haven in the house of a Mr William Griffiths. Here Parsons and
some of the other priests who had come over from Rome that
summer presently foregathered and were able to spend a few
weeks unwinding and comparing notes – relating 'one to the other
the mercies that God had showed them in the time of their being
abroad in the country, what shires, towns, houses they had visited,
what success they had had, what perils they had escaped, what
disposition they found in themselves and others for the time to
come'.

It was agreed, among other things, that a recruiting drive for
the foreign seminaries should be started in the universities and two
priests were detailed to work among the undergraduates. Parsons
had decided to send Campion up to Lancashire where, surrounded
by a predominantly sympathetic population, his chances of survival
might be better. He also wanted him to write something in Latin
which could be circulated at Oxford where Campion's memory
was still green, and in the Catholic houses of the North he would
have greater leisure for literary composition and more 'commodity
of books'.

After the party at Uxbridge broke up, Parsons himself went
back to London. He was fully aware of the risk he was running
and laid his plans accordingly. 'Though I have many places in
London where I can stay,' he wrote to his friend Father Agazzari
in November, 'yet in none of them do I remain beyond two days,
owing to the extremely careful searches that have been made to
capture me. I think, however, that by the Grace of God I am
sufficiently safe from them owing to the precaution I take, and
am going to take, of being in different places from early morning
till late at night.' But as the pressure on the Catholic laity increased
Parsons knew that he might not always be able to rely on his
friends for shelter and he acquired a house of his own on the
north bank of the Thames near Blackfriars which he used as his
headquarters, as a storage place for books, vestments and the other

paraphernalia of his trade, and as a refuge for other priests in time of need.

From his base in the capital Robert Parsons had, in fact, now taken over effective control of the Mission's operations. Such was the reputation of the Society of Jesus and the force of his own personality, that the secular priests co-operated willingly and seemed only too ready to follow his lead. All the same, Parsons was feeling the strain of his position and told Agazzari that the burden was more than he could easily support without fresh help. Apart from the purely practical considerations, he was anxious to consolidate the predominance of Jesuit over secular priest and continued to press for a new draft of at least five men from the society. One of these, he stipulated, should be a Spaniard, a first-rate man and especially qualified to resolve complicated questions of conscience. He also wanted fresh reserves from the English college – a supply of 'numerous soldiers, courageous for the battle'. Until these reinforcements arrived, Parsons was prepared to carry on as best he could. After celebrating Mass and preaching, sometimes twice in one day, 'I struggle with almost unending business', he wrote. 'This consists mainly in solving cases of conscience which occur, in directing other priests to suitable places and occupations, in reconciling schismatics to the Church, in writing letters to those who are tempted at times in the course of this persecution, in trying to arrange temporal aid for the support of those who are in prison and in want. For every day they send to me, laying bare their needs. In short, the burdens of this kind are so many that, unless I perceived clearly that the honour of God required what we are doing, and that very badly, I should not hesitate to say that I am weary.'

Weary though he might be, during that winter Parsons was to add yet another task to his already overwhelming work-load. In spite of all the government's efforts to suppress it, book-running – the illegal importation of works of Catholic propaganda and devotion from Continental presses – was still going on, but Parsons had conceived the bold idea of publicising the Mission's activities by setting up his own underground press in or near London. The technical problems involved in putting this idea into practice were formidable – a suitably private place had to be found to house the press, printers and binders recruited and supplies of paper and type got together without arousing suspicion. Although never a man to minimise technical problems, Parsons was not easily discouraged by them, and during the course of November 1580 he set about contriving ways and means. Through the good offices of one of George Gilbert's young men, he got the loan of Mr Brooksby's house at Greenstreet, lying between the then outlying suburban villages of East Ham and Barking. Another of his contacts, the printer Stephen Brinkley, came with seven workmen to manage the press and Parsons himself was the author of the first work to be printed – *A Brief Discourse containing certain reasons why Catholics refuse to go to Church.*

Even so, there were, as Parsons remarked, 'very great difficulties in carrying out the project'. To start with, all the equipment had to be carried the six or seven miles from London, and the press itself had to be worked so that Mr Brooksby should remain in ignorance of what was going on. Then the local parish authorities began to cause trouble. Ironically enough they wanted to know why the occupants of Greenstreet House did not come to church. Parsons and the faithful George Gilbert, who was with him, had one very bad scare when a rumour reached them that the press had been discovered, due, so Parsons believed, to 'an incautious purchase of paper'. One of Brinkley's men was arrested and, to make matters worse, Parsons had begun to have serious doubts about the reliability of his servant, Robert Alfield. But at last the book was ready for distribution and the press could be dismantled.

No sooner had this been done than the first official counterblasts to Campion's Bragge appeared on the streets. Brinkley, coming to report that all was safe, found Parsons worried and depressed. Neither of the two replies to Campion – one written by the Puritan William Charke and the other by a more orthodox churchman Meredith Hanmer – were particularly startling, but both contained accusations which wanted answering. Brinkley offered to set up the press again, but there was now nowhere to put it and Parsons was increasingly anxious about the intentions of the servant Alfield. The situation was saved by Francis Browne, brother of Lord Montague, who offered the loan of a house and servants. Parsons was able to send Alfield away on a visit to his father, and ten days later appeared *A Brief Censure upon two books written in answer to Mr. Edmund Campion's offer of a disputation.* Another book or pamphlet produced by the secret press was *A Discoverie of John Nichols* – an exposure by Parsons of a somewhat dubious individual, originally a Protestant minister, who had spent some time at the English college in Rome and who was now being much petted and paraded by the government as a notable convert to Protestantism.

The difficulties of this form of publishing did not, of course, end with printing and binding. The books had to be distributed 'so that what is written may reach the hands of all'. The usual method was to make up parcels of fifty or a hundred copies at some central clearing house and pass them on to the missionary priests, who circulated them among the faithful on their travels. This, however, was not the only way in which they were brought to the notice of the public. According to Parsons, as soon as one of the regular searches for proscribed literature was under way, numbers of young gentlemen would be standing 'ready to distribute other copies at night in the dwellings of the heretics, in the workshops as well as in the palaces of the nobles, in the Court and about the streets, so that the Catholics alone may not be charged with being in possession of them'. No doubt this prank appealed strongly to the young gentlemen, but it would have done nothing to endear them to the authorities, trying unsuccessfully to track down the source of this new material being produced under their noses. For although Parsons and Brinkley tried to camouflage their activities – the *Brief Discourse* alleged itself to have been printed at Douai – any knowledgeable printer could recognise English paper and English type.

A very much harder line was now being taken against all Catholics and in his letter to Agazzari of 17 November, Parsons reported that 'the violence of the persecution, which is now inflicted on the Catholics throughout the whole kingdom, is most intense and it is of a kind that has not been heard of since the conversion of England. Everywhere there are being dragged to prison, noblemen and those of humble birth, men, women and even children ... and in proclamations as well as in discourses and sermons they are made infamous in the eyes of the people under the name of traitors and rebels.' This new wave of severity, in which a considerable number of the better-known recusants were being rounded up and gaoled without the option, was due in part to the troubles in Ireland – Mendoza told Philip of Spain in October that over the past six weeks 'more than five hundred Catholic English gentlemen have been imprisoned for fear that they might rise in consequence of the news from Ireland' – in part to a fresh crisis situation beginning to build up in Scotland and in part, of course, to the disturbing resurgence of confidence visible among the Catholics themselves.

The government's biggest guns were trained on the priests who had brought this resurgence about and on the laymen suspected of associating with them, but in spite of increasingly fierce proclamations about the consequences which could be expected by those caught maintaining, harbouring, and succouring Jesuits and other seminary priests, and the revival currently being enjoyed by the ancient trade of informer, the two most wanted men in the country continued to prove irritatingly slippery customers. Campion, 'the wandering vagrant', after a slow and difficult journey had reached the comparative sanctuary of the north-west. Parsons, 'the lurking wolf', going about his business in the capital, seemed to bear a charmed life. Ralph Sherwin was taken on 13 November, the very day after he had been staying with Parsons, and Edward Rishton and a group of gentlemen from Lancashire were arrested when the Red Rose public house in Holborn was raided. Parsons was expected at this gathering, in fact he was on his way, but although he knew the district well and had been there only a few days before, he failed to find the house – possibly because he enquired for it by its other name, the Red Lion. Next day he heard that the door had been shut and 'the secretary Walsingham's men within it that were sent to apprehend me'. A little later he was visiting a house in Tothill Fields when the searchers arrived and only escaped 'by running into the haymow'.

When Parliament met on 16 January 1581, the fact had to be faced that the Queen's gradualist policy was no longer working. Those of her advisers who had never concealed their disapproval of this policy were not sorry to have been proved right. Everyone was agreed that the anti-Catholic legislation which, in general outline, had remained unaltered since 1559, must now be strengthened. The only area of disagreement lay in the nature and extent of the changes and it soon became evident that Elizabeth was not going to be stampeded into panic measures. She would certainly have had little sympathy with the Puritan divine who was gloomily convinced that the world was going mad and Anti-christ resorting to every extreme 'that he may with wolf-like ferocity devour the sheep of Christ'. The Queen clung to her belief that consciences were not to be forced and to her refusal 'to make windows into men's hearts and secret thoughts'. Ten years earlier she had vetoed a bill making it compulsory to take the Anglican communion at stated intervals. In 1572 and 1576 she had squashed attempts to reintroduce it, and she would have nothing to do with it now.

But if interfering with men's secret thoughts was one thing, permitting foreign interference and open defiance of her laws was quite another, as Sir Walter Mildmay, one of the government's spokesmen in the Commons, made clear. After referring to the 'implacable malice of the Pope and his confederates' which so far, thanks to the 'almighty power of God', had proved ineffectual, Sir Walter went on to warn his audience that 'seeing our enemies sleep not, it behoveth us also not to be careless'. The enemies of the Protestant state would if they could 'procure the sparks of the flames that have been so terrible in other countries to fly over into England and kindle as great a fire here'. Meanwhile, the Pope was resorting to underhand methods of encouraging undutiful subjects to defy their Queen. 'The obstinate and stiff-necked Papist is so far from being reformed as he hath gotten stomach to go backwards and to show his disobedience, not only in arrogant words but also in contemptuous deeds. To confirm them herein, and to increase their numbers, you see how the Pope hath and doth comfort their hollow hearts with absolutions, dispensations, reconciliations and such other things of Rome. You see how lately he hath sent hither a sort of hypocrites, naming themselves Jesuits, a rabble of vagrant friars newly sprung up and coming through the world to trouble the Church of God; whose principal errand is, by creeping into the houses and familiarities of men of behaviour and reputation, not only to corrupt the realm with false doctrine, but also, under that pretence, to stir sedition.' As a result, not merely the old, hard-core recusants but 'many, very many' who had previously been willing to conform were now refusing to come to church, and this, of course, was the really worrying thing.

Having outlined the problem, Sir Walter turned to the question of a solution. The Queen, he pointed out, had been extraordinarily patient over a long period, but since the Catholics had not responded to 'favourable and gentle manner of dealing' it was time 'to look more narrowly and straitly to them, lest ... they prove dangerous members ... in the entrails of our Commonwealth'. This represented the feeling of the entire House. Indeed, the Commons' only complaint was that the Queen had been patient for far too long. A committee, consisting of all the Privy Councillors and fifty-seven members of the Lower House, was appointed and began work immediately on drafting a bill entitled 'For obedience to the Queen's Majesty against the see of Rome', which received its first reading on 8 February. The Commons were then informed that the Lords were also considering a bill along the same lines as their own, but a good deal milder in its provisions.

Since both Houses were united in their desire to see more stringent penalties imposed on Catholic recusancy, they agreed to join forces. If, as seemed only too probable in the light of past experience, the Queen were to baulk at the last moment, Parliament's only hope of putting pressure on her lay in presenting a common front. After several meetings between the representatives of both Houses, a longer and amended version of the Commons' bill emerged and was read for the first time on 18 February. Among other things, it made the saying of Mass a felony and therefore subject to the death penalty. Anyone hearing Mass would now become liable to six months in gaol for a first offence and the pains of praemunire – loss of all goods and imprisonment during the Queen's pleasure – for the second. The recusancy fines were raised from the old flat rate of twelve pence to a staggering £20 for a first offence, £40 for the second, £100 for the third and after that praemunire.

If the bill had passed into law in this form and if it had been rigorously enforced, it would undoubtedly have gone a long way towards eradicating Catholicism in England by making life intolerable even for its peaceful and loyal adherents. This, as Professor Neale has pointed out, was undoubtedly what it was planned to do. There seems no reason to doubt, either, that this is what the three great advisory bodies – Council, Lords and Commons – wanted to happen. Certainly there is no indication that there were any dissenting voices. It did not happen because the Queen would not have it, or so all the available evidence suggests. After 18 February there was silence for nine days – a period presumably taken up with intensive consultations at Court. Then came another flurry of meetings between the parliamentary committees and on 4 March a third version of the bill was laid before the Commons. It was this version which presently reached the Statute Book as the 'Act to retain the Queen's Majesty's subjects in their due obedience' and which represented the limits Elizabeth was prepared to go to.

The bill as enacted was a good deal harsher than any previous anti-Catholic legislation but the earlier drafts had been significantly toned down. The section dealing with the missionaries and their undesirable activities was framed as an extension of the Act of 1571, which had made it a treasonable offence either to reconcile or be reconciled to Rome through the influence of *Regnans in Excelsis* or any similiar pronouncement. This statute was now to apply to the missionary priests and their converts. In future, any person attempting to 'absolve, persuade or withdraw' any of the Queen's subjects from their 'natural obedience', or who persuaded them *'for that intent'* to leave the Church of England for the Church of Rome were to be adjudged as traitors. Any person who allowed himself to be so persuaded, or who promised obedience to the 'pretended authority of the See of Rome' was to suffer as in cases of high treason. Anyone aiding, abetting or concealing such persons would be guilty of misprision of treason. The addition of the words 'for that intent' in the final draft of the bill emphasised the Queen's stubbornly secular approach to the whole problem and allowed for some elasticity in the interpretation of the law – at least this is probably what she intended. In practice, however, it seems to have made little difference to those who were tried under the Act, since the courts persisted in regarding the fact of reconciliation to Rome as automatically involving a withdrawal of allegiance. This is certainly what the Commons had intended and in view of the Pope's attitude was not entirely unreasonable.

The most dramatic difference between the Act as originally envisaged by Parliament and the Act which received the royal assent lay in the sharp distinction drawn between the crime of becoming a Catholic (or rather of becoming one again) and the crime of being a Catholic. The former, to all intents and purposes, was now the treason of adhering to the Queen's enemies; the latter could still be compounded for with fines and imprisonment. For saying Mass the price had risen to a fine of two hundred marks and a year in gaol, for hearing Mass a fine of one hundred marks and a year in gaol, for the luxury of refusing to go to church a fine of £20 a month. Anyone over the age of sixteen who was absent for twelve months must produce two sureties in the sum of at least £200 until such time as they did conform. This was galloping inflation in the cost of salvation and could quickly prove ruinous when enforced, but it was a good deal better than it had been before the Queen's intervention.

Another bill passed by the 1581 session of Parliament was the Act against seditious words and rumours uttered against the Queen's most excellent Majesty. Hitherto the penalty for slandering the sovereign had been the loss of both ears and three months in gaol, but with the option of a fine in lieu of ears. The new bill withdrew the option and increased the term of imprisonment to last during the Queen's pleasure. To repeat such an overheard slander (as distinct from inventing one) had previously involved one ear and one month in gaol, again with the option of a fine instead of an ear. Now that option was to disappear as well, and the term in gaol increased to three years. A repetition of either offence would now become a felony. Under the old law the punishment for writing or printing a slander against the sovereign had been the loss of the right hand, as the Puritan hero John Stubbs had recently discovered. Under the new law this, too, became a felony. Oddly enough, opposition to this savage measure came from the Commons. Not that they objected to the savagery, but they could see that it would be a two-edged weapon – one which could be turned against outspoken critics from the Puritan left as easily as against the Catholic right. In Professor Neale's felicitous phrase, 'they had visions of an earless *élite* of godly men, languishing for years in prison'.

The House therefore set about amending the bill and scaling down the penalties. Thomas Norton, that scourge of popery, inserted a clause which would have made it a seditious rumour to affirm that the doctrine taught by the Church of England was heretical or schismatic. If Norton had succeeded in getting this clause past the Queen he would, in theory at least, have imposed an ideological orthodoxy as rigid as that of any modern totalitarian state. In fact, of course, he did not. After a period of deadlock and a good deal of huffing and puffing between the Lords and Commons, a compromise was arrived at. Norton's addition had to be sacrificed, but the Commons succeeded in restoring the optional fines and in reducing the terms of imprisonment to six months and three months respectively. Second offences remained felonies, as did the writing or printing of slanderous material, but the left-wingers were able to get in a qualifying 'with malicious intent' which, they hoped, would protect all but the rashest of the godly. The only response the missionaries could make to the challenge of the new legislation was to redouble their efforts, in an attempt to increase their flocks to the point where no prison could hold them. It was a forlorn hope but Robert Parsons' letters are full of the cheerful resignation with which the Catholics of England faced the prospect of increased hardship and 'perpetual imprisonment'.

In the spring of 1581 the drama of the first Jesuit mission had begun to move towards its climax. Parliament rose on 18 March and about a week later Parsons received the manuscript of Campion's book. This work, which contained 'Ten Reasons for the confidence with which Edmund Campion offered his adversaries to dispute on behalf of the Faith' and which is usually referred to as the *Decem Rationes*, ran to about 20,000 words. The main thread of Campion's argument – and the one least likely to endear him to his adversaries – was that the Protestants knew their position to be intellectually indefensible and were therefore obliged to depend on brute force rather than reasoned disputation. Since the book was intended for a learned public, it bristled with quotations and references. Parsons, knowing that Campion had been working almost entirely from memory and that the smallest error would be joyfully pounced on, commissioned one of his lay contacts, Thomas Fitzherbert of Sywnnerton, to verify the text as far as he could without arousing suspicion. Even taking this precaution, and knowing the dangers involved, Parsons decided that Campion ought to come south to superintend the printing of this important and complicated piece of work, but as an added safeguard he was to stay at public inns instead of Catholic houses on the journey.

Meanwhile, Parsons turned to grapple with the problem of setting up the secret press again. Stephen Brinkley offered to act 'as prefect of the printers' for the third time and a priest, William Maurice, began to buy paper and other essentials. But the greatest difficulty, as always, was to find a safe base for their operations. At last, 'having searched very diligently', Parsons was put in touch with a widow willing to lend her house 'which stood in the middle of a wood, twenty miles from London'. This was Stonor Park near Henley and Parsons and his team moved in towards the end of April. They were only just in time, for one evening not long afterwards, Father William Hartley, one of the priests deputed by the Uxbridge conference to work at the university, happened to mention while visiting Stonor that he had heard in Oxford that the servant of Roland Jenks, a Catholic bookbinder, had gone over to the enemy and betrayed his master.

This was a bad blow, as Parsons had very recently employed Jenks at his house at Blackfriars. First thing next morning he sent a messenger to London, but he was too late – the house had already been raided and its contents seized. Worse than the loss of his property was the news that during the search Alexander Bryant, a Douai priest and close friend of Parsons, had been found hiding in a nearby house and arrested. Bryant's special connection with Parsons was evidently known to the authorities, for he was at once singled out for special treatment. After a week in prison, where he was deprived of food and drink, Bryant was transferred to the Tower and tortured with unusual severity – as well as being repeatedly racked, needles were thrust under his nails in an attempt to wring from him 'by the pain and terror of the same' details of the whereabouts of Parsons and the secret press.

Campion had arrived from the north when the news of Bryant's sufferings reached Stonor, and he and Parsons sat up together nearly all one night discussing what they would do if they were taken. With incredible fortitude Bryant had remained silent and the printing of the *Decem Rationes* proceeded without incident, although slowly because of the limited supply of type available. It was ready by the end of June and William Hartley undertook the dangerous business of distributing it at Oxford. In a feat of considerable daring and ingenuity several hundred copies were planted on the benches in St Mary's Church, where a formal Academic Exercise was being held, and not surprisingly caused a sensation.

As soon as Hartley had reported the success of his mission, the party at Stonor broke up. Campion was ready to leave on 11 July, intending to return to Lancashire where he had left his books and belongings and then to make his way to Norfolk. First, though, he wanted Parsons' permission to accept an urgent and long-standing invitation to visit Lyford Grange, which lay in the Vale of the White Horse between Wantage and Abingdon. The mention of Lyford set alarm bells ringing in Parsons' head. Ever since the capture of Alexander Bryant he seems to have had a presentiment that time was running out and Lyford was just the sort of place most likely to prove a death trap. Its owner, Mr Yate, a noted recusant was in gaol and his mother lived in the house with a community of eight ex-Brigittine nuns. There were two priests, Fathers Ford and Collington, in constant attendance, so Campion's visit was scarcely necessary from the spiritual point of view.

On the other hand, it was not easy to refuse. Mr Yate had written to Campion from prison, begging him to go and see his mother and Campion himself was very persuasive. He may well have pointed out that neither he nor Parsons were in England for their health but to bring aid and comfort to the oppressed Catholics whatever the circumstances. Parsons' every instinct told him that Campion should get out of the neighbourhood of Oxford as soon as possible, and it went badly against the grain of his practical commonsense to put the whole of their mission at risk for the sake of a piece of sentiment. But in the end he gave way, only stipulating that the visit to Lyford should not last more than one night. As an added precaution, he put the lay-brother, Ralph Emerson, in charge, ordering him to see that this programme was carried out. The two friends then said goodbye and Parsons returned to London, although he would now be without the invaluable support of George Gilbert. The hunt had grown too hot for that enterprising young gentleman and Parsons had been forced to send him abroad to safety.

Contrary to Parsons' forebodings, Campion's overnight stay at Lyford passed off quietly. His hostess and her companions were, of course, in a flutter of delight at seeing him and reluctant to let him go, but Campion kept his promise and immediately after dinner on Wednesday, 12 July, he and Emerson rode away, accompanied by Father Collington, one of Mrs Yate's resident chaplains who was to escort them on the first stage of their journey. All might have been well if, later that day, a party of Catholics had not arrived to call on the ladies. There was bitter disappointment when they discovered how narrowly they had missed the treat of hearing the glamorous Father Campion. Then someone had a bright idea. The travellers could not have gone far. Surely it would be possible to catch up with them and beg Campion to return, just for a few days? Thomas Ford, the other priest at Lyford, who should have known better, set off at once on this extremely ill-advised errand. He found Campion at an inn near

Oxford where already a considerable number of people with more enthusiasm than sense had come out from the university to meet him and try and persuade him to preach.

When Ford's proposition was put to him, Campion explained that he was acting under obedience and that Ralph Emerson was now his superior. Everyone present then combined to make an impassioned assault on Ralph. Father Parsons, they pointed out, had not realized there would be such a large company in urgent need of spiritual consolation; he certainly could not have intended that so many hungry souls should be sent empty away. Sturdy little Ralph Emerson was not proof against this sort of argument. Before he knew where he was, he found himself agreeing to ride on alone to Lancashire to attend to the unfinished business there, thus sparing the Father the dangers and fatigue of the journey. Campion should stay at Lyford, where he would be among friends, until the following Sunday and then go direct to Norfolk to wait for Ralph in another 'safe' house.

But on the following day, as Campion and the other two priests retraced their steps along the narrow Berkshire lanes, through the fields of standing corn, someone else was planning to pay a visit to Lyford. George Elliot was not untypical of that class of person who found in the laying of information a ready-made solution to their personal and financial problems. Although neither his character nor past career would bear too close an inspection – he is said to have been in prison facing a charge of murder when he wrote to the Earl of Leicester offering his services – Elliot had at one time been a Catholic and had worked in various Catholic households, both useful qualifications for a priest-catcher. In its campaign against the missionary priests, the government was obliged to rely heavily on informers and could not afford to be over-fussy about their antecedents – at least someone in Elliot's position would have a strong motive for giving satisfaction. Accordingly he was let out of gaol to begin a startlingly successful career as one of those 'false brethren' who constituted by far the greatest single danger to the Catholic population.

Whether or not it was pure chance that Elliot should have been pursuing his avocation in and round Oxford just at the time when Campion was in the neighbourhood is uncertain, but after 12 July anyone with any Catholic connections could scarcely have failed to pick up his scent. Quite apart from this, Lyford, just as Robert

Parsons had foreseen, was an obvious target for one of Elliot's profession. When he presented himself there on Sunday 16 July, following his usual simple but effective routine of posing as a devout member of the faithful eager to hear Mass, he gained admission without difficulty; Mrs Yate's cook, who had known him in the days when he had been steward to Mr Roper of Orpington, whispering that he would be lucky enough to hear Father Campion preach. Elliot just had time to send his companion, one David Jenkins, to find a magistrate before proceeding decorously to the chapel, where a congregation of some sixty people was assembled. He sat through the Mass and Campion's sermon on the all too appropriate text 'Jerusalem, Jerusalem, thou that killest the prophets'. Elliot, Judas Elliot, as he was to become known, then took his leave with more haste than courtesy, refusing a pressing invitation to stay to dinner.

This in itself should have aroused suspicion but in the general euphoria of the moment no one seems to have taken any particular notice of the stranger's abrupt departure – besides Father Campion would be setting out for Norfolk as soon as he had eaten. Considering the identity of her guest, Mrs Yate's security arrangements were remarkably casual. Only one look-out had been posted, and while the company was still at the dinner table he came panting in with the horrifying information that the house was surrounded by armed men. Campion wanted to be allowed to take his chance outside. He might even now be able to slip through the cordon and in any case if he were taken, the searchers would probably be satisfied. But his hosts would not hear of such a thing and the three priests were hustled away into a secret place opening out of one of the upper rooms just as the first hammering fell on the front door.

To begin with the search party, which was made up of local men dragged from their normal Sunday pursuits, showed no great enthusiasm for their task. They found nothing and were only too willing to call off the hunt. Once outside, they had no hesitation in giving Elliot a piece of their collective mind for wasting their time on a fool's errand and making trouble for them with their neighbours. But Elliot was not going to be cheated of his triumph by a parcel of ignorant yokels. Did they really expect to find Campion, the notorious Jesuit and traitor, hiding under a bed or keeping company with the rest of the family, he demanded scornfully. Or were they perhaps all secret papists, conspiring to aid the Queen's enemies? This was fighting talk, but when Elliot flourished his royal warrant and insisted on a more thorough search being made the magistrate, much as he may have resented taking orders from this jumped-up jack-in-office, had no choice but to obey. At their second attempt the posse uncovered several likely hiding places, but no priests. It was growing dark by this time and operations were suspended until the following day, Elliot and a select band of helpers remaining on guard.

Mrs Yate had her bed made up in a room close to the priests' hole and when all was quiet Campion came out to speak to her and some of her companions – nobody at Lyford can have felt like sleeping that night. The noise disturbed the searchers, who came to investigate, but Campion was able to get back unseen. Next morning it all began again – the examining of every cupboard, closet and chimney, tapping the wainscot for hollow sounds, hacking at suspicious plaster, tearing up the floorboards, but still nothing. Not even the most zealous priest-catcher could complain of lack of co-operation now and tension in the house mounted unbearably as it began to look as if the miracle was going to happen. Then, just as Elliot prepared sulkily to admit defeat, someone – was it Elliot himself? – looked up and noticed a chink of light over the stairwell in a place where no chink of light should have been. A section of the wall was opened up with a crowbar and there were the three priests in a space just large enough for them to lie side by side.

Humphrey Forster of Aldermaston, Sheriff of Berkshire for the year 1581, had been away from home that eventful weekend, but the news that Campion was taken brought him hurrying to Lyford. The sheriff seems to have been a trifle embarrassed by the size of the fish which had been landed and he sent to the Council for instructions on how to proceed. After three days, during which time Campion remained at Lyford being treated with careful respect by his captors, orders arrived that the male prisoners – in addition to the three priests, nine laymen were in custody – should be brought to London under strong guard. The journey took them through Abingdon and Henley, where Robert Parsons had once more taken refuge. He was dissuaded from going in person to see the procession pass by but sent his servant Alfield, who reported that Campion seemed well and in good spirits. The third and last halt was at Colnbrook and then came the ride through London to the Tower. The authorities were naturally eager to show off their prize to his maximum disadvantage and Campion was placed at the head of the cavalcade, 'on a very tall horse, without cloak on his back, his arms tied behind his loins, and his feet confined by a rope beneath his horse's belly.... Around the hair of his head they encircled an inscription written in great big capital letters: EDMUND CAMPION, THE SEDITIOUS JESUIT.' Although the great majority of the people who lined the streets found this spectacle eminently satisfactory, there was a more thoughtful element who were not entirely happy at seeing a man of Campion's calibre and reputation for scholarship being treated like a common criminal, or his case so blatantly pre-judged.

In the four months which elapsed between his arrest and trial, Campion was alternately offered life, liberty and preferment if he would change his religion, and racked to extort confessions and names. According to the rack-master, who should have been a connoisseur in such matters, Campion did not possess quite the iron physical courage of Alexander Bryant and some information was wrung from him. At a Council meeting held on 4 August a letter was drafted to Sir Henry Nevill and Ralph Warcoppe instructing them 'to repair unto the Lady Stonor's house and to enter into the same, and there to make diligent search and enquire for certain Latin books dispersed abroad in Oxford at the last Commencement, which Edmund Campion upon his examination hath confessed to have been there printed in a wood, and also for such other English books as of late have been published for the maintenance of popery, printed also there as it is thought by one Parsons, a Jesuit, and others; and further, for the press and other instruments of printing, etc., thought also to be there remaining.'

In the raid on Stonor the press was seized and the priest William Hartley, the printer Stephen Brinkley and four of his assistants, and a member of the Stonor family arrested and carried off to London. But Robert Parsons' phenomenal luck still held. He had just left Stonor to visit a house near Windsor and when news of this latest disaster reached him, he retreated to Michelgrove in Sussex. There he was unexpectedly offered an opportunity of crossing to France with a party of Catholic refugees. Parsons had to make a difficult decision and make it quickly. He was now on the run and if he stayed in England his capture could only be a matter of weeks, perhaps days. Once across the Channel, he would be able to make a detailed report to his Superiors without fear of his letters falling into the wrong hands. He could also discuss the needs of the Mission with William Allen in person, and Parsons was becoming more and more convinced that the Jesuit mission could not be maintained 'unless there were someone to be agent beyond the seas for many matters'. Then there was the secret press. Parsons believed that the value of keeping up a steady flow of Catholic books could not be underestimated and it might well be months before production could be started again in England. He had two or three manuscripts in preparation, and in France he could get on with the work of printing without delay. Of the reinforcements he had begged from the Society in Rome, Fathers Heywood and Holt had now arrived and should be able to carry on for a while. From the practical point of view, the arguments in favour of his going, for a time at least, were overwhelming. On the other hand, Parsons knew that it would look as if he were deserting his post and was worried about the possible effect on morale. All the same, the issue was never in doubt. Edmund Campion could serve the cause by dying nobly a martyr's death. Robert Parsons' vein of earthy, peasant commonsense told him that he could serve it best by staying alive.

He left England sometime between 13 and 21 August and was to devote the rest of his life to working unceasingly for the hopeless dream of the Great Enterprise. He never did return and died at last, in 1610, far from the green hills of his native West Country, a lonely, embittered man with the sour taste of failure in his mouth.

All my joints to tremble for fear

'It makes my heart leap for joy to think we have such a jewel.
It makes all my joints to tremble for fear when I consider the
loss of such a jewel.'

George Ireland, the House of Commons, February 1585

T H E execution of Edmund Campion is generally accepted today
as an act of judicial murder. Certainly there can be little doubt
that Campion and the thirteen others arraigned with him in Westminster Hall were not guilty as charged and that their trial was
rigged as ruthlessly as in any modern 'purge', but in 1581 the
English government was less concerned with observing the niceties
of fair play than with questions of national survival. There had,
in fact, been some indecision in government circles over the best
way of proceeding against Campion – by far their most important
capture so far. In the first draft of the indictment he was charged
with having traitorously pretended to have power to absolve the
Queen's subjects from their natural obedience, with the intention
of withdrawing 'the said subjects of the said Queen from the
religion now by her supreme authority established within this
realm of England to the Roman religion, and to move the same
subjects of the said Queen to promise obedience to the pretensed
authority of the Roman See to be used within the dominions of the
said Queen'. Before the trial came on, however, these charges were
dropped and it was decided instead to invoke the old Treason
Statute of 1352.

Another, far more wholesale indictment was drawn up charging
William Allen and Robert Parsons in their absence, Edmund
Campion and (presumably as an afterthought since their names
were added in the margin) the dozen assorted priests then in
custody and the layman Henry Orton with having conspired
together in Rome and Rheims to imagine, contrive and compass
not merely the deposition of the Queen but her death and final

destruction. They were also accused of having planned 'to incite, raise and make sedition' in the realm, 'to procure and set up insurrection and rebellion' against the Queen, and 'to change and alter according to their will and pleasure the government of the said realm, and to invite, procure and induce divers strangers and aliens ... to invade the realm and to raise, carry on and make war against the said Queen'.

The reasons which lay behind this somewhat startling change of plan are conjectural but they were probably not unconnected with Elizabeth's extreme sensitivity over measures which could be construed as religious persecution for its own sake and her equally extreme reluctance to regard all her Catholic subjects as traitors, or even to appear to do so. Added to and arising from this was the official determination to discredit the missionary priests – especially those fabled monsters the Jesuits – as thoroughly as possible in the public mind. If the government had stuck to its original plan and prosecuted Campion under the 1581 Act now on the statute book, they would have had a better case in law and it would probably have been the wiser decision, but it made very little difference in the end. His life was equally forfeit either way, and either way the Catholic propaganda machine was bound to present him as a martyr for religion.

Campion himself certainly had no doubts on the matter. When the customary question, whether he had anything to say why sentence should not be passed, was put to him by the Lord Chief Justice, he replied: '... if our religion do make us traitors, we are worthy to be condemned; but otherwise are and have been as true subjects as ever the Queen had. In condemning us you condemn all your own ancestors – all the ancient priests, bishops and kings – all that was once the glory of England, the island of saints, and the most devoted child of the See of Peter. For what have we taught, however you may qualify it with the odious name of treason, that they did not uniformly teach? To be condemned with these old lights – not of England only, but of the world – by their degenerate descendants, is both gladness and glory to us. God lives; posterity will live: their judgement is not so liable to corruption as that of those who are now going to sentence us to death.'

Campion's death provoked a positive barrage of pamphlets, tracts and 'True Accounts' which kept the printers working overtime on both sides of the Channel. It also brought into sharp focus the perennial argument as to whether the English Catholics and the missionary priests were being persecuted for their religion, as the Catholics maintained; or whether they were being punished as ordinary law-breakers and traitors respectively, as the English government maintained. This is an old controversy and an unfruitful one, based as it is on the false premise that religion and politics could be treated as separate issues. If this ever had been possible in the past, *Regnans in Excelsis* and papal intervention in Ireland had effectively put an end to any hope that it might become possible again in the foreseeable future.

In any ideological conflict, however, public opinion is of paramount importance. This was as true of the sixteenth century as of the twentieth, and in 1583 the English government felt impelled to issue an explanation and justification of its use of torture in the interrogation of captured priests – a matter which was being made much of by Catholic propagandists, despite the fact that no contemporary Catholic regime had a particularly clean record when it came to the use of physical barbarity on prisoners. *A Declaration of Favourable Dealing by Her Majesty's Commissioners for the Examination of Certain Traitors* was probably written by Thomas Norton, one of the commissioners concerned with the examination of Edmund Campion. It pointed out that torture was legal in certain cases and affirmed that it was never applied in matters of conscience, but only to uncover treasonable practices. Nor was it used 'at adventure', but only where there were reasons for believing the prisoner was concealing evidence. Also in 1583 appeared *The Execution of Justice in England, not for Religion but for Treason*, a twenty-page pamphlet written by Lord Burghley and spelling out the official attitude to the missionary priests.

Burghley's own religious convictions were slightly left of centre but in *The Execution of Justice* his approach, like the Queen's, was strictly secular and political. England's quarrel was not with Roman Catholicism as such but with the Pope's claims of supremacy in temporal matters. No national ruler, whatever his creed, who lived in the real world could accept the right of another state to interfere in any way with the exercise of his sovereign power. No national ruler did accept it. Even the Catholic Mary Tudor had forbidden the entrance of certain papal bulls and had refused to allow the Pope to replace her favourite Cardinal Pole. Burghley regarded the excommunication of Elizabeth as a declaration of war, the invasion of Ireland as an act of unprovoked aggression. *Regnans in Excelsis* had invited the Queen's subjects to rebel against her – indeed it had laid a duty on them to do so. The fact that the *Explanatio*, which had recently fallen into the government's hands, temporarily absolved the English Catholics of that duty made things no better – it merely enabled them to continue to enjoy the benefits accruing to loyal subjects while waiting for a favourable opportunity to rise up and bite the hand that was feeding them.

The principal result of the *Explanatio*, although curiously enough Lord Burghley failed to exploit this valuable propaganda point, was to cast serious doubt on the credibility of all Catholic protestations of loyalty, such as those made by Edmund Campion on the scaffold. As far as the Jesuit and seminary priests were concerned, Burghley maintained they were being prosecuted not because they were Roman Catholics, not even because they were unable to give satisfactory answers to the so-called Bloody Questions – did they believe that the Pope had power to depose the Queen? – in the event of a foreign invasion to enforce the deposition, would they fight on the Pope's side? – but because they were traitors found guilty under the normal processes of the law. The missionaries were Englishmen born who had chosen to transfer their allegiance to the Queen's avowed enemies. They were infiltrating the realm in disguise, using their religious proselytising as a cloak to conceal their real purpose, which was to sow sedition, win subjects from their allegiance and practise conspiracies 'for the procurement and maintenance of the rebellion and wars against her Majesty and her realm'.

In reply to those critics who objected that since the priests had come unarmed as simple scholars and schoolmasters it would have been enough to correct them without 'capital pain', Burghley asked: 'Shall no subject that is a spial and explorer for the rebel or enemy against his natural prince be taken and punished as a traitor because he is not found with armour or weapon, but yet is taken in his disguised apparel, with scrolls and writings, or other manifest tokens, to prove him a spy for traitors, after he hath wandered secretly in his sovereign's camp, region, court or city?' The Lord Treasurer had no doubt in his own mind that, if 'reason and experience' were to be used in dealing with such adversaries, 'all these and suchlike are to be punished as traitors', because no

right-minded person could deny that 'the actions of all these are
necessary accessories and adherents proper to further and continue
all rebellions and wars'. And if anyone maintained that 'none are
traitors that are not armed', then 'they will make Judas no traitor
that came to Christ without armour, colouring his treason with
a kiss'.

The Catholic answer to *The Execution of Justice* appeared in
the following year. In *A True, Sincere and Modest Defence of
English Catholics,* William Allen was at pains to refute accusations
of treachery against the mission and to insist on its irreproachably
non-political character. He had little difficulty in demolishing the
case against Edmund Campion and argued that no priest could
properly be convicted under the old treason laws, but only under
those passed since 1559 which made matters of conscience into
treason. He also dismissed all assertions that the English Catholics
were not being persecuted for their faith as 'a very notorious
untruth', challenging anyone to deny that 'most prisons in England
be full at this day and have been for years, of honourable and
honest persons not to be touched with any treason or other offence
in the world' except their faith. As far as *Regnans in Excelsis* was
concerned, Allen maintained that neither he nor the English
Catholics at large had ever 'procured our Queen's excommunication; we have sought the mitigation thereof; we have done our
allegiance notwithstanding; we have answered, when we were
forced unto it, with such humility and respect to her Majesty
and council, as you see, no man can charge us of any attempt
against the realm or the prince's person'.

At the same time, Allen admitted his belief in the justice of
spiritual supremacy over temporal and that the Pope had the right,
in certain circumstances, to depose a reigning sovereign. 'Therefore,' he went on, 'let no man marvel that in case of heresy the
Sovereign loseth his superiority and right over his people and
kingdom: which cannot be a lawful Christian state or commonwealth without due obedience to Christ's and the Church's laws.'
There was nothing new about this. The papacy had claimed the
right of deposition for centuries and had occasionally exercised it
with varying degrees of success but, wrote William Allen, to claim,
as Burghley had done, that while Popes were 'suffered to make
and unmake kings at their pleasure' no monarch could sit securely
on his throne was nonsense – 'a bugge fit only to fright babes'.

No Catholic prince, against whom the same power could equally be applied, was in the least worried by it. Allen omitted to add, however, that no Catholic prince was currently in the least danger of being deposed. The *True and Modest Defence* ended with an eloquent plea for some measure of toleration for the English Catholics, conveniently ignoring the fact that there was no toleration for Protestants in Catholic countries, except in those cases where the executive was too weak to prevent it.

Neither side, of course, was being completely honest. In their anxiety to create a favourable public image neither side could afford to be completely honest. As a result, neither the picture of the sinister, lurking priest indoctrinating the gullible with superstitious nonsense and poisoning their minds against their lawful sovereign in such time as he could spare from plotting murder and treachery; nor that of a saintly, disinterested priesthood administering spiritual consolation to an oppressed majority before being cruelly and unjustly butchered represents anything like the truth. The truth, as usual, lay somewhere in the large grey area between these starkly black and white alternatives.

The basic dishonesty of the official English attitude lay in its stubborn insistence that the Catholics, both lay and priestly, were not in any sense being persecuted for their religious beliefs. In an age when it was axiomatic that religious disunity was the first step on the road to national disunity and from thence to civil war and anarchy, religious deviants of all kinds inevitably suffered for their beliefs. At a time when national security was being threatened by international Catholicism, pressure on the native Catholic population inevitably intensified. At least in England persecution remained on a political basis, though this was a matter of regret to those who equated Roman Catholicism and all its works with Anti-Christ.

The basic dishonesty of the Catholic position lay in its determined attempt to have things both ways – its vocal indignation that such men as Edmund Campion should be smeared with 'the odious name of traitor', while at the same time refusing to face the uncomfortable fact that no orthodox, believing Roman Catholic could logically accept the bastard, heretic and excommunicated Elizabeth as his lawful sovereign. A very few, notably Nicholas Sander, did have the sort of three-o'clock-in-the-morning courage which could look squarely at the problem and then make the choice of allegiance which conscience dictated. The rest either postponed a decision until circumstances had made it for them, or else slid gratefully through whatever legalistic loopholes the Vatican was able to provide. In the event, after the normal, illogical fashion of the human race, the vast majority of those Englishmen who also happened to be Roman Catholics were and remained loyal subjects of the crown – thus vindicating the Queen's confidence that habits of national and personal loyalty would always prove stronger than loyalty to any creed.

As front-line combatants in the battle for hearts and minds, the missionary priests occupied a special category and although the vast majority of them were undoubtedly as uninterested and uninvolved in politics as they professed to be, it was neither reasonable nor realistic to expect the English government to regard them in isolation from the wider political scene. It is, in fact, possible to over-sentimentalise the missionary priests. While their courage and their devotion is not in question, they were all grown men who came to England of their own free will with the openly avowed intention of propagating and practising a system of belief and a form of worship forbidden by law, all of them knowing exactly what they could expect if they were caught. It also needs to be remembered that although only a very few were traitors in the accepted sense – in the sense of being actively engaged in plotting the destruction of the state by direct means – indirectly the success of their mission must necessarily have led to the overthrow of the Protestant constitution. William Allen, though he tried conscientiously to keep his various interests in watertight compartments, was by the early eighties deeply committed to plans for overthrowing the Protestant state by whatever direct means appeared to offer the best chance of success. Had a Catholic army ever managed to establish a bridgehead on English soil, the priests would not have been able to stand aside. They were ear-marked for the important role of directing the consciences of Catholics – in other words, of helping to organise the rising of English Catholics which would be a vital part of any attempt to enforce *Regnans in Excelsis*.

It is not, therefore, surprising that the Protestant state regarded the missionaries as a fifth column 'who privily felt the minds of men, spread abroad that princes excommunicate were to be deposed, and whispered in corners that such princes as professed not the Romish religion had forfeited their regal title and authority....

that the Bishop of Rome hath supreme authority and absolute power over the whole world, yea even in temporal matters; that the magistrates of England were no lawful magistrates ... yea, that whatsoever was done by the Queen's authority since the time that the Bull declaratory of Pius Quintus was published against her, was by the laws of God and man altogether void and to be esteemed as of no validity'. Of course the Protestant state over-reacted, but states which feel themselves threatened have a habit of over-reacting, especially to danger which appears to come from within the body politic.

Lord Burghley summed the matter up neatly enough when he remarked that 'where the factious party of the Pope ... do falsely allege that a number of persons whom they term as martyrs have died for defence of the Catholic religion, the same in very truth may manifestly appear to have died (if they so will have it) as martyrs for the Pope'. If the Elizabethan establishment had had the courage and far-sightedness to content itself with merely restraining and deporting the missionaries; if the papacy had had the wisdom and far-sightedness to confine its efforts to win England back to Rome by spiritual means alone, both sides would have emerged from the struggle with a cleaner record. But over an issue so clouded with emotion, an issue which, beneath all the long words, the justification and rationalisation, was concerned with such basic human drives as fear, anger and aggression, any attempt to pass moral judgements on either side is a somewhat pointless exercise.

Conditioned as we are to thinking of the Elizabethan era as one of the most notable success stories of history, it is fatally easy to forget that that was seldom the way it looked to thinking Elizabethans, and at the beginning of the 1580s thinking Elizabethan observers of the international scene had more excuse than usual for feeling pessimistic about the future. The decade had opened with the Spanish annexation of Portugal, an event which alarmingly increased the already alarming power and wealth of Spain. It gave King Philip control of the entire Iberian peninsula, with the use of Portuguese ports and the Portuguese navy. It gave him the revenues of Portugal's colonial empire in the east to add to those of his own colonial empire in the west. It made him, on paper at least, the richest and most powerful monarch the world had ever seen. In France the increasing influence and popularity of the Holy

League, an ultra-Catholic and pro-Spanish faction led by Mary Stuart's cousin the Duke of Guise, boded no good to Protestants anywhere but to English Protestants in particular it threatened danger in an acute form.

Trouble was brewing even nearer home in Scotland, where Mary Stuart's son James, having reached his teens, was becoming another factor to be reckoned with. In 1579 a dispute over the title and estates of the Lennox earldom brought James's cousin Esmé Stuart, the seigneur d'Aubigny, an ardent Catholic and client of the Duke of Guise, across from France – ostensibly to stake his claim to the Lennox patrimony but actually bearing an unadvertised commission from his patron to win young James's affection and revitalise the French party in Scotland. Not surprisingly, young James, who had been brought up according to sound Calvinistic principles, found the companionship of his good-looking, Frenchified kinsman an altogether delightful novelty. Within a matter of months d'Aubigny, or the Duke of Lennox as he soon became and his henchman, Captain James Stewart, later Earl of Arran, had established their ascendancy. Within a couple of years they had engineered the downfall of the unlikeable but reliably pro-English Regent Morton and the eclipse of the English party which had held power in Edinburgh ever since the last remaining adherents of Mary Stuart had been eradicated in the aftermath of St Bartholomew.

This ominous turn of events on the other side of the vulnerable postern gate aroused the liveliest suspicions in London but Elizabeth, preoccupied with the hectic courtship she was currently conducting with the French King's brother, was unwilling to attempt the eviction of Lennox by force. She could not afford to offend France while she was bargaining for an alliance to counter-balance the weight of Spain; nor would she risk alienating Scottish national feelings and perhaps driving the adolescent James irretrievably into the arms of his mother's relations. Thrifty as ever, she was equally reluctant to try bribery on a scale likely to be effective – at least not until she could feel assured of an adequate return for her money. For the time being, therefore, there was little to be done but listen unconvinced to Lennox's private protestations of good-will and watch his flirtation with the Elders of the Kirk while awaiting developments. From her past experience of the way in which Scottish affairs were not infrequently conducted, the Queen of England may have felt that it would not be long before there were developments of an interesting nature north of the Border.

To the political wing of the English Catholic exiles, lacking similar valuable experience, the apparent success of the Duke of Lennox opened up a wide range of exciting possibilities. In October 1581, Robert Parsons, now established with his printing press at Rouen, wrote to the General of the Jesuits '... the greatest hope we have lies in Scotland, on which country depends the conversion not only of England but of all the lands in the North. For the right to the kingdom of England belongs to the Queen of Scotland and her son (after the death of this woman who now reigns) and some hopes have now begun to be conceived of this son of hers, especially now that the Earl of Morton has been executed, if sufficient contact were made with him while he still gives evidence of great obedience to his mother and before he is confirmed in heresy'. Even before he was obliged to leave England Parsons had sent one of the missionaries, Father Watts, up to Scotland to carry out a preliminary reconnaissance. Watts' first report was encouraging. He had been received by several of the nobility and had even been presented to James.

By the time this report arrived Parsons had crossed to France and the Spanish ambassador in London had taken a hand. Watts was instructed to go back to Scotland 'to try to get a private interview with d'Aubigny, and tell him that, if the King would submit to the Roman Catholic Church, many of the English nobles and a great part of the population would at once side with him and have him declared heir to the English crown and release his mother'. Watts proceeded cautiously – he was not entirely sure of Lennox with his French connections nor of the sincerity of the Scottish nobles. Towards the end of October he told Mendoza that the best argument to bring about James's conversion – apart, of course, from its being the true road to salvation – was to show him 'that it was the only means by which he could become a powerful King, uniting the crowns of Scotland, England and Ireland' and this, as Mendoza remarked in a dispatch to Philip, could only be achieved 'by his gaining the sympathy of so mighty a monarch as your Majesty'.

Whether James would rise to the bait or not remained in doubt but throughout the winter of 1581-2 plans were being laid for a Catholic *coup d'état* in Scotland to be followed by an invasion of

England by way of 'the border. The threads of this elaborate conspiracy stretched from Mendoza at the Court of St James's to Mary Queen of Scots in her prison at Sheffield Castle, from Lennox at Holyrood across the North Sea to the Duke of Guise, Robert Parsons, William Allen and the Spanish and papal representatives in France, while two Jesuit fathers, Holt and Creighton, commuted between London, Edinburgh and Paris bearing letters and messages, promises and suggestions. Progress was slow at first – there was a good deal of mutual distrust to be overcome, distances were considerable and the need for secrecy meant that no corners could be cut – but in April 1582 Father William Creighton arrived from Scotland with a letter for Juan Bautista de Tassis, Spanish ambassador in Paris, from the Duke of Lennox.

Lennox, encouraged by Creighton's confident assurances of support, had finally agreed to commit himself to the 'design' which the Pope and the King of Spain had in hand 'for the restoration of the Catholic religion and the liberation of the Queen of Scotland' – providing he was guaranteed adequate backing, and he had listed his requirements in a memorandum to be passed on by Creighton to the appropriate quarters. Lennox's ideas of what constituted adequate backing were optimistic – an army of 20,000 men, preferably Spaniards, Italians, Germans and Swiss, paid for eighteen months, together with a number of pioneers, plenty of munitions and artillery plus the sum of 20,000 crowns. When de Tassis was visited by Creighton and Robert Parsons he at once raised his eyebrows at the size of these demands but was hastily reassured that Lennox would leave such matters to be settled by the Duke of Guise, who was of the opinion that six to eight thousand infantry would be ample. Guise himself was full of enthusiasm for the project and proposed making a diversionary landing on the coast of Sussex 'to put the whole kingdom into confusion'.

Robert Parsons went on to tell de Tassis that the English Catholics were eager for the design to be carried out, and that if arms were taken up in Scotland 'with a well grounded prospect of success', they would come flocking to join the invading army. The North and 'all that part which borders upon Scotland' was full of Catholics, and if the Pope would name some influential person for the great bishopric of Durham (Parsons had William Allen in mind) he would be able to raise the people. There were many other persons who would do the same in other districts, since England was 'so full of Catholics that it could not be believed'.

Having just spent over a year in England, Parsons could reasonably be accepted as an authority but de Tassis, who seems to have possessed rather more commonsense than his colleague in London, was not entirely convinced. 'When I asked him what security they have for all this,' he wrote to Philip, 'and whether any of the principal men had formed a confederation for this object and given each other some security of signatures, as the custom is, he answered me that he knew all this from what many of them had declared when he had treated with them of their consciences.' If the ambassador thought this an evasive answer, he was careful not to actually say so and, having received no briefing from Spain, listened to his visitors 'with a friendly countenance', trying 'neither to divert them in any way from what they propose, nor yet to give them encouragement' but showing himself 'desirous, as a Christian, that everything should succeed as they are planning it'.

Apparently undismayed by this, the two Jesuits went away to spend the next six weeks putting the final touches to the invasion plan. Several conferences were held in which the Duke of Guise, William Allen, the Archbishop of Glasgow, Mary Stuart's agent in Paris, the papal nuncio and even the sceptical de Tassis took part. Snags such as the fact that the mercenary army to be landed in Scotland, whether six or twenty thousand strong, existed only on paper; that the Duke of Guise, despite his soubriquet of King of Paris, was not King of France, and that Henri III, poor creature though he might be, would certainly warn Queen Elizabeth of any Guisard plot against her the moment he heard about it, were brushed aside. But even the most optimistic of the conspirators could not ignore the fact that no action of any kind would be possible until the Pope and the King of Spain had been persuaded to disgorge something more substantial than fair words. Accordingly, at the end of May, Creighton set off for Rome and Parsons for Lisbon, where Philip was then in residence.

Before anything concrete had resulted from either of these missions, the inevitable happened in Scotland. Discreetly prodded by the English government, the Kirk and the Protestant lords decided that Lennox had had a long enough run for his money. On 22 August James was kidnapped by the earls of Angus, Gowrie and Mar in the so-called Raid of Ruthven, and James Stewart, Earl of Arran, was arrested. Lennox holed up for a time in the fortress of Dumbarton but was finally obliged to apply to Queen Elizabeth for a safe conduct to return to France by way of England. The Duke was out of the game and by the following spring he was dead.

The Raid of Ruthven came as a bad blow to the Franco-Spanish plotters, but they were not discouraged for long. On 4 May 1583, de Tassis was reporting to Philip, 'It appears to me that Hercules (code name of the Duke of Guise), seeing matters in Scotland altered, and with but small probability of promptly assuming a position favourable for the plans that had been formed, has now turned his eyes towards the English Catholics, to see whether the affair might not be commenced there.... I understand that he has the matter in such train as may ensure his success, and in such case it would be very necessary that he should have at hand the funds for immediate wants, and particularly for one object which I dare not venture to mention here, but which if it be effected will make a noise in the world, and if not, may be safely mentioned another time.'

In a letter to the Cardinal of Como dated two days before, the papal nuncio Castelli had been rather more explicit. 'The Duke of Guise and the Duke of Mayenne,' he wrote, 'have told me that they have a plan for killing the Queen of England by the hand of a Catholic, though not one outwardly, who is near her person and is ill-affected towards her for having put to death some of his Catholic relations. This man, it seems, sent word of this to the Queen of Scotland, but she refused to attend to it. He was however sent hither, and they have agreed to give him, if he escapes, or else his sons, 100,000 francs.... The Duke asks for no assistance from our Lord [the Pope] for this affair; but when the time comes he will go to a place of his near the sea to await the event and then cross over on a sudden into England. As to putting to death that wicked woman, I said to him that I will not write about it to our Lord the Pope (nor do I) nor tell your most illustrious lordship to inform him of it; because, though I believe our Lord the Pope would be glad that God should punish in any way whatever that enemy of His, still it would be unfitting that His Vicar should procure it by these means. The Duke was satisfied; but later on he added that for the enterprise of England, which in this case would be much more easy, it will be necessary to have here in readiness money to enlist some troops to follow him.'

Castelli reported that Guise estimated his requirements at 100,000 to 80,000 crowns, adding, 'God grant that with this small sum that great kingdom may be gained'.

The Cardinal of Como replied on 23 May: 'I have reported to our Lord the Pope what your lordship has written to me in cipher about the affairs of England, and since his Holiness cannot but think it good that this kingdom should be in some way or other relieved from oppression and restored to God and our holy religion, his Holiness says that, in the event of the matter being effected, there is no doubt that the 80,000 crowns will be, as your lordship says, very well employed.' In the event, of course, this projected 'deed of violence', as de Tassis cautiously phrased it in another dispatch to Philip at the end of June, was not mentioned again. Philip was disappointed, but not surprised.

It was not the first time that this particular method of solving the English problem had been suggested. Three years earlier, the Welshman Humphrey Ely had visited Madrid on behalf of a group of anonymous English noblemen, to seek a ruling from the papal nuncio there as to whether or not they would incur sin by carrying out a plan to murder the Queen. The nuncio, Cardinal Sega, gave it as his opinion that they need have no qualms, adding that in any case he was sure the Pope would grant them a retrospective absolution. However, to make assurance doubly sure, he referred the matter to Rome, at the same time asking for absolution for himself if it was felt that he had gone too far. On 12 December 1580, the Cardinal of Como, who as papal Secretary of State could speak with peculiar authority, conveyed the official feeling on the subject of assassination in a letter to Sega. 'Since that guilty woman of England rules over two such noble kingdoms of Christendom,' he wrote, 'and is the cause of so much injury to the Catholic faith, and loss of so many million souls, there is no doubt that whosoever sends her out of the world with the pious intention of doing God service, not only does not sin but gains merit, especially having regard to the sentence pronounced against her by Pius V of holy memory. And so, if those English nobles decide actually to undertake so glorious a work, your lordship can assure them that they do not commit any sin. We trust in God also that they will escape danger. As far as concerns your lordship, in case you have incurred any irregularity, the Pope bestows upon you his holy benediction.'

Quite apart from the dubious moral position of a spiritual leader who condones murder as being a justifiable means to a desired end, Pope Gregory was committing yet another of the numerous tactical errors made by the papacy in its campaign against Elizabeth. The English government was not, of course, in a position to tap the confidential correspondence of papal nuncios, but it had other sources of information and was in little doubt that the Holy Father would cheerfully have pinned a medal on anyone who succeeded in killing the Queen. In 1581 a renegade priest named Tyrrel confessed to having personally heard the Pope say that such a deed would be 'a good work', although it should be carried out without bringing discredit on his reputation.

Popes, being human, can be wrong-headed – they are not normally fools and it was outstandingly foolish to hand over to one's enemy, gift-wrapped, such a first-class propaganda weapon. The explanation lies partly in the fact that the Vatican was still relying on reports and recommendations supplied by the English exiles – both of which were more remarkable for wishful thinking than for accuracy. A memorandum of 1583, attributed to William Allen, presented a picture of England where two-thirds of the population were Catholic sympathisers, either open or secret, living in fear and slavery, who would 'seize the first opportunity to help chastise their adversaries, whose intolerable yoke they hate more than if they were Turks' and who had learned 'to detest their domestic heretic more than any foreign prince'. Another such document of 1582, attributed to Robert Parsons, declared that all the Catholics in England would welcome Mary Stuart as their Queen and went on to state unblushingly that there was never a prince as universally hated in England as Elizabeth. If Gregory believed even half these reports he had some reason for thinking that murder might well prove the quickest and cheapest method of achieving results.

Meanwhile, throughout the summer and autumn of 1583, plans for the reconstructed 'holy enterprise' were being worked out in Paris. Although James regained his freedom of action in June and had recalled the Earl of Arran, Parsons and Allen both advised that, while the state of Scotland and the King's religious intentions remained so uncertain, a direct invasion of England offered the best chance of success. A Spanish force of about 5,000 men, drawn from the Duke of Parma's army in the Netherlands, commanded by the Duke of Guise and accompanied by all the English exiles, was to land at the Pile of Fouldrey on the Lancashire coast where it would be joined by a further force of 20,000 native Catholics. It would then proceed to liberate Mary Stuart and, unspecified but implicit, dispose of Elizabeth Tudor in some convenient but permanent fashion. This, in outline, was the scheme laid before the Pope by Robert Parsons in September, and William Allen wrote to Rome urging 'that now was the time for acting, that there had never been a like opportunity, nor would such a chance ever recur'. The Pope was sympathetic and ready to be co-operative, but he would not produce any cash until he was certain of the King of Spain. Without the King of Spain's word not a soldier would embark and the King of Spain, while paying lip-service to the idea, remained notably lukewarm. At last, in October, he definitely withdrew his support and the whole house of cards collapsed.

Ever since the spring of 1580 the English government, and especially Principal Secretary of State Francis Walsingham, had been watching the situation in Scotland and France with close attention and considerable anxiety. Walsingham, whose nose for such matters was acutely sensitive, was convinced that 'some great and hidden treason not yet discovered' was being hatched, but although he worried at the problem for nearly three years, using every source of information – official and unofficial – that was open to him, hard news proved surprisingly hard to come by. Rumours there were in plenty, and enough clues to confirm suspicions that a conspiracy involving Mary Queen of Scots, the Catholic faction in Scotland, the Jesuits, the Papacy and either France or Spain – perhaps both – aimed at destroying Elizabeth and setting Mary on the throne did indeed exist.

In October 1581 a letter from Mary to the Archbishop of Glasgow in Paris was intercepted and revealed that she knew all about certain 'designs' of her cousin the Duke of Guise. It did not, unfortunately, reveal what those designs were. In May of the following year one of Mendoza's messengers, disguised as a dentist, was picked up near the border. The 'dentist', who was probably Father Watts, managed to bribe his way out of trouble, but left behind a looking-glass with letters addressed to the Duke of Lennox hidden in the back. In March 1583, the Jesuit Holt was arrested in Scotland at the instigation of Walsingham's agents but, much to Walsingham's annoyance, was released by the Scots before anything useful could be got out of him.

By piecing together such scraps of information as he had been able to collect, Walsingham had come to the conclusion that the key to the puzzle would be found in France. In a sense, of course, he was right but, rather surprisingly for one with his intimate knowledge of French affairs, he failed to take account of the antipathy which existed between the Guise faction and the King of France. Not realising that the conspirators were taking a good deal of trouble to keep Henri III and his ambassador in ignorance of their intentions, Walsingham settled down to watch the French embassy like puss at a mousehole. Although the immediate results of this surveillance were disappointing, it was information received from a member of the embassy staff which finally put the Secretary of State on the right track by drawing his attention to the suspicious behaviour of one Francis Throckmorton, who was one of the Queen of Scots' chief agents and who seemed curiously shy of being seen by daylight. Walsingham therefore extended his operations to include a watch on Throckmorton's movements and by early November 1583 had collected enough evidence to justify an arrest. Throckmorton was taken at his house by Paul's Wharf where a number of incriminating papers were also seized.

At his preliminary examination before the Council he tried to brazen things out, but later, after two sessions on the rack, he broke down and confessed all he knew. It was not everything – he had not been in on the conspiracy from the beginning and had acted chiefly as a subordinate carrying out orders from abroad – but it was quite enough to enable Walsingham to set about unravelling the mystery which had defeated him for so long. It was also enough to show him that it was the Spanish, not the French, ambassador who had been abusing his diplomatic privileges and in the New Year Bernardino de Mendoza was summoned before the Council and informed that he was no longer *persona grata* with the Queen. His departure, in a flurry of mutual umbrage, did not, in fact, have much effect on Anglo-Spanish relations – certainly his presence in England had done nothing to improve them. What did bring the inevitable confrontation perceptibly closer was another, this time a successful, murder plot. On 1 July 1584, William of Orange was shot three times at close range as he was going up the stairs of his house in Delft by a Burgundian, Balthazar Gerard, generally believed to have been an agent of the King of Spain.

With the death of Orange, Dutch resistance, already under severe pressure from the efficient and energetic Duke of Parma, would almost certainly collapse – unless help came from outside – and Elizabeth was brought face to face with the issue she had been successfully evading for nearly twenty years. Should she stand aside and see the remainder of Flanders, Holland and Zeeland swallowed up, and the whole of the North Sea coastline with the great ports of Antwerp and Flushing fall into Spanish hands; or should she embroil herself in a Continental war which would not only cost her a great deal of money she could ill afford, but provide the King of Spain with a cast-iron *casus belli* any time he cared to use it?

While the Queen and her Council wrestled with the political and financial problems raised by William's death, other people were looking at it from a more personal angle. Two of the great Protestant leaders – Admiral Coligny and the Prince of Orange – had been murdered in cold blood by Catholic fanatics. Now only Elizabeth was left. But for how long? The previous October a young Catholic gentleman named Somerville, or Somerfield, had set out for London from Warwickshire with the declared intention of shooting the Queen and seeing her head set on a pole, 'for she was a serpent and a viper'. There is no reason to believe that Somerville was part of any larger scheme and no doubt he was more than a little mad, but that did not necessarily make him any the less dangerous, as the twentieth century has every reason to know. It only needed one madman, one fanatic armed with knife or pistol, to get within range for a few seconds and the whole elaborate structure of Elizabethan England would have been destroyed, literally, at a stroke. There would be no Parliament – it was automatically dissolved by the sovereign's death – no Council, no lords lieutenant, no judges, no magistrates, no royal officials of any kind – their commissions all expired with the sovereign. There would, in fact, have been no authority anywhere until the heir-at-law took possession of the throne – and that heir was the Queen of Scotland.

To a nation still digesting the alarming disclosures of what has become known for convenience sake as the Throckmorton Plot, news of the assassination in Delft came as a forcible reminder not of how much depended on Elizabeth's life – the nation had been living with that uneasy knowledge and worrying about it at intervals for twenty-six years – but of how terrifyingly that life might be cut off, and of whom would stand to benefit. To brush aside the Queen's danger just because she happened to survive is to miss the point entirely. The danger was real enough; there were enough shady characters slipping to and fro between England and the Continent during those years with little to lose and everything, including a martyr's crown, to gain by a single 'deed of violence'. Elizabeth was not assassinated but she certainly *could* have been. That she escaped was due in part to the remarkable ineptitude of her ill-wishers, in part to the unsleeping vigilance of Francis Walsingham.

The Council, who knew more than most about the inside story, took the threat very seriously indeed and regarded it as so immediate that they were not prepared to wait for Parliament to act. In September 1584 they embarked on dramatic and unprecedented measures to try and safeguard the Queen by removing the principal motive for her murder. To this end an association of 'natural-born subjects of this realm of England' was to be set up, dedicated to avenging with their 'whole powers, bodies and lives' any attempt on the life of their 'most gracious sovereign lady Queen Elizabeth'. The bond which members of this association were to sign went through several drafts, but in its final form – the form in which it was circulated through the towns and shires that autumn and winter – it was a straightforward invitation to lynch law. The signatories, and there were tens of thousands of them, bound themselves by their solemn oath and 'in the presence of the everlasting God' not merely never to accept any pretended successor 'by whom or for whom any such detestable act shall be attempted or committed', but 'to prosecute such person or persons unto death and to act the utmost revenge upon them'. In other words, in the event of Elizabeth's untimely end, Mary Stuart was to be killed out of hand – whether she had been an accessory before the fact or not.

The Bond of Association was a naked appeal to the most primitive instincts of its signatories, a statement of intent to meet violence with violence, and, as undoubtedly its authors hoped it would, it had the effect of hardening and canalising national feeling. When Parliament met at the end of November, members found some difficulty in containing their loyalty, their patriotism and their fury. Sir Walter Mildmay, speaking on the 28th, scarcely needed to remind his audience that 'through the goodness of Almighty

God by the ministry of this our gracious Queen we have enjoyed peace now full twenty-six years, the like whereof, so long together, hath not been seen in any age; the commodities whereof may appear sufficiently by comparing the blessedness of this our happy peace with the miserable state of our neighbours, long afflicted with cruel wars'. Nor did he need to chill their blood any further by spelling out the consequences of a successful 'sacred enterprise', further details of which had just come to light from documents found in the possession of Father Creighton, captured at sea by the Dutch acting on a tip-off from Walsingham. Quite as clearly as Sir Walter members of the House of Commons could visualise the 'devastation of whole countries, sacking, spoiling and burning of cities and towns and villages, murdering of all kind of people without respect of person, age or sex, and so the ruin, subversion and conquest of this noble realm'.

Against this looming horror a double line of defence was planned – first to provide for the Queen's safety by making it clear in the strongest possible terms that the Catholic heiress would not survive to enjoy an inheritance seized for her by violent means and, second, to extirpate once and for all those 'malicious, raging runagates' the Jesuits and seminary priests. The passage of the Act for the Queen's Safety resolved itself, in outline, into a struggle between a majority of the Commons who wanted the Bond of Association to be given the force of law on the one hand, and on the other, the Queen herself who 'would not consent that anyone should be punished for the fault of another' or that anything should reach the statute book 'that should be repugnant to the Law of God or the Law of Nature, or grievous to the conscience of any of her good subjects, or that should not abide the view of the world, as well enemies as friends'.

Apart from the ethical considerations involved, Elizabeth was clearly anxious that nothing should be done which might prejudice the ultimate right of Mary Stuart's son to the reversion of the English crown. As the Bond of Association was worded, any person that might any way claim by or from a 'pretended successor' would have been included in the wholesale vendetta. Looking into the future, it seems that Elizabeth had already begun to regard James as her natural heir. In the short term it would obviously have been extremely unwise to take legislative action which might have the effect of driving him into the arms of the Catholic powers.

But the House of Commons – whose feelings for the Queen are probably best summed up in words of a member for a Wiltshire borough who was moved to exclaim, 'It makes my heart leap for joy to think we have such a jewel. It makes all my joints to tremble for fear when I consider the loss of such a jewel.' – were thinking with their hearts and not their heads. They were obsessed with one basic issue – or rather two interrelated basic issues – how best to protect their 'jewel' and how best to protect themselves if they should lose her.

A compromise still had to be hammered out when, early in February 1585, came the shock revelations of the 'Parry Plot'. Sir Edmund Neville, himself strongly suspected of sympathising with the enemy, accused one William Parry, Doctor at Law, with having propounded to him an amiable scheme for collecting a party of ten horsemen 'to set upon the Queen as she rode abroad to take the air, and to kill her'. Dr Parry had at one time been employed by Lord Burghley as a secret service agent and in that capacity had gone abroad to try and penetrate 'the dangerous practices devised and attempted against her Majesty by her disloyal subjects and other malicious persons in foreign parts'. In the course of his duties he had, so he said, encountered Thomas Morgan, one of Mary Stuart's agents in France, who suggested to him that he should undertake Elizabeth's murder. Parry had replied that this 'might easily be done, if it might appear to be lawful', and had then written off to Rome requesting papal approval for his 'Design' and a plenary pardon. He returned to England in January 1584 and at once made a full report to the Queen, who heard him 'without being daunted', and proceeded to grant him various marks of favour. Certain of his past misdeeds were forgiven and he was actually sitting in the Parliament of 1584 as member for Queenborough. In December, though, he had electrified the House by making a speech in defence of the Jesuits, for which error of taste he had been committed to the serjeant's ward by his outraged colleagues and only released after his own abject apologies and the Queen's personal intervention.

When Parry was arrested he began by denying 'with great and vehement protestations' that he had been planning the Queen's destruction, but after a confrontation with Edmund Neville and a further night's reflection he decided to make a full confession, without the added incentive of torture. He admitted all the facts but swore that his intentions had been of the best, that he had never meant any harm to come to the Queen – on the contrary, he had been trying to uncover further dangerous designs against her life. Precisely what Dr Parry's intentions were, remain unclear. Some of the early part of his story is corroborated by independent evidence and he may have been speaking the truth, in which case his only crime was over-enthusiasm. But he was no longer in the government service and it was dangerous to the point of being suicidal for a private individual even to mention a murder plot to anyone without authority from above. Also, if he was acting the part of *agent provocateur* on his own initiative, it seems odd that he did not unburden himself to Francis Walsingham in private, as he was given every opportunity to do at his first examination. Perhaps, as Holinshed's Chronicle grimly suggests, he had been practising 'at sundry times to have executed his most devilish purpose and determination; yet covering the same so much as in him lay with a veil and pretence of great loyalty unto her Majesty'.

William Parry remains something of an enigma. 'A man of very mean and base parentage but of a most proud and insolent spirit, bearing himself always far above the measure of his fortune after he had long led a wasteful and dissolute life', he was a typical product of the strange twilight world which existed just beneath the surface of Elizabethan society – a world of spies, adventurers and soldiers-of-fortune living on their wits, ready to sell their services and their souls to the highest bidder, resorting to straightforward crime when times were bad, hobnobbing with the great when their luck was in. Parry may have been suffering from delusions of grandeur. He may have been a double agent. He may quite simply have wanted money. We are never likely to know for certain.

To the general public, by far the most startling disclosure of the Parry Plot was the letter addressed to Parry by the Cardinal of Como and produced in evidence at his trial. This remarkable document, the English translation of which, printed by Holinshed, corresponds with the Italian draft preserved in the Vatican archives, added still more fuel to the furnace of popular fury. '... his Holiness doth exhort you to persevere, and to bring to effect that which you have promised' the Cardinal had written. 'And to the end you may be so much the more holpen by that good Spirit which hath moved you thereunto, he granteth unto you his blessing, plenary indulgence, and remission of all your sins, according to your request. Assuring you, that beside the merit that you shall receive therefore in heaven, his holiness will further make himself debtor, to acknowledge your deservings in the best manner that he can.... Put therefore your most holy and honourable purposes in execution, and attend your safety.'

The discovery of a potential assassin in their very midst raised the already feverish temperature of the Commons, and two overwrought members petitioned the Queen to allow them to devise an especially horrible kind of penalty to fit Parry's 'most horrible kind of treason'. Elizabeth thanked them for their concern, but refused their request. She would not agree to any dealing other than 'the ordinary course of law'. Nor had this most recent scare in any way modified her resolve not to be stampeded into allowing the law of the jungle to become the law of England. The Queen had strong feelings about the necessity of observing proper decorum in the public conduct of affairs, and by legalising murder she would achieve nothing except to advertise her insecurity to the world; no Act of Parliament, however draconian, was ever going to deter the kind of mentality set on winning the halo of a tyrannicide. Neither would Elizabeth have anything to do with the proposals, painstakingly drafted by Lord Burghley, providing for an Interregnum in case of her sudden death. These proposals included provision for a sovereign parliament – a revolutionary concept which revolted the Queen. And again, as her coldly sceptical mind would have told her, no such arrangements, however painstakingly worked out, would have the slightest hope of averting civil war if she died before the Catholic heiress.

The Act for the Queen's Safety as finally passed was a much emasculated version of the notorious Bond. In the event of invasion, rebellion or plot against the state, a panel of commissioners, privy councillors and others, was empowered to hold an enquiry into the facts. Then, and only then, might the members of the association pursue and wreak vengeance upon any person judged by the commissioners to have been privy to such an outrage. In the event of a successful attempt on the Queen's life, the 'pretended successor', unnamed but no prizes were being offered for guessing her identity, was to be declared disabled. The heirs of such a successor were exempted unless, of course, also judged 'assenting and privy'. There would be no Interregnum, no Grand

Council or sovereign parliament, nothing, in fact, to prevent the country from sliding into anarchy and darkness.

There can be no question but that Elizabeth knew the risk she was running, both for herself and for England; that if an assassin's bullet found her while Mary Stuart still lived, she would leave behind a reputation for criminal negligence which nothing would ever erase. But, as so often before, she preferred to back her own judgement, her own instinctive flair, against all the sound, logical advice she was being offered. Stubbornly she preferred to trust in God, or providence, to hope to ride out the storm, to gamble on survival. She had, after all, been gambling on survival since her teens. As so often before, events, or luck, were to prove her judgement, or instinct, a better guide than the soundest, most logical advice available.

The Act for the Queen's Safety served its purpose. It provided a respectable legal framework for the subsequent proceedings against Mary Stuart. It did nothing to prejudice the final, peaceful accession of James, and it kept him quiet in the meantime. But in 1585 it needed a strong head not to succumb to the prevailing atmosphere of panic, an iron will to resist the pressure of emotional blackmail. Fortunately for England's reputation among the nations and before posterity, Elizabeth Tudor's courage and self-confidence were equal to the occasion. Years before she had told an obstreperous House of Commons, 'I will never by violence be constrained to do anything', and she had meant just precisely what she said.

CHAPTER TEN

So long as that devilish woman lives

'So long as that devilish woman lives, neither her Majesty must make account to continue in quiet possession of her crown, nor her faithful servants assure themselves of safety of their lives.'

Francis Walsingham, London, January 1572

T H E second piece of business which engaged the attention of the Parliament of 1584-5 was a bill against Jesuits, seminary priests and other such like disobedient persons. In the opinion of Thomas Digges, the member for Southampton, 'these hellhounds cladding themselves with the glorious name of Jesus, and such wretched souls as they bewitch with their wicked doctrine' were the only real danger to the Queen, since, as he wrote in a Discourse on the subject, 'they are fully persuaded her Majesty's life is the only stay why their Roman kingdom is not again established here'. Thomas Digges was by no means alone in his opinions and there were those who wanted the bill to include a clause 'that whosoever should teach the Romish religion should be as a traitor, because between the Queen and the Pope there can be no communion'. This motion was, however, rejected. It would confuse treason with heresy and give colour to the Catholic accusation that the Protestants were trying to stamp out Catholicism by foul means because they could not confute its doctrine in a fair fight.

The Act which presently received the royal assent was designed to keep the missionary priests within bounds by 'letting them find how dangerous it shall be for them to come here or once to put their foot on land within any her Majesty's dominions'. It laid down that any priest ordained by the authority of Rome since the first year of the Queen's reign must leave the country within forty days. Any such priest who disobeyed this order or who came into England in future would automatically be guilty of high treason. Any layman who 'willingly and wittingly' received, comforted or maintained a priest would now be guilty of felony; any 'home Papist' who sent money to the English colleges and seminaries abroad would become liable to the penalties of praemunire; anyone sending a child to be educated at a Catholic school abroad could be fined £100 for each offence; anyone knowing the whereabouts of a priest who failed to lay information within twelve days could be fined and imprisoned at the Queen's pleasure.

The government took immediate advantage of the forty-day moratorium by rounding up a number of priests being held in custody and sending them into exile, among them Father Jasper Heywood, who had taken over from Robert Parsons as superior of the Jesuits in 1581, two other Jesuits, Fathers Bosgrave and Hart, and Edward Rishton, one of the party which came from Rheims in 1580. The new law was the logical expression of the fear of a threatened society of the enemy within its gates – a fear which most contemporary Western societies have experienced to some degree. But this latest attempt to expel from the state such members who acknowledged allegiance to a power dedicated to its overthrow did not have any immediately noticeable deterrent effect on the missionary priests. As long as there continued to be a supply of determined men irrevocably committed to the task of saving other men's souls, and equally immutably convinced that not only were they helping to atone for their country's sins in the eyes of God but also incidentally earning their own eternal reward by their sufferings on earth, no man-made law ever would deter them.

William Allen's brother Gabriel, returning to Rheims from England in March 1583, reported that during the three years he had been away 'never a day passed but he had the opportunity of hearing Mass'. Gabriel Allen had spent a month in London waiting for a passage to France and had visited nearly all the Catholic prisoners, both lay and priestly, excepting those in the Tower which he wisely 'did not venture to go near'. In prisons like the Marshalsea, he told his brother, the inmates were able to say Mass every day and visitors were allowed in from time to time for conference, confession or communion. More surprisingly, the priests were 'allowed to go out every day to different parts of the city, and attend to the spiritual needs of the Catholics, on condition that they return to the prison at night'.

Gabriel's experiences reinforced William Allen's long-held conviction that no attention should be paid to those faint-hearts who cried aloud or whispered that the priests should be reserved 'for more seasonable times'. 'We have not to wait till things are better,' he wrote energetically, 'but to make them better, and we must buy back happier times from the Almighty ... by zeal, labour and blood, especially that of priests.' And so the priests continued to offer themselves as willing sacrifices. Just as no Act of Parliament could terrify them, no physical barriers existed which could keep them out – there were too many stretches of lonely coastline where a ship's boat could be beached on a dark night.

During the first half of the 1580s the organisation of this cross-Channel 'underground railway' was in the capable hands of Robert Parsons, working in conjunction with William Allen at the college at Rheims. 'We have shared the business between us,' wrote Parsons to the Spanish Jesuit Pedro de Ribadeneira in September 1584, 'he sending me priests from the Seminary, and I arranging, to the best of my power, for their safe transport to England. To do this and a number of other things required for the equipment of this spiritual war, I am obliged to maintain a modest establishment at Rouen, which is a most convenient town on account of its nearness to the sea, so that from there some can make trips to the coast to arrange for boats to convey people across (for they cannot use either the public boats or the ordinary ports that are well known).' Just how many priests Parsons was handling does not appear to be recorded but, according to his own estimate, there were nearly three hundred missionaries labouring in the vineyard at this time. Of these the vast majority were secular priests – the number of Jesuits either at work or in prison in England at any one time during the 1580s could be counted on the fingers of one hand.

Two members of the Society who did pass through the 'modest establishment' at Rouen were Father William Weston and Ralph Emerson, who embarked at Dieppe on 8 September 1584, together with Henry Hubert, a layman and an old friend of Weston's. William Weston, born at Maidstone in 1550, was yet another Oxford man whose conscience had taken him on the well-trodden pilgrim road to Rome via Douai. His early years in the priesthood were spent in Spain and he was at Seville when the summons 'to go to England and work there for the salvation of souls' reached him. Ralph Emerson was, of course, the former companion of Edmund Campion who had escaped capture at the time of Campion's arrest. He had since been in Scotland with the Jesuit William Holt and was now returning to England to distribute a consignment of 'books, written in English, both on spiritual and devotional matters, and on matters of controversy' – the writing, printing and dissemination of which remained one of Robert Parsons' special concerns.

Despite the intense alarm and resentment building up over the political activities of the Society of Jesus, the fact remained that the Jesuit Mission in England had recently diminished almost to vanishing point. Jasper Heywood had not been a great success as Superior and during the first eight months of 1584 there appears to have been only one inexperienced priest still at liberty. The ever practical Superiors of the Order questioned whether, in present circumstances, any useful purpose would be served by sending over more suitably qualified men, always in short supply, but the combined pressure exerted by William Allen and Robert Parsons had persuaded the Father General to make another effort. Parsons thought highly of William Weston and was hopeful that 'he would win much success'. Being, however, a firm believer in the maxim that God helps those who help themselves, he had gone to considerable trouble, borrowing money for the purpose, to ensure that his colleague's mission should get off to the best possible start.

'Father William Weston and Ralph left here ten days ago with all they required for going on board,' he wrote to the General on 15 September. 'I arranged for a special boat to be at their disposal and managed also that an English gentleman [this was Henry Hubert or Hubbard], who was staying here and has properties on the English coast, should enter the country with them, for the sole purpose of guiding them safely to his house: afterwards he and his servant will come back. They are very well equipped for the journey – that is to say, they are well primed with information, well clothed, have seventy crowns in their purse ... and all their expenses are paid until they reach the boat. The cost of the boat and the gentleman's expenses I am also paying. We are obliged to do all this so that they may cross safely, as I hope in God they will do, since the gentleman will go with them as far as London, where there are many houses now fitted up to receive them.'

The journey, thus efficiently provided for, went smoothly and Weston sent Parsons a letter from the boat in such good spirits that he broke into Greek verse. The party made landfall on the East Anglian coast, between Yarmouth and Lowestoft, where Hubert's estates lay, and Weston and Hubert went ashore to take shelter in a safe house in the neighbourhood. 'In the meantime,' Weston was to write in the autobiography which describes his adventures, 'Ralph stayed in the boat with our baggage – it was our plan to send him a horse secretly, under cover of night, and collect our possessions.... This was done very quickly. So far all had gone well, and he joined us with his valuable burden safe and entire. The next day, after we had made arrangements for their conveyance by river, Ralph put the cases of books aboard a light boat and sailed with them to Norwich – the starting-place for the freight-waggons and carriers that take the merchandise of the district to London. Meanwhile we got on our horses, and making our way by comfortable stages, arrived in London ahead of him.'

In London Henry Hubert, who had taken every precaution to keep his return from France a secret, got a nasty fright when an acquaintance came up to him and greeted him by name 'in the open street', but Weston, whose face was not known, felt brave enough to go to the carrier terminus at Bishopsgate to await Emerson's arrival. In the end, to his great relief, he ran into him in the middle of the road. Ralph himself was safe but his news was bad – the precious cases of books had been detained by a suspicious official and the difficult decision of whether to take the coward's way out and abandon them or run the obvious risk of trying to reclaim their property now had to be faced. 'Whatever we did, we were in trouble,' Weston wrote. After a good deal of anxious discussion, Ralph's devotion to duty won the day and, feeling that if necessary he could 'bribe his way through', he went back to the inn where the books were impounded, only to find that the worst had already happened. The cases had been opened and the moment Emerson appeared he was arrested and taken before the magistrates. He was questioned closely about the books but luckily no one seems to have suspected his connection with William Weston. All the same, Ralph, who was to spend the next twenty years in prison, was now definitely out of the picture and his 'mis-adventure' came as a bad blow to his companions, who had been relying on him to vouch for them to their fellow Catholics.

Parsons had given Weston an introduction to a Mrs Bellamy,

who had once sheltered him at her house near Harrow, and he
and Hubert now decided to ride out and see her. Weston had some
'tokens' to prove his identity, but even when these had been handed
over, 'secretly, as had to be done on such an occasion', he met
with blank denial. Mrs Bellamy did not know what her visitor was
talking about, she had never set eyes on Father Parsons, had never
even heard of him. Weston saw that nothing was to be gained by
persisting. 'Besides,' he wrote, 'I suspected I might be treading on
unsafe ground, and feared that we might have made a mistake
either about the house or about the lady, or that the situation
might have altered, as it so often does in the present troubled state
of the country. So giving the rein to our horses, Henry and I rode
off, taking a different road from that by which we had come.'
It was just as well that they did take this simple precaution, for
it subsequently transpired that there had been a spy in Mrs Bellamy's
house who followed them to try and discover their identity.

Back in London, the two men took stock of their position. It
was not encouraging. Both fully realised the danger of staying too
long at a public inn where awkward questions might be asked
at any moment. In fact, their chances of survival were negligible
unless they could make contact with the Catholic underground,
and their recent experience with Mrs Bellamy had been a frightening indication of the prevailing mood of acute suspicion of all
strangers. One other possible line of approach remained open.
When Henry Hubert fled to France he had left his pregnant wife
behind and had been told that she had gone into hiding at a
friend's house until her child was born – a device often resorted
to by Catholic mothers-to-be in order to avoid the necessity of
presenting their babies for baptism at the parish church.

Although they were not even certain that Mrs Hubert was still
in the same retreat, it seemed worth trying to find her and, as
Hubert himself was by this time scared of his own shadow – 'every
house and building appeared suspect and unsafe to him' – William
Weston set off alone to make enquiries. At first he was greeted
with the same distrust and flat denial. No one at the house had
heard of Mrs Hubert, she was not there and never had been. However, 'from one or two indications', Weston felt fairly certain that
he had come to the right place and 'became rather more daring'.
Eventually his persistence paid off and as soon as the family were
convinced of his *bona fides*, they lavished on him 'every courtesy

and attention their kindness could suggest'. Henry Hubert was fetched for a reunion with his wife while Weston was taken in charge by a fellow priest and given facilities to start work.

William Weston was to remain at liberty for just under two years, during which time he fulfilled all Parsons' hopes by 'doing wonders and ... giving great edification to all'. His most notable convert was Philip Howard, Earl of Arundel and son of the Duke of Norfolk executed for his part in the Ridolfi Plot. Probably his most notable exploit was when he penetrated into the Tower with, not surprisingly, 'a feeling of great trepidation', to spend a whole day in conference with Jasper Heywood shortly before the latter's banishment. William Weston was a brave man and a modest one, although he had a somewhat dubious enthusiasm for exorcising evil spirits. After several narrow escapes he was finally captured in London on 3 August 1586, but fortunately for the continuity of the Jesuit Mission, Fathers Garnet and Southwell had arrived three weeks earlier and were able to take over.

Garnet and Southwell, like Parsons and Campion before them, formed a powerful combination of talent. Southwell, the poet, had all Campion's charm, his other-worldly sweetness of nature, his eagerness for martyrdom (or unhealthy preoccupation with death), and his felicity of language. 'Our ship may be tossed about and grind upon the rocks,' he wrote to the Rector of the English college in Rome in December 1586, 'but it cannot go to pieces or be sunk. We live on in the midst of storms, with but little security for the body. Yet, if they do carry us off, they will only be taking us to life and to rest. Even in shipwreck we shall be blessed.... Christ's soldiers fight under most favourable terms; for if the enemy defeat them he crowns them, and if he let them alone, he is himself defeated: while they are in life they save the souls of others, and in death they win salvation for their own souls ... in the midst of dangers it is marvellous what joy of heart I feel, reflecting under whose name and in what cause I am enlisted. For though the flesh be weak, and this corruptible body drag down the soul, still our blood if shed will ransom souls.... Assuredly it is not unpleasant to die that virtue may spring to life in many souls, and vices receive their deathblow.' In fact, Southwell evaded capture for six years and was not executed until 1594.

Henry Garnet, a Derbyshire man, whose special interests were music and mathematics, proved an even more slippery and resourceful customer than Parsons had been and survived for a record twenty years, only coming to grief in the aftermath of the Gunpowder Plot. Like Parsons he operated a secret press. Like Parsons he organised an efficient system for meeting and helping new priests as they came in from France and Flanders before posting them to districts where they were most needed. As a result, he wrote, 'many persons who saw a seminary priest hardly once a year, now have one all the time and most eagerly welcome any others no matter where they come from'.

Another Jesuit, arriving in the crisis year of 1588 and who might (in some respects) be described as the James Bond of the missionary priests, was John Gerard. Gerard, landing on the Norfolk coast with three companions one wet November night, made effective use of his knowledge of the technical terms of hunting and falconry as a cover – especially when in the company of those Protestant gentlemen 'who had practically no other conversation except, perhaps, obscene subjects or rant against the saints and the Catholic faith'. He proved an exceptionally tough and enterprising campaigner, but was eventually caught in the spring of 1594 as a result of information received. Taken to the Tower, he was tortured by 'the manacles' – that is, hung up by the wrists – in an attempt to get him to betray Garnet's whereabouts among other things, and Gerard, in his autobiography, has left a detailed description both of the mechanics of this particular form of persuasion and of what it felt like.

'They took me to a big upright pillar,' he wrote, 'one of the wooden posts which held the roof of this huge underground chamber. Driven in to the top of it were iron staples for supporting heavy weights. Then they put my wrists into iron gauntlets and ordered me to climb two or three wicker steps. My arms were then lifted up and an iron bar was passed through the rings of one gauntlet, then through the staple and rings of the second gauntlet. This done, they fastened the bar with a pin to prevent it slipping, and then, removing the wicker steps one by one from under my feet, they left me hanging by my hands and arms fastened above my head.' Gerard was a tall, heavy man and the tips of his toes still touched the floor. As he had been suspended from the highest staple in the pillar, the earthen floor beneath him had to be scraped away. 'Hanging like this,' he went on, 'I began to pray. The gentlemen standing around asked me whether I was willing to confess now. "I cannot and I will not," I answered. But I could hardly utter the words, such a gripping pain came over me. It was worst in my chest and belly, my hands and arms. All the blood in my body seemed to rush up into my arms and hands and I thought that blood was oozing out from the ends of my fingers and the pores of my skin. But it was only a sensation caused by my flesh swelling above the irons holding them. The pain was so intense that I thought I could not possibly endure it.'

He did, however, more than once, without uttering a syllable the authorities wanted to hear. Some people, as has been remarked, are torturable and some are not. Gerard's career, in fact, was far from over. After recovering from his ordeal, he achieved the rare distinction of escaping from the Tower. He remained at work in England until 1606 when he was smuggled out of the country by the Spanish ambassador, and died in Rome at a ripe old age on 27 July 1637.

In spite of the Act of 1584, by no means all the missionaries captured after this date were executed as traitors. Weston, for example, survived to tell the tale of his adventures and his twenty years in prison (he was released and deported in James's reign, as was Ralph Emerson), and there were communities of priests in most of the London prisons, as well as at special centres like Wisbech, living as guests of her Majesty under far from intolerable conditions by contemporary standards. Those with the necessary funds could and did bribe their warders to carry messages and allow them special privileges – this was how Gerard managed his escape. Some converted their warders and they were generally able to practise their religion, say or hear Mass regularly and receive visitors. Gerard, referring to the time he spent in the Clink, makes the illuminating remark that 'after a few months we had, by God's grace, everything so arranged that I was able to perform there all the tasks of a Jesuit priest, and provided only I could have stayed on in this prison, I should never have wanted to have my liberty again in England'. Not all prisoners, of course, were so fortunate or so well organised, but few sixteenth-century governments would have gone to the trouble and expense of keeping such potentially dangerous enemies of the state alive under any conditions.

Apart, however, from the obvious undesirability of giving the Catholic cause too many martyrs – the alacrity and cheerfulness with which the victims went to the scaffold was liable to move some standers-by to speculate 'that such an extraordinary contempt of death cannot but proceed from above' – neither the Queen nor the nation (with the exception of the lunatic fringe), would have tolerated a bloodbath on the standard Continental pattern. The statistics show that, roughly speaking, the number of deaths went up and down with the political barometer. In 1581, four priests were executed; in 1582, eleven priests; in 1583, two priests and two laymen; in 1584, six priests and three laymen; in 1585, two priests and two laymen; in 1586, twelve priests and three laymen; in 1587, six priests; and in 1588, the Armada year, twenty-one priests and ten laymen. There was another peak in the early 1590s, also a time of acute international tension, but after that executions fell off noticeably. It is estimated that altogether some two hundred and fifty people died as a more or less direct result of their religious proclivities during the forty-four years of Elizabeth's reign, and this includes about fifty who died in prison. It was enough, but it was no bloodbath in any sixteenth-century book.

No statistics, of course, can measure individual human suffering, such as those of the priests who fell into the clutches of that legendary monster and sadist Richard Topcliffe, 'old and hoary and a veteran in evil', who for a time held a special licence from the Council to torture suspects in private in his own house. All the same, in circumstances which naturally tend to bring such individuals from out of the woodwork, it is surprising and gratifying to know that Topcliffe, who enjoyed his work, was the exception rather than the rule. According to the accounts of the priests themselves, prison officials were often openly sympathetic and found the whole business nauseating. Nevertheless it went on – a necessary weapon it was felt – and the twentieth century has little to teach the sixteenth when it comes to the techniques of breaking down a prisoner's resistance.

'Some,' wrote Robert Southwell in his *Humble Supplication to her Majesty*, 'besides their tortures, have been forced to lie continually booted and clothed many weeks together, pined in their diet, consumed with vermin, and almost stifled with stench. Some have been watched and kept from sleep, till they were past the use of reason, and then examined upon the advantage, when they could scarcely give account of their own names.' Apart from the rack, which could dislocate the victim's joints by stretching him between wooden rollers, and the manacles, the most common forms of physical torture seem to have been 'Little Ease', a dungeon so constructed that its inmate could neither stand nor lie, and 'The Scavenger's Daughter', an iron ring which rolled victims into a ball and so crushed them 'that the blood sprouted out at divers parts of their bodies'. Some, too, as Robert Southwell delicately put it, 'have been tortured in such parts, as is almost a torture to Christian ears to hear it'. Not unnaturally, much useful information was obtained by these methods.

While the brunt of the attack was borne by the priests, the laity – or at any rate that section of the laity which was actively involved with the Mission – could suffer acutely from harassment, anxiety and mental stress, as evidenced by William Weston's early adventures. In general, though, it was their property and their liberty which were at risk rather than their lives, and contemporary Catholic propagandists weaken their own case by hysterical overstatement. Despite the fact that the penal laws had become progressively more severe, the situation had not altered fundamentally. Even in the seventies and eighties those Catholics who managed to avoid drawing undue attention to themselves and, above all, kept out of politics, do not appear to have experienced worse inconvenience than that of any disadvantaged minority in any society.

Among the professional classes, probably as good an example as any is that of the lawyer Edmund Plowden, who never made any secret of his religious opinions but who remained much esteemed among his colleagues and published two volumes of reports or 'Commentaries' which became a standard legal text book. As treasurer of his Inn, the Middle Temple, he had much to do with the building of the Middle Temple Hall and earned a respectful posthumous tribute from William Camden. 'In England died this year [1584] no man more worthy to be remembered than Edmund Plowden, who as he was singularly well learned in the Common Laws of England, whereof he deserved well by his Writings, so for Integrity of Life he was second to no man of his Profession.' At the same time, Plowden never became a serjeant-at-law, never in fact advanced beyond the status of 'un Apprentice de la Comen Ley', when in happier circumstances a man of his quality could have confidently expected to hold high office. He could, so the tradition goes, have become lord chancellor, if only he had not been a Catholic.

Few known recusants escaped the notice of the authorities at some time in their lives – Edmund Plowden was no exception. Some were bound over in their own recognisance to be of good behaviour and appear before the Council when summoned; some were confined within narrow geographical limits; but even those who went to gaol were occasionally released, either temporarily or permanently, on compassionate or other grounds. Sir John Southworth was let out in March 1586 to go to Bath to take the waters, but he was alleged to have broken the terms of his parole by associating with Catholics and was re-arrested in May. John Talbot of Grafton was allowed to leave the house in Surrey where he was confined to go to his home in Worcestershire to settle some private business, and William Tyrwhitt in Kent received a similar licence for a journey to Lincolnshire. In 1585, Lady Lovell and her son were released from prison and granted immunity from further prosecution on the intervention of the Queen herself. There were many petitioners for clemency, and the degree of success they achieved seems to have depended on the amount of influence they or their relatives could command and, of course, on the nature of their offence.

If the penal laws had ever been rigorously and uniformly enforced, the picture would have been very different and life would have become intolerable for the most well-behaved and peaceable Catholics. This, however, was probably never the government's intention – it was certainly never the Queen's – and even if it had been, the thing could not have been done. The executive could pounce punitively on an isolated centre of disaffection in any part of the country at need, as in 1569, and from time to time individual bishops or lords lieutenant would mount search and destroy missions in selected areas, but the sort of administrative machinery necessary for keeping all of the Catholic population under an iron hand all of the time simply did not exist.

The fine of twenty pounds a month for non-attendance at church is a case in point. If this had been levied on anything like a systematic basis, it would quickly have bankrupted the small gentry families which formed the solid core of Catholic recusancy. In 1586 a report on the working of the 1581 Act brought to light the disturbing facts that some recusants were escaping indictment altogether through the corruptness of juries, and that some 'being indicted are winked at by justices in respect of kindred or friendship'. Others were going untouched through the inefficiency, deliberate or otherwise, of clerks of assize and sheriffs 'who do not their duties in orderly sending out process, or in forbearing to apprehend the offender, when they may, or in committing some error or other whereby the execution of the law is deferred'. As a result of this deplorable state of affairs, the report concluded gloomily, 'many are encouraged to offend and to make small account of the pains set down against them'. In 1587 Parliament made an attempt to close the more obvious loopholes, but even so it has been estimated that less than two hundred people were actually paying the dreaded monthly fine during the period 1581 to 1593.

Generalisations about the English Catholics under Elizabeth are not made any easier by the fact that no one really knows how many of them there were. Estimates, or rather informed guesses, vary from between two and three per cent by one authority to from 750,000 to 1,000,000 by another, out of a total population of three and a half to four millions at the end of the reign. It does seem, though, that the spiritual revival brought about by the efforts of the Douai and Jesuit missionaries had reached and passed its peak by 1584. What might be termed the 'second wave' of the Jesuit invasion went some way towards stabilising the situation – in the 1590s the government was sufficiently alarmed by the numbers of priests still being sheltered in private houses to bring in further anti-Catholic legislation – but by the second half of the 1580s the continual pressure, the continual sense of insecurity, the threat as well as the actuality of imprisonment with all its attendant discomforts and inconveniences, the threat as well as the actuality of crippling fines and distraint on lands and chattels, were having their inevitable effect.

There were other forces at work too. Civil disobedience never sat easily on the shoulders of what was an essentially law-abiding section of the community and, as the international crisis worsened, the imputation of disloyalty hurt a class with a long and honourable record of service to king and country worst of all. It is scarcely surprising, therefore, that even those Catholics who had clung most staunchly to the faith of their ancestors should have begun to seek a compromise way out of the agonising dilemma they were trapped in, and that the slide into outward conformity should have gathered momentum. Especially as the Catholic community became more and more rent by internal dissension. Those unfortunates whose consciences, fears of hell fire, or plain stubbornness would not allow them release simply lay low and waited out the siege as best they could, trying to avoid prosecution by such stratagems as temporarily leaving home, cultivating local officialdom (churchwardens and even searchers could often be either bribed or overawed), and pleading excuses like ill-health or being 'out of charity' with a neighbour to avoid going to church. In many places, especially in country districts, Catholics and Protestants lived quite comfortably together, but the saying 'a Catholic always pays his debts', which became current at this time, was probably due not so much to superior moral rectitude as to the fact that no Catholic who might at any time have to depend heavily on the goodwill of his neighbours, could afford to make a single unnecessary enemy.

With so many imponderables to be taken into account, the only honest answer to the question 'what was it like to be a Catholic during Elizabeth's reign?' must be 'it depended'. It depended on an individual family's degree of commitment to their religious faith, on their standing in the community, on the climate of local opinion, on the zeal or lack of it shown by the local ecclesiastical and civil authorities, and, of course, on the international situation. This seldom remained static for long, and by the end of 1585 there had been a number of developments. On the credit side, Anglo-Scottish relations, after six years of instability, were once again on a firm basis. King James, having finally made up his mind on which side his bread was buttered, had signed a treaty with Elizabeth agreeing not to attack England and to go to her assistance if she were attacked. In return, James accepted an annual pension of £4,000 from the English crown (he had wanted £5,000 but Elizabeth refused to part with a penny more), and a tacit assurance that nothing would be done by Parliament to prejudice his right to the succession.

Also on the credit side, though this was not immediately apparent, Elizabeth's arch-enemy, Pope Gregory XIII, had died to be replaced by Sixtus V, who was privately sceptical about the chances of the Holy Enterprise and who disapproved of assassination as a weapon of war. In France, too, things had changed. Elizabeth's former suitor, the Duke of Anjou, was dead and, as Henri III for the most obvious of reasons would never father children, the Huguenot leader, Henri of Navarre, had now become heir to the French throne. This was too much for the Duke of Guise and his Holy League, and in January 1585 they concluded a secret treaty with Spain by the terms of which Guise became King Philip's pensioner to the tune of 50,000 crowns a month in return for his promise to ensure, by whatever force of arms proved necessary, that Henri of Navarre should never enjoy his inheritance.

It was spring before the English government first got wind of the Treaty of Joinville and it needed nobody to explain that if this meant the bellicose duke would now be kept busy at home, it also meant that Philip now had nothing to fear from French inter-ference in whatever foreign adventures he might be contemplating. It meant, in fact, that France and Spain had reached the sort of understanding which England had most reason to fear: especially as by the end of the year a state of open, if undeclared warfare existed between England and Spain. In May, Philip had seized all English shipping in Spanish ports. In August, Elizabeth had at last stepped over the brink by taking the Dutch under her pro-tection and despatching an expeditionary force to the Netherlands. In September, that enthusiastic private entrepreneur Francis Drake was unleashed to 'annoy the King of Spain' on his own coast as only he knew how, before going off to pay another of his un-welcome visits to the Caribbean. By the winter, the King of Spain had become sufficiently annoyed to begin giving serious considera-tion to plans for solving the English problem once and for all, and instructed his veteran naval commander, the Marquis of Santa Cruz, to draw up detailed estimates of the forces that would be required for such an undertaking.

One other thing which happened in 1585 was the departure to Rome of William Allen and Robert Parsons. Ostensibly the pur-pose of Allen's journey was to discuss the increasingly serious financial position of the seminary at Rheims, and that of Parsons to prepare for taking his final vows in the Society of Jesus. No doubt these were both perfectly valid reasons, but they did not prevent both men from concentrating their energies over the next three years on working to promote a Spanish invasion of England by all the means at their joint disposal. William Allen had travelled a long and stony road since that autumn day in 1568, when he had started his modestly optimistic venture at Douai for the reconversion of his countrymen by peaceful persuasion.

By the early spring of 1586, the international situation could hardly have looked much blacker from the point of view of William Allen's countrymen. With the King of France apparently the helpless puppet of the King of Spain's hired bullies, with the King of Spain's army in the Netherlands apparently sweeping all before it, England, not for the last time in her history, stood alone with nothing but the hard-pressed Dutch rebels and the equally hard-pressed French Huguenots between her and an inexorably advancing Spanish tide which would soon be lapping the shores of Western Europe from Gibraltar to the Elbe. No one in England realised all the grim implications of this situation more clearly than Francis Walsingham, who maintained listening posts in every European capital.

In some circles Francis Walsingham has the reputation of a sixteenth-century Lavrenti Beria. Somewhat closer inspection reveals the disappointing reality of a conscientious, over-worked and under-staffed government official, frequently in poor health and much given to physicking himself, who combined the functions of Home and Foreign Secretaries with those of head of MI5 and the Special Branch. It is on his performance in the latter capacities that Walsingham's notoriety depends but, in fact, there were probably never more than about a dozen full-time professional agents on his pay-roll at any given moment. Reliable spies, always in short supply, tended to come expensive and it was not until 1582 that Walsingham first began to receive any sort of regular budget for this side of his work. It started at a grudging £750 per annum and was gradually increased to £2,000 by 1588, two years before his death. In the early days most of the cost of maintaining a secret service is said to have come from its founder's own pocket.

Nevertheless, by the mid-eighties, Francis Walsingham had built up a formidable and far-reaching intelligence network. He drew his information from a wide range of sources. Much of it came in through normal diplomatic channels. Queen Elizabeth's representatives in France and elsewhere were all expected to set up their own intelligence services (this was an important part of the job for the ambassadors of every first-class power), and there was always at least one servant or secretary or minor official in every Court or great man's household ready to part with gossip and sometimes even with hard news if the price was right. Walsingham could also rely on the friendly offices of Dutch, French and German Protestant leaders. As well as these official and semi-official sources, he made use of an unknown but quite considerable number of free-lance news-gatherers scattered all over Europe. These included merchants, traders, businessmen, commercial agents, licensed travellers and petty functionaries who would pass on any interesting items which happened to come their way.

From a list drawn up after his death, it seems that Walsingham was in the habit of receiving information from twelve places in France, nine in Germany, four in Italy (he had even penetrated the English college at Rome), four in Spain, three in the Low Countries and from as far afield as Constantinople, Algiers and Tripoli. In addition to his foreign network he had four regular agents in England, engaged on tracking the movements of the Jesuit and seminary priests. One way and another, it would probably be no exaggeration to say that very little went on in Catholic circles either at home or abroad during the 1580s which did not, sooner or later, come to the notice of that 'most subtle searcher of secrets', Sir Francis Walsingham.

By modern standards, Queen Elizabeth's secret service was a pitifully haphazard and amateurish affair. Its agents, both full and part-time, were a floating population of greatly varying ability and trustworthiness, working individually and often, without doubt, working for both sides. Many of their reports were sheer guess-work, many were very likely sheer invention. The service owed its remarkable record of success to the skill and flair which enabled Francis Walsingham to sort out the mass of apparently unrelated material which flowed through his office, piece it together and make from it a coherent whole. It was a task which needed not only endless patience but an instinct for spotting and interpreting the single relevant fact or sentence in an agent's report. Walsingham had the patience. He developed the instinct slowly by un-remitting hard work and concentration, helped by the fact that he was motivated throughout by a deep sense of the righteousness of his cause – sincere convictions were after all by no means a Catholic monopoly. Walsingham held distinctly left-wing views which, despite the valuable services he rendered her, was why the Queen never really liked him. He was noted by William Camden to be 'a most sharp maintainer of the purer religion', and he undoubtedly believed that in his labours he was fighting Anti-Christ and all his works.

High on the list of these works Walsingham numbered Mary

Queen of Scots. 'So long as that devilish woman lives,' he had written to Leicester in January 1572, 'neither her Majesty must make account to continue in quiet possession of her crown, nor her faithful servants assure themselves of safety of their lives.' Nothing which had happened since the unravelling of the Ridolfi Plot had caused Walsingham to alter that opinion. The unravelling of the Throckmorton Plot, his own first major *coup*, left him in no doubt that Mary had been as deeply involved in the one as in the other. Francis Throckmorton, like the Duke of Norfolk before him, had learned on the scaffold that he who supped with the Queen of Scotland needed a long spoon indeed, but the Queen of Scotland herself was apparently once more to escape unscathed the consequences of her misdeeds – almost, but on this occasion not quite.

Ever since the first few months after her arrival in England Mary had been living under the guardianship of George Talbot, Earl of Shrewsbury, in one or other of that much-tried nobleman's mansions in the North Midlands. Her freedom of movement had, it is true, been restricted, but she was served by a retinue of her own servants and friends more than thirty strong, and dined as befitted a queen beneath a cloth of estate, her 'diet' and entertainment costing Queen Elizabeth £52 a week and, according to Shrewsbury, a good deal more out of his own pocket. No other viable solution to the problem (apart from the one favoured by the House of Commons) had suggested itself over the years, but during the early eighties Elizabeth, in the search for a solution to the problem of James, had made a prolonged and apparently genuine effort to find some way by which mother and son might be reunited and reign jointly in Scotland. The negotiations foundered, as they were bound to do, on the two Queens' ineradicable mutual distrust and on the virtual impossibility of devising adequate safeguards against Mary's repudiation of any undertakings given while a prisoner the moment she regained her liberty. Mary was outwardly all complaisance – indeed the initiative for this round of peace talks had come from her – but that did not prevent her from taking an equally active interest in the progress of the Guise/Mendoza plans to free her by force of arms and place her in her own right on another and infinitely more attractive throne.

Just how seriously the Queen of England and her advisers took these negotiations with Mary, or whether they ever really believed in James's much vaunted (by Mary and her friends) 'devotion' to his mother and her cause is difficult to say. Elizabeth may have hoped that by using the bait of the succession it would be possible, now that James was reaching maturity, to proposition him into taking over responsibility for his volatile parent. But James himself presently put an end to any such optimistic thoughts by making it perfectly plain that he was not interested in sharing his throne with anybody, and that his only concern about his mother's future was that England should continue to bear the odium and expense of keeping her safely out of the way. The arrest of Francis Throckmorton and Father Creighton, the assassination of Orange, and the breaking of the Parry murder plot all combined to extinguish the last spark of hope of reaching a negotiated settlement with the Queen of Scots. The curtain had come down and already the scene shifters were setting the stage for the last act of her tragedy.

To Francis Walsingham one of the most disturbing revelations of the Throckmorton affair had been the extent of Mary's foreign correspondence and the ease with which she was apparently able to send and receive uncensored letters in the large and laxly organised Shrewsbury establishments. By the summer of 1584 a reverberating three-cornered row between the earl, his formidable countess (better known as Bess of Hardwick), and their royal guest in which, at least so far as the two ladies were concerned, no holds of any kind were barred, had provided an unexceptionable excuse for making a change.

After an interim period of six months a new custodian was appointed and Mary quickly discovered that her circumstances had altered in more ways than one. Sir Amyas Paulet was no great nobleman, though he was accustomed to high society, having been Queen Elizabeth's ambassador in France. More important he was a man of strict Puritanical principles and a close and trusted friend of Francis Walsingham. He treated Mary with scrupulous respect but, like John Knox before him, was immune to her famous charm and unmoved by tantrums. Paulet took his responsibilities very seriously and wrote to Walsingham in July: 'Whereas it hath pleased her Majesty to commit unto me the charge, as well as the safe keeping of this Queen, I will never ask pardon if she depart out of my hands by any treacherous slight or cunning device, because I must confess that the same cannot come to pass without some gross negligence or rather traitorous carelessness.... My conscience beareth me witness,' he went on, 'and my doing I hope shall testify for me, that as I have been very careful and curious to perform every syllable contained in my instructions with all preciseness and severity, so I have done all my endeavour to make these people and their friends to know that if it were possible I would not be deceived by them.'

Paulet's instructions had been drafted by Walsingham and were extremely detailed – there was to be no communication between Mary's household and his own, except in his presence; none of Mary's servants were to leave the house without a guard; no strangers were to be admitted on any pretext whatever, and special attention was to be paid to the comings and goings of 'laundresses, coachmen and the like'. 'I have (I thank God) reformed no small number of abuses of dangerous consequence,' wrote Paulet, 'and experience doth inform me daily of other such new faults as might carry great peril, which I omit not to redress by little and little as I may.' Throughout the spring and summer of 1585 Walsingham and Paulet were engaged in methodically stopping the earths. By the autumn they felt satisfied that Mary had been effectively isolated from her undesirable friends, and in the New Year Paulet was able to report that it was impossible for a piece of paper as big as his finger to be conveyed without his knowledge. Walsingham had completed the first part of his plan. It was now time to put stage two into operation, and the Secretary of State had the means ready to his hand.

In December 1585, a Catholic exile named Gilbert Gifford had come over from France entrusted by Thomas Morgan with the task of trying to find a way of evading Paulet's unceasing vigilance and reopening a secret channel of communication with Mary. Gifford was arrested on his arrival at Rye and at once sent up to Walsingham in London. He may or may not have already been in Walsingham's employment – to a suspicious mind his appearance looks just a little too pat to be entirely coincidental. At any rate he spent some time in secret conference with the Secretary and, so far as is known, raised no difficulties when certain suggestions were put to him.

Walsingham, it appeared, was as interested as Thomas Morgan in setting up Mary's private post office again. This time, though, it would be a supervised private post office. The arrangements discussed between Gifford, Walsingham and Walsingham's confidential secretary, Thomas Phelippes, were ingenious but essentially simple. The Queen of Scots was now established at Chartley Manor in Staffordshire, and beer for the household was delivered once a week from the town of Burton. With the connivance of the brewer, letters could be carried in and out in a watertight box small enough to be inserted into the bunghole of a beer barrel. Gifford's part was to collect Mary's personal mail from the French Embassy, where it arrived by diplomatic bag. He passed it on to Thomas Phelippes, an expert linguist and genius with codes. While Phelippes copied and deciphered the letters, Gifford travelled by leisurely stages to Chartley where the originals were returned to him by Paulet. Gifford handed the letters to the brewer and the brewer, unknown to Gifford, took them back to Paulet who checked that nothing had been added to the package. It was then delivered as arranged. The outgoing post would work in reverse order. The trap looked foolproof. Walsingham hoped it would prove a death trap.

The first trial delivery was made on 16 January 1586 and went without a hitch. Mary, naturally delighted to have made contact once more with the world of intrigue which was her life-line, and fatally unsuspicious, gave orders that the backlog of clandestine correspondence which had been piling up at the French embassy should be sent on to her forthwith. Eighteen years ago Francis Knollys had written of the Queen of Scotland, 'she hath courage enough to hold out as long as any foot of hope may be left unto her'. She had not changed.

To begin with the person who derived most benefit from this unusual postal service was the brewer of Burton, code-named 'the honest man'. He was, of course, being handsomely paid for his trouble by both sides but, as a man of sound business instincts, it soon occurred to him to raise the price of his invaluable beer. Paulet considered 'the honest man's' demands both peremptory and unreasonable, but had to give in to them 'or lose his service'.

Meanwhile, an exceptional amount of overtime was being worked in Walsingham's office as letters, twenty-one packets of them 'great and small', some of which had been waiting delivery for nearly two years, started to flow out of the French ambassador's private coffers. There were letters from the Queen of Scots' agents in the Low Countries, from Thomas Morgan and the Archbishop of

Glasgow in Paris, from Charles Paget and Sir Francis Englefield, both prominent figures in the exiled community, from Robert Parsons, from the Duke of Guise and the Duke of Parma. They provided a complete picture of everything Mary's partisans in Europe had been doing and saying on her behalf since the time of the Throckmorton Plot. It was the sort of windfall any secret service chief dreams of, but although it filled many gaps in his knowledge and gave him much interesting information to be filed away for future use, it did not in general terms tell Walsingham anything that he had not already known or guessed.

By the middle of May, Mary's replies were coming back. In them she made it perfectly clear that she was completely identified with the purpose of the Enterprise, that she would welcome an invasion and was willing and eager to seize her cousin's throne. They provided helpful corroborative evidence that Mary had no scruples about conspiring against the state, but again they told Walsingham very little that he and his mistress did not already know. From past experience the Secretary also knew that the only hope of getting Elizabeth to proceed against Mary would be to confront her with irrefutable proof that the Queen of Scots had brought herself within the scope of the 1585 Act. From past experience of Mary and her friends he had little doubt that sooner or later such proof would be forthcoming. In the meantime, the beer barrels were providing him with a first-rate listening post.

The genesis of the Babington Plot, like that of most of its predecessors, is complicated and more than somewhat obscure. As usual a good many equivocal personalities were involved, and in the labyrinth of spy and counter-spy, double agent and *agent provocateur*, it is far from clear at this distance in time who was double-crossing who. It is also evident that this was often far from clear at the time. In outline, though, the plot was the same mixture as before – a rising of English Catholics, aided by an invading army financed jointly by Spain and the Pope, to release Mary, depose Elizabeth and replace her by Mary, and re-establish the Catholic faith.

Two things, however, give this particular affair a distinctive character. One was the fact that the assassination as well as the deposition of Elizabeth was an integral part of the plan from the beginning. (Some conspirators had been less explicit on this point, but whether any conspirators, having once succeeded in deposing

Elizabeth, would then have gone to the trouble or the risk of keeping her alive is hardly worth debating.) The other fact was that this time Elizabeth's government, thanks to its increasingly efficient secret service, was in a position to follow developments from an early stage.

The two chief protagonists in England were a priest named John Ballard and Anthony Babington. Both Ballard and Babington were already known to Walsingham who had begun to keep an eye on their movements in May. Ballard was in the habit of associating with a group of ardent young Catholic gentlemen who hung about the fringes of the Court, and the most prominent figure in this group was Anthony Babington – a young man of good family with a good deal more money than sense, handsome, gay, charming, conceited and cowardly. He had first made Mary's acquaintance in the days when he had been a page in the Earl of Shrewsbury's household and had since acquired the reputation among Mary's friends in France of being one of her staunchest adherents. He was, therefore, the obvious person to organise the actual rescue operation and act as her liaison officer.

Towards the end of June 1586, Mary received a letter from Thomas Morgan through the beer barrel post advising her to write a friendly letter to Babington. This she promptly did and Babington's reply contained a lengthy exposition of the plans afoot for her liberation. As far as Walsingham was concerned the most interesting paragraph came towards the end. 'For the despatch of the usurper,' wrote Babington, 'from the obedience of whom we are by the excommunication of her made free, there be six noble gentlemen all my private friends, who for the zeal they bear unto the Catholic cause and your majesty's service will undertake that tragical execution. It resteth that according to their good deserts and your majesty's bounty their heroical attempt may be honourably rewarded in them if they escape with life, or in their posterity and that so much I may be able by your majesty's authority to assure them.'

This was what Walsingham had been waiting for. Everything now depended on Mary's reply and Thomas Phelippes was sent up to Chartley to be ready to decipher it the moment it emerged from the beer barrel. First came a brief acknowledgement with the promise of more to follow. 'We attend her very heart at the next,' reported Phelippes. On 17 July it came. It was a very long

letter. After warmly commending Babington and his suggestions
in general terms, Mary proceeded to offer the conspirators much
sound practical advice on how 'to ground substantially this enterprise and to bring it to good success'. She had, after all, become
quite an expert on such matters by now. She also knew that if
anything went wrong this time, the consequences were likely to
be disastrous, not only for Babington and his friends, but for
herself. In the circumstances, she was understandably anxious that
there should be no security leaks and that no detail of the preliminary staff work should be overlooked. 'Affairs being thus
prepared,' she went on, 'and forces in readiness both without and
within the realm, then shall it be time to set the six gentlemen
to work, taking order, upon the accomplishing of their design, I
may be suddenly transported out of this place, and that all your
forces in the same time be on the field to meet me in tarrying
for the arrival of the foreign aid, which then must be hastened
with all diligence.'

If this did not sign Mary's death warrant then nothing would,
but Walsingham, in his natural anxiety to make a clean sweep
of the culprits, either instructed or allowed Phelippes to add a
postscript asking for 'the names and qualities of the six gentlemen'
before the letter was sent on to its destination. He thus provided
useful ammunition for all those partisans of Mary who were later
to insist that she had been framed.

As it happened it was a waste of effort, for Babington never
replied. Already events were slipping out of his precarious control
and he contemplated flight. On 2 August Walsingham decided it
would be dangerous to wait any longer and the arrests began.
Babington himself was taken in the house of that same Mrs Bellamy
who had once sheltered Father Parsons and been so suspicious of
William Weston. By the end of September the fourteen known
conspirators had been tried, condemned and executed amid heartfelt rejoicing on the part of the citizenry of London – rejoicing
manifested by 'public bonfires, ringing of bells, feastings in the
streets, singing of psalms and such like'. All that now remained
was to ensure that the 'wicked murderess' herself, the 'bosom
serpent', the 'monstrous and huge dragon' came to her just deserts.
This, as no doubt Francis Walsingham and his colleagues had
foreseen, proved a good deal easier said than done. It took, in
fact, six months of concentrated hard work, with Elizabeth fighting

a determined rearguard action throughout and trying everyone's patience to its limit.

'I would to God,' Walsingham was moved to lament at one point, 'her Majesty could be content to refer these things to them that can best judge of them, as other Princes do.'

Mary's trial finally came on at Fotheringay Castle in October before a panel of thirty-six distinguished commissioners, as provided by the Act for the Queen's Safety. She defended herself with courage, eloquence and dignity. She denied, as she was bound to do, all knowledge of the conspiracy but, in the face of Babington's evidence and that of her own secretaries (who had had no hesitation in betraying their mistress), quite apart from the other evidence so patiently amassed by Walsingham, her denials were regarded as no more than a matter of form. The commissioners would have proceeded to judgement, had they not been suddenly called back to London by royal command. There, in the Star Chamber, all the evidence was solemnly passed in review, Mary's two secretaries, Nau and Curle, were produced and repeated the statements they had previously given in writing. After this the assembled commissioners unanimously gave their sentence, finding the Queen of Scots 'not only accessory and privy to the conspiracy but also an imaginer and compasser of her Majesty's destruction'.

Two further formalities now had to be observed – the sentence must be publicly proclaimed, as laid down in the 1585 Act, and Elizabeth must sign the warrant for Mary's execution. Parliament had already been summoned, 'to make the burden better borne and the world abroad better satisfied', as Lord Burghley put it, and after two postponements the session opened on 29 October. It was an extraordinary session. All normal business went by the board while both Houses, united as seldom before and seldom since, combined to exert the last ounce of pressure on their obstinate sovereign lady. Elizabeth had won some notable battles of will with Parliament in the past and she could no doubt have won again – when she had made up her mind on a matter of principle she was immovable – but on this occasion her battle was with herself. It was not until the beginning of December that she finally agreed to have the sentence published under the Great Seal and once more bonfires were lit, bells rung and psalms (and most probably other things as well) sung in the streets of London. Another two months, though, had gone by before Elizabeth could bring herself to sign the warrant and the Queen of Scots went to her predestined end in the Great Hall at Fotheringay.

That Elizabeth's indecision and distress during this period were both genuine and agonising there need be no question. But her extreme, apparently perverse reluctance to authorise the execution of her deadliest enemy is, on the face of it, difficult to comprehend. So difficult, in fact, that some people have dismissed it as mere play-acting. Possibly there was some play-acting. Elizabeth always was a consummate actress, 'a princess who can act any part she pleases', and she knew she was presenting the Catholic world with a first-rate propaganda weapon.

'What will they not now say,' she exclaimed, 'when it shall be spread that for the safety of her life a maiden Queen could be content to spill the blood even of her own kinswoman?'

Elizabeth suffered from a most un-Tudor-like squeamishness when it came to spilling the blood of her kinsfolk, but it is not really likely that humanitarian considerations were weighing very heavily on her this time. Mary had been a nuisance and a source of anxiety for nearly thirty years. For nearly fifteen years she had been a source of ever-increasing danger both to England and to Elizabeth.

'I am not so void of judgement as not to see mine own peril,' the Queen had told Parliament in November, 'nor yet so ignorant as not to know it were in nature a foolish course to cherish a sword to cut mine own throat; nor so careless as not to weigh that my life daily is in hazard.'

All the same, if she could have found a way even then of keeping Mary alive, she would undoubtedly have done so. Once Mary was dead, Philip of Spain would have no excuse left for postponing the Enterprise. With Mary on the English throne, the Guise family would become all-powerful and their attitude to Spain was not likely to remain subservient; but once Mary was dead, Philip need have no qualms that he would be spending Spanish blood and Spanish gold to bring about the close Anglo-French alliance it had always been the cornerstone of his policy to avoid. To the Catholic King himself, to the Duke of Parma commanding a magnificent fighting instrument in the Netherlands, to Pope Sixtus in Rome, to the clamorous English expatriates all over Europe, it would then indeed appear 'God's obvious design' to bestow upon him the crowns of England and Scotland. Elizabeth, looking into a future dark with

the threat of war and the terror of the unknown, had every reason
to hesitate before she removed the cause of any lingering doubt
in Philip's mind about the Almighty's intentions.

Probably, though, more than all the solid political considerations,
more than her inherent dread of committing herself to any irrevoc-
able course of action, more than any scruples of compassion for her
cousin and sister queen, the aspect of Mary's end which upset
Elizabeth most and lay beneath her irrational, hysterical reaction
after the deed had been done, was the superstitious revulsion of
one who has violated a sacred mystery. To the sixteenth-century
mind there was something unutterably atrocious in the notion of
subjecting God's anointed to earthly trial and judicial execution.
To one of Elizabeth's background and temperament it was the
ultimate tabu – hence her desperate, eleventh-hour attempt to shift
the terrible responsibility onto the shoulders of men who had, after
all, taken a solemn oath to pursue the 'pretended successor' unto
death, once she had been found guilty by due process of the law.

The rights and wrongs of the Queen of Scots have been exhaus-
tively rehearsed over the centuries – literally rivers of ink and
forests of paper have been consumed in the process. But Elizabeth
Tudor and Mary Stuart were trapped by history in a life-and-death
struggle over which they had very little control – cousins foredoomed to enmity by their blood and birth. It is, therefore, as
futile to blame Elizabeth for her treatment of Mary as it is to
blame Mary for her endless intrigues; to blame her for being the
sort of woman she was – constitutionally incapable of ever seeing
anyone's point of view but her own. That Mary had coveted
Elizabeth's throne since the days when she quartered the English
royal arms with her own is not really in question. Just how deeply
she was involved in the plots to seize that throne by violence
will no doubt always remain a matter of debate. But by 1586 Mary's
guilt or innocence had long ceased to have any relevance. The
mere fact of her existence was now intolerable and England quite
simply could no longer hold the rival queen. Her presence had
become a gangrenous sore which the nation must slough off or
perish. This was the tragedy of Mary Stuart.

Epilogue. There is only one Christ Jesus

'There is only one Christ Jesus and one faith: the rest is dispute about trifles.'

Elizabeth I, Queen of England

I F the defeat of King Philip's invincible Armada proved to the satisfaction of Queen Elizabeth's subjects that God was an Englishman (as indeed they had always suspected), it also proved, to the relief of the other European nations, that he was not a Spaniard. Although the indecisive running battle in the Channel did not really prove anything else, this in itself was enough to take the heat out of the long struggle for power which had been fought in the freezing Flanders mud, on the waters of the Spanish main, in the fever-ridden swamps of Central America, and in manor houses hidden in the green depths of the English country-side. But to the English Catholics the heat and the heart had gone out of the fight sixteen months before the sails were sighted off the Lizard. They could have accepted and welcomed the peaceful accession of Mary Stuart with clear consciences, but no one except the extreme right-wing lunatic fringe would for a moment have accepted Philip of Spain – despite his descent from John of Gaunt. After 1587 the struggle became simply one for survival; a struggle to hand on the tiny, obstinate spark of faith to each succeeding genera-tion until the memory of old wrongs and old fears had faded and Englishmen at last realised that the two creeds could live together side by side without threatening each other with extinction, or – to put it more brutally – until they realised that it no longer mattered very much.

It is tempting and easy for a materialistic age to dismiss the whole conflict as a useless, sterile waste of time, but to do so is surely to miss the point entirely. The men and women of sixteenth-century England did not regard it as a waste of time. To them the reality of the living God was a vital part of their lives, even if many of them were content to keep him for Sundays and to worship him as the Establishment thought best. To us perhaps the worst aspect is the terrible, unnecessary human suffering, the waste of lives, the tragedy of a situation in which men who could have fulfilled themselves by rendering valuable services to the community were instead condemned to be butchered on the scaffold, to rot in prison or eat their hearts out in exile.

William Allen, who misunderstood the mood of his own countrymen so profoundly that he could issue a bitter personal attack on the Queen on the eve of the Armada, urging his fellow Catholics as they valued their immortal souls not to fight for 'an infamous, depraved, accursed, excommunicate heretic, the very shame of her sex and princely name; the chief spectacle of sin and abomination in this our age; and the only poison, calamity and destruction of our noble Church and Country', understood very well the nature of his own predicament. 'Thou knowest, good Lord,' he wrote, 'how often we have lamented together, that for our sins we should be constrained to spend either all, or most, of our serviceable years out of our natural country, to which they are most due, and to which in all ages past they should have been most grateful; and that our offices should be acceptable, and our lives and services agreeable to strangers, and not to our dearest at home.' But neither Allen and the other exiles, nor the victims of rope and knife and rack, ever for a moment believed their sorrows and torments were a waste.

Deeply as many individual Catholics suffered, it is as well to remember that it might all have been very much worse. All the seeds of religious hysteria were present, and if the Queen had for one moment relaxed her iron grip on the fanatical left-wing element, which was strong – especially in the eighties – in the House of Commons and within the Church of England itself, then there might well have been some very nasty scenes indeed. As it was, at no time, not even when a Catholic invasion fleet was in the Channel, within sight of the coast, were the English Catholics ever in danger of Protestant mob violence. In spite of a continual jeremiad that the Queen's fatal tendency to lenience, her wilful blindness to the full extent of the papist menace would certainly bring disaster upon her and upon the godly, Elizabeth continued to refuse to regard her subjects as Protestants and Catholics. To her they were all Englishmen, good, bad and indifferent. She was right, of course, and when the moment of crisis came, they rose to her as Englishmen, first, last and always. Perhaps the saddest irony of all is that when the defeat of the Sacred Enterprise was spread abroad the English students in the college at Rome cheered aloud at the news.

Of course it was all a tragic waste, but no one living in the twentieth century should need to be told that when man's aggressive instincts become sublimated in devotion to a cause, when passions become mixed with politics, the result is inevitably suffering, bloodshed and, above all else, waste. The pity of it is that more people could not have agreed with Queen Elizabeth when she remarked, 'There is only one Christ Jesus and one faith: the rest is dispute about trifles.'

Notes on Sources

As this book is written by a non-specialist for other non-specialists it would have been pretentious to include the full apparatus of notes and bibliography. Any specialists who should happen to read it will, of course, immediately recognise the material used but for those general readers who may be interested, the following is an indication of the sources I have drawn upon most heavily.

General Surveys

The dust of this ancient battle has only recently begun to settle and consequently it is only within the present century that dispassionate general surveys have begun to appear. Generally acknowledged as the foremost of these is *England and the Catholic Church under Queen Elizabeth* by A. O. Meyer, translated by J. R. McKee, first published in 1916 and re-issued with an introduction by John Bossy in 1967. Two modern accounts from the Catholic point of view are *The English Catholics in the Reign of Elizabeth* by J. H. Pollen (1920) which takes the story up to 1580, and *The Reformation in England*, Vol. 3 by Philip Hughes (1954). *Papists and Puritans* by Patrick McGrath (1967) deals, as the title suggests, with both types of Elizabethan non-conformity.

For the Reformation movement in general, *The English Reformation to 1558* by T. M. Parker, Oxford, 1950, covers the early stages clearly and concisely. Two wider modern surveys are *The Reformation* by Owen Chadwick, Vol. 3 of The Pelican History of the Church, revised edition published in 1968, and *The English Reformation* by A. G. Dickens, revised edition issued in The Fontana Library in 1967. An older but still objective account is *The English Church in the reigns of Elizabeth and James I* by Walter H. Frere (1904). Two other still older histories from the Protestant and Catholic viewpoints respectively are *The Annals of the Reformation* by John Strype in four volumes, Oxford, 1824, and Charles Dodd's *The Church History of England from*

1500 to the year 1688, edited by Mark A. Tierney in five volumes (1839-43). Both are valuable for the printed documents they contain.

For the political background which is an inseparable part of the story of the Elizabethan Catholics *Before the Armada, the Growth of English Foreign Policy 1485-1588* by R. B. Wernham (1966) is a general survey, while *The Shaping of the Elizabethan Regime* by Wallace MacCaffrey (1969) deals with a specific period in detail. See also *Elizabeth I and the Unity of England* by Joel Hurstfield (1960). William Camden's *History of the most renowned and virtuous Princess Elizabeth, late Queen of England* (1630) is the nearest thing we have to a contemporary political history of the reign and is invaluable as a source. Indispensable for anyone writing about Elizabethan politics are Conyers Read's two great studies of Elizabethan statesmen: *Mr Secretary Walsingham and the Policy of Queen Elizabeth* (1925) and *Mr Secretary Cecil and Queen Elizabeth* (1955) followed by *Lord Burghley and Queen Elizabeth* (1960). For proceedings in Parliament I have leaned heavily and gratefully on Professor J. E. Neale's classic *Elizabeth I and her Parliaments* (1953 and 1957).

The above are not, of course, all the general histories I have consulted but they were the most relevant for my particular purpose.

PROLOGUE

The Queen of Scots' own recollections of her flight into England are preserved in *Memorials of Mary Stuart* by Claude Nau, ed. J. Stevenson, Edinburgh, 1883. See also *The Life of Mary Queen of Scots* by Agnes Strickland, Vol. 2 (1873) and, of course, the latest biography *Mary Queen of Scots* by Antonia Fraser (1969). The letters of Richard Lowther and Francis Knollys are to be found in the *Calendar of State Papers Relating to Scotland and Mary Queen of Scots*, Vol. 2. The Spanish Ambassador's comments are in the *C.S.P. Spanish, Elizabeth*, Vol. 2. William Camden's *History* describes the English government's reactions and many of the documents are printed in *The Fall of Mary Stuart* by F. A. Mumby (1921).

CHAPTER ONE

The descriptions of Elizabeth as princess are in the *Calendar of State Papers, Venetian*, Vol. 6, Pt. 2, and the reports of the Italian agent in London, Il Schifanoya, which are an invaluable source for the first year of the reign, appear in *C.S.P. Venetian*, Vol. 7. For foreign affairs with special reference to France see *C.S.P., Foreign, Elizabeth*, Vol. 1 and *A Full View of the Public Transactions in the Reign of Queen Elizabeth*, ed. Patrick Forbes (1740); for Rome *Anglo-Roman Relations 1558-1565* C. G. Bayne, Oxford, 1913; for Spain *C.S.P. Spanish, Elizabeth*, Vol. 1 and *Documents from Simancas Relating to the Reign of Queen Elizabeth* T. Gonzalez, ed. Spencer Hall (1865). For the Parliament of 1559 see *Elizabeth I and her Parliaments*, Vol. 1, J. E. Neale and for the point of view of the reformers in particular, Strype's *Annals* Vol. 1, Pt. 2 and the *Zurich Letters*, Vol. 7, ed. H. Robinson, Parker Society, Cambridge, 1846.

CHAPTER TWO

For the Protestant view on the fate of the Marian Bishops see Strype, Vol. 1, Pts. 1 and 2. For a contemporary Catholic account see *The Rise and Growth of the Anglican Schism* by Nicholas Sander with a Continuation by Edward Rishton, trans. and ed. by David Lewis (1877). Two relatively modern studies of the religious settlement are, from the Anglican viewpoint, *The Elizabethan Clergy, and the Settlement of Religion, 1558-64* by Henry Gee, Oxford, 1898 and, from the Catholic side, *The Elizabethan Religious Settlement, a study of contemporary documents* by H. N. Birt (1907). Another contemporary Catholic appraisal – the Report prepared by Nicholas Sander for Cardinal Moroni – is printed in *Miscellanea* Vol. 1, Catholic Record Society (1905). For an account of the Catholic emigrés and of the propaganda war see *The English Catholic Refugees on the Continent* by Peter Guilday, New York, 1914, and *Elizabethan Recusant Prose, 1559-1582*, A. C. Southern (1950). For the provisions of the Acts of Supremacy and Uniformity see *The Tudor Constitution: Documents and Commentary* by G. R. Elton, Cambridge, 1960 and also McGrath, *Papists and Puritans*. The Oath of Supremacy is printed in Gee. Catholic reaction to the new order in England can be found in *C.S.P.,*

Rome, Vol. 1 and the activities of King Philip's ambassador in *C.S.P., Spanish, Eliz.*, Vol. 1. For the survey of Justices of the Peace, see *Letters from the Bishops to the Privy Council, 1564*, ed. Mary Bateson, Miscellany, Camden Society Vol. 53, N.S. (1895).

There is only one relatively modern biography of William Allen, *An Elizabethan Cardinal* by Martin Haile (1914), written from the Catholic viewpoint. For the founding of the Seminary at Douai see *First and Second Diaries of the English College, Douai*, edited and with a valuable Historical Introduction by T. F. Knox (1878), also *Letters and Memorials of William Allen*, ed. T. F. Knox (1882).

For Mary Stuart's first widowhood, see Nicholas Throckmorton's dispatches in the *C.S.P. Foreign, Elizabeth*, Vols. 3 and 4; for the English intervention in Scotland in 1559-60 the *C.S.P. Scottish* Vol. 1 and Read's *Mr Secretary Cecil*. Maitland's account of his interview with Elizabeth is printed in *A Letter from Mary Queen of Scots to the Duke of Guise, Jan. 1562* by J. H. Pollen, Scot. Hist. Soc. xliii (1904). Other documents relating to this period are also printed in *Elizabeth and Mary Stuart: The Beginning of the Feud* by F. A. Mumby, Boston, 1914.

The dispatches of Guerau de Spes are printed in the *C.S.P. Spanish, Eliz.* Vol. 2. See also *Mr Secretary Cecil* for the crisis of 1569. Many of the documents relating to the Rising in the North are printed in *Memorials of the Rebellion of 1569*, ed. Cuthbert Sharp (1840). A modern, Catholic study of the Ridolfi affair is *The Dangerous Queen* by Francis Edwards (1964). See also *The Marvellous Chance* by Francis Edwards (1968). Documents — letters, depositions and confessions are printed in *Collection of State Papers ... left by William Cecil, Lord Burghley* ed. Samuel Haynes and William Murdin, Vol. 2 (1740-59) and in *Illustrations of British History* by E. Lodge (1838).

The Bull *Regnans in Excelsis* is printed in Camden and also in J. H. Pollen's *The English Catholics in the Reign of Elizabeth*. Bishop Jewel's counter-blast — 'A view of a seditious Bull' — can be found in *The Works of John Jewel*, 4th portion, Parker Society (1850).

For the Parliaments of 1571 and 1572 and the resulting legislation see Neale, *Elizabeth I and her Parliaments*, Vol. 1 and McGrath, *Papists and Puritans*.

CHAPTER FIVE

See Strype for the general reaction of St Bartholomew and Murdin for the plan to send Mary back to Scotland. *The Catholic Laity in Elizabethan England, 1558-1603* by W. R. Trimble, Harvard University Press, 1964 contains a useful survey of the conditions under which the English Catholics lived. There is a wealth of more detailed information in the *Acts of the Privy Council*, ed. J. R. Dasent (1890-1907), in the *State Papers, Domestic, Elizabeth* preserved at the Public Record Office and in the Cecil Papers at Hatfield House (see the Historical Manuscripts Commission Reports). More material still, which is outside the scope of this book, has been printed in the various *Miscellanea* of the Catholic Record Society, in *Recusant History* and in the Journals and Proceedings of a number of county Archaeological Societies.

For the continuing success of William Allen's foundation at Douai see the *First and Second Diaries of the English College*.

Sources for the story of Cuthbert Mayne are *A Briefe Historie of the Glorious Martyrdom of XII Reverend Priests* by William Allen ed. J. H. Pollen (1908), *The Troubles of Our Catholic Forefathers* by John Morris (1872) and the *Acts of the Privy Council*. See also *Sir Richard Grenville of the Revenge* by A. L. Rowse (1937). For other and later martyrs see *Memoirs of the Missionary Priests* by Richard Challoner ed. J. H. Pollen (1923), *Lives of the English Martyrs* by Bede Camm (1905) and *Unpublished Documents Relating to the English Martyrs, 1584-1603*, ed. J. H. Pollen, Catholic Record Society, Vol. 5 (1908).

CHAPTER SIX

For foreign affairs in the 1570s see the *C.S.P. Foreign*, Vols. 8, 9 and 11, also *C.S.P. Spanish, Elizabeth*, Vol. 2, Read's *Mr Secretary Walsingham* and R. B. Wernham's *Before the Armada*. The troubles afflicting the Seminary at Douai in the late 1570s are chronicled in the *First and Second Diaries of the English College*. For the founding of the English College at Rome and its early teething troubles see above – also Robert Parsons' account of Domestical Difficulties in *Miscellanea* Vol. 2, Catholic Record Society (1906), the *Letters and Memorials of Father Robert Parsons*, ed. L. Hicks, Catholic Record Society No. 39 (1942) and, for the daily life at the College, *The English Romayne Life* by Anthony Munday, printed in the Harleian Miscellany, VII (1746).

CHAPTER SEVEN

For the Jesuits see *Records of the English Province of the Society of Jesus*, ed. Henry Foley (1877-1884). The standard biography of Edmund Campion is still *Edmund Campion* by Richard Simpson (1867) which prints a number of letters and documents, but see also *Edmund Campion* by Evelyn Waugh (1935). There is, oddly enough, no biography of the able, complex and controversial Robert Parsons. His own fragmentary Memoirs are printed in *Miscellanea* 2 and 4, Catholic Record Society (1906 and 1907) and there is a valuable Introduction by Leo Hicks to the *Letters and Memorials*. Campion's *Bragge* is printed in Simpson and also in Pollen's *The English Catholics in the Reign of Elizabeth*.

CHAPTER EIGHT

See above for the adventures of Campion and Parsons. See Neale, *Elizabeth I and her Parliaments*, Vol. 1 for the Parliament of 1581.

CHAPTER NINE

See Simpson for the trial of Edmund Campion. Lord Burghley's Execution of Justice is printed in *Somers Tracts*, in the *Harleian Miscellany* and in Holinshed's *Chronicle*. William Allen's True Sincere and Modest Defence of the English Catholics is printed in The Catholic Library No. 2 (1914). See also *The Execution of Justice by William Cecil and A True, Sincere and Modest Defence of English Catholics by William Allen*, ed. Robert M. Kingdon, New York, 1964. For the Lennox-Guise-Throckmorton affair see Read's *Mr Secretary Walsingham*, the *C.S.P. Scottish*, Vol. 6,

C.S.P., Spanish, Elizabeth, Vol. 3, *The Letters and Memorials of William Allen* and the *Letters and Memorials of Father Robert Parsons*. The official account of the Throckmorton Plot is printed in the *Harleian Miscellany*, Vol. 3. For the Bond of Association and the Parliament of 1584-5 see Neale's *Elizabeth I and her Parliaments*, Vol. 2. For the Parry Plot see Read's *Mr Secretary Walsingham*, Holinshed's *Chronicle* and William Camden's *History*; also *An Elizabethan Problem* by L. Hicks (1964) and *The Strange Case of Dr William Parry – the Career of Agent-Provocateur* by L. Hicks, *Studies*, Dublin, 1948.

CHAPTER TEN

See Neale's *Elizabeth I and her Parliaments*, Vol. 2 for the Parliaments of 1585 and 1586. For the 'second wave' of the Jesuit invasion see *Letters and Memorials of Robert Parsons*, also *John Gerard – The Autobiography of an Elizabethan*, trans. and ed. Philip Caraman, Longmans Green, 1951, and *William Weston – The Autobiography of an Elizabethan*, trans. and ed. Philip Caraman, Longmans Green, 1955. For the laity at this period, see Trimble's *The Catholic Laity in Elizabethan England* and for Robert Southwell, J. H. Pollen's *English Martyrs*. There is a full account of the Babington affair in *Mary Queen of Scots and the Babington Plot* by J. H. Pollen, Scot. Hist. Soc. 3rd series, iii (1922). See also Read's *Mr Secretary Walsingham* and *The Letter-Books of Sir Amias Paulet* by John Morris (1874).

EPILOGUE

The Defeat of the Spanish Armada by Garrett Mattingly (1959) is an outstanding modern account. William Allen's *Admonition to the Nobility and People of England and Ireland* which, although he may not have written it himself, was issued in his name, was reprinted in 1842. For Catholic plans for the succession see *Letters and Memorials of William Allen* and *Letters and Memorials of Robert Parsons*.

Index